THE COMPLETE **IDIOT'S** GUIDE® TO

a Career in Computer Programming

by Jesse Liberty

que®

A Division of Macmillan Computer Publishing
201 W. 103rd Street, Indianapolis, IN 46290

The Complete Idiot's Guide to a Career in Computer Programming

Copyright © 1999 by *Que*

International Standard Book Number: 0-7897-1995-9

Library of Congress Catalog Card Number: 99-63041

Printed in the United States of America

First Printing: *May 1999*

01   00   99   4   3   2

Trademarks

Warning and Disclaimer

Executive Editor
Angie Wethington

Acquisitions Editor
Stephanie McComb

Development Editor
Gregory Harris

Technical Editor
Donald Xie

Managing Editor
Thomas Hayes

Project Editor
Leah C. Kirkpatrick

Copy Editor
Victoria Elzey

Indexer
Mary Gammons

Proofreader
Maribeth Echard

Interior Design
Nathan Clement

Cover Design
Michael Freeland

Illustrator
Judd Winick

Copy Writer
Eric Borgert

Layout Technicians
Lisa England
Tricia Flodder

Contents at a Glance

Contents

About the Author

Jesse Liberty has been a Distinguished Software Engineer for AT&T and a Vice President of Citibank. Today he is the President of Liberty Associates, Inc. (http://www.libertyassociates.com), which provides contract-programming as well as training, mentoring, and consulting in object-oriented analysis and design.

Jesse is the author of a dozen books on object-oriented analysis and design and computer programming, and he has taught programming and design to more than 20,000 students at onsite classes and on the Internet.

Dedication

This book is dedicated to Johann Gutenberg and Adam Smith.

Acknowledgments

I'd like to thank many people at Que who have shepherded this book and supported it as it came to fruition. Special thanks to Stephanie McComb, and also to Tracy Dunkelberger, and Holly Allender. Thanks also to Donald Xie, Gregory Harris, Leah Kirkpatrick, and Victoria Elzey.

As always, I must thank my wife, Stacey Liberty, and my children, Robin and Rachel, who supported, encouraged, and tolerated me in this endeavor. And my dog Milo and cat Fred, who talked over the issues with me and never once disagreed with my ideas.

This book literally could not have been possible without the contribution, support, and assistance of Sally Silver, president of Sally Silver Companies. Sally is one of the great stars of the industry, and her assistance here and in so many ways is greatly appreciated.

Tell Us What You Think!

As the reader of this book, *you* are our most important critic and commentator. We value your opinion and want to know what we're doing right, what we could do better, what areas you'd like to see us publish in, and any other words of wisdom you're willing to pass our way.

As a Publisher for Que, I welcome your comments. You can fax, email, or write me directly to let me know what you did or didn't like about this book—as well as what we can do to make our books stronger.

Please note that I cannot help you with technical problems related to the topic of this book, and that due to the high volume of mail I receive, I might not be able to reply to every message.

When you write, please be sure to include this book's title and author as well as your name and phone or fax number. I will carefully review your comments and share them with the author and editors who worked on the book.

Fax: (317) 581-4666

Email: gwiegand@mcp.com

Mail: Greg Wiegand
          Que
          201 West 103rd Street
          Indianapolis, IN 46290 USA

Introduction

You're certainly no idiot, but there are times when the complexity of software makes you feel like one. You know there is a lot to learn, and you suspect it is very complex, perhaps even overly technical. Yet, somehow you find it appealing, and you know that some people are making lots of money at programming computers. The question is: Is this a good opportunity for you?

Can you do it? Are there really jobs available that you could get if only you knew how? How do you get started?

This book is not simply a tutorial on how to program computers. It will, however, guide you through the maze of jargon, and will provide a road map on how to get from where you are to where you want to be.

This book is for people new to the computer market or folks wanting to apply their skills to a new position. I do assume you already know how to use a computer to do word processing, for example, or to use a spreadsheet. I cover a number of programming languages for which there is great market demand. You need never have written a program before. Perhaps you're not even quite sure what programming is. That's fine; I'll teach you what you need to know.

Along the way, I'll discuss the opportunities in the industry and how you can get your first job. I'll offer tips on putting together a résumé, handling an interview, and getting the experience you need. I'll also teach you what the different jobs are, tell you what they pay, and discuss how to decide which is right for you.

You can't learn to program without understanding some of the technology, and I'll introduce you to the various approaches and techniques, and give you the information you need to decide which language is right for you. In short, this book provides an overview of the entire industry and serves as a guide to getting started; it doesn't substitute for a complete course in programming, but it does tell you how to structure your course to get where you want to go.

I do not assume you are a math whiz, a techno-geek, or a computer hobbyist. If you are, great, you'll be way ahead; but there is no need to worry if this is the first book you've ever read about programming and if you've never been good at math. There are only two requirements to excel at programming: You must be bright and you must be motivated. The best programmers I know started out at musicians, social workers, psychologists, writers, waiters, and taxi drivers.

What I do assume is that you are interested in finding a new career in programming because you have heard that it is fun, interesting, and lucrative. It is all of that and more, and here's the dirty little secret: It isn't that hard to get started. The opportunities are dumbfounding. We'll cover this in detail later in the book, but let me give you one small statistic to whet your appetite: According to a study by the Bureau of Labor Statistics, by the year 2005 there will be over two million new jobs for software professionals!

Conventions

The Complete Idiot's Guide to a Career in Computer Programming is organized to help you get your programming career off to a flying start. In doing so, the book uses the following conventions:

➤ **Bold** indicates text you type, items you select, click, and press.

➤ You see `monospace` type for URLs, onscreen messages, and command output.

➤ Any words that are being defined or emphasized appear in *italic*.

Also, be sure to watch for these features:

Check This Out!

There are "Check This Out" sections throughout the book. I use them to point out things that are noteworthy, stuff to be leery of, great tips—basically, they are full of information that adds to your understanding of programming and maybe even make you say "Wow!"

Geek Speak

Everyone knows that technical subjects sometimes leave you scratching your head wondering what that long-winded explanation just meant. Well, have no fear. I provide "Geek Speak" boxes to highlight terms, methods, or brainy stuff that you don't necessarily need to know, but that definitely helps you make more sense out of programming.

Notes

The "Note" boxes are used as a catchall to pass along cross-references pointing you to other sections of the book, provide interesting facts, or for anything else I feel you should take a look at.

A Word About Microsoft

This book is focused on where the career opportunities are, and you can't write a book such as this without focusing on technology by Microsoft. Whether you think Microsoft is the "evil empire" or the greatest entrepreneurial endeavor of our time, you simply can't ignore it. As they used to say about IBM, it isn't the competition, it is the environment.

Over the past six to eight years, I've become almost 100% focused on Microsoft technology and tools. You will find a distinct bias in this book toward Microsoft products such as Visual C++, Visual InterDev, SQL Server, and so forth, as well as Microsoft technology, including COM, ActiveX, ASP, and DNA. (You need not know what any of these are just yet; suffice it to say that they are all part of Microsoft's approach to solving development problems.)

There are other ways to approach these issues, but Microsoft is spending billions of dollars a year developing these products, the market is following their lead, and I believe strongly that this is where the best employment opportunities lie. The lessons in this book will also apply across platforms and with other technologies, but the examples are decidedly influenced by Microsoft. This may be because it is what I know best (and when all you have is a hammer, the whole world looks like a nail), but it is also because I think it is the right approach if your goal is to make money as a professional developer.

Part 1

Careers in Software

Sometimes it looks like the new gold rush: So many people are making so much money in software. Are there really still good jobs waiting for you, or is it too late? (Don't worry—if it were, we wouldn't have published this book!) This section explores the opportunities and tells you what you'll need to learn in order to compete for the best jobs.

Chapter 1

Market Opportunity

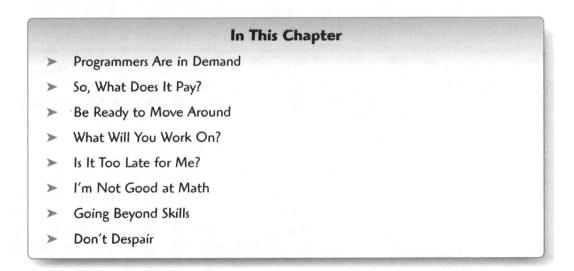

In This Chapter

- ➤ Programmers Are in Demand
- ➤ So, What Does It Pay?
- ➤ Be Ready to Move Around
- ➤ What Will You Work On?
- ➤ Is It Too Late for Me?
- ➤ I'm Not Good at Math
- ➤ Going Beyond Skills
- ➤ Don't Despair

Programmers Are in Demand

Computers have revolutionized the way the world handles information. As the information technology field grows, the programmers who design and maintain systems have become all the more vital. According to the Information Technology Association of America, there is a tremendous shortage of software professionals. That's good news if you're looking for work. Demand is high and supply is low, and that is driving up compensation to record levels.

Right now there are more than 1.5 million computer-related jobs in America, with nearly 340,000 jobs available for which there are no qualified applicants. The shortage is so severe that Congress has nearly doubled the number of H-1B visas given to foreign software professionals to 115,000 over the next three years.

Even so, experts predict that the shortage will grow worse in coming years. The demand for software professionals is higher and expected to be more sustained than for any other job category in America. In fact, according to the Bureau of Labor Statistics, computer scientists, computer engineers, and systems analysts are expected to be the three fastest growing occupations through 2006! (I'll explain these three job titles later in this chapter, but essentially they all mean the same thing: people who write software for a living.)

In short, it is a great time to be a programmer; the demand is skyrocketing and that brings elevated salaries and favorable working conditions.

So, What Does It Pay?

This is the single most important question, so, of course, it is the hardest to answer and no one really wants to talk about it.

One reason for the reluctance to discuss salary is that the range of compensation is surprisingly large, varying by some estimates from $20,000 through $200,000 per year. The vast majority of programmers, however, fall within a somewhat narrower band of $40,000–$100,000, with the average hovering just under $60,000 nationwide. Fully 10% of software engineers earn more than $80,000, and a few highly gifted programmers make a lot more.

The big money, of course, is in leading software projects, where salaries start at $100,000 and go up quickly. It is not unusual for a Chief Technology Officer to command a quarter of a million dollars a year, or more.

The Good Kind of Rate Increase

According to a 1998 report in *Information Week*, programmer salaries are skyrocketing at an annual rate of increase of more than 14%, at a time when workers in other fields are seeing an average 3–4% increase.

Starting salaries are high as well. In 1997, the Bureau of Labor Statistics reported starting salaries for computer programmers in a range from $38,000 to more than $67,000, depending on specific skills and area of the country.

Various factors contribute to actual salaries. For example, location is a tremendous factor; where you live and work greatly influences your earning potential.

For example, the average salary in the Southwest is nearly $80,000 a year, whereas the average in the Midwest is closer to $50,000. The best salaries appear to be in the technology centers: Silicon Valley, Boston, New York, Atlanta, and so forth. In some of these areas, salaries are routinely supplemented by sign-on and annual bonuses and additional incentives, including stock options.

Nearly 56% of the engineers who responded to a survey by *Software Development Magazine* said they expect to receive a bonus beyond their normal salary, with fully 23% expecting that bonus to be in the $5,000 to $10,000 range.

The highest-demand programmers are those who work in object-oriented languages such as C++ and those who can develop Web-based database applications. This is where the market is, and focusing on C++, Java, and database programming is probably your best bet for a lucrative career.

Overall, the highest incomes go to independent consultants. According to a survey in *Software Development Magazine*, consultant annual incomes range from $25,000 up to $800,000, with an average compensation of more than $85,000. Consultants, however, take on additional risks and generally receive fewer benefits; for example, they almost never receive stock options, health insurance, or similar benefits.

Job Satisfaction

In a survey by *Information Week*, 69% of programmers said they were "satisfied" or "very satisfied" with their current level of compensation. Interestingly, in that same survey, salary came third in importance to the vast majority of programmers.

The most important areas of concern when evaluating job satisfaction were the challenge of the work and the atmosphere of the company. These were followed by the more prosaic concerns about salary and opportunity for promotion, the ability to receive in-house training, and then traditional benefits such as time off and flexible schedules.

Software development positions come in a great variety of sizes and conditions. There are programmers working alone, in small teams of three or four, in larger teams of eight to ten, or on huge development teams, with dozens of developers, managers, team leaders, and even vice presidents.

Software development has so permeated our society that you can find just about any working conditions to meet your style, needs, and priorities. In general, the cushy jobs in large, well-financed companies pay moderately well but offer little chance to strike it rich. The folks who are working 70-hour weeks, sleeping on futons on their cubicle floor, and coding in large warehouses with little in the way of perks besides a constant flow of caffeinated beverages are the programmers who are betting that their stock options will one day be worth millions. It is a classic risk/benefit tradeoff, and you can pick your level of risk to match your personality and long-term aspirations.

Be Ready to Move Around

Unlike traditional careers, software professionals move around a great deal, from job to job and from company to company. A *Software Development Magazine* survey found that the majority of respondents worked for their current employer for fewer than five years, and fully 20% had been at their current job for less than a year.

It is not uncommon for a software engineer to change jobs every two years; and, frankly, some employers are skeptical of any engineer who has been in a single job for most of his or her career. The reasoning goes something like this: "The best people are in enough demand to be attracted from one job to another. Why was this person stuck at one place for so long?"

It is also a truism in the industry that it is far easier to increase your salary by changing jobs than it is to do so through routine promotions and raises.

Be Ready to Work Hard

All this money doesn't come easily; over 80% of the industry reports working more than 40 hours per week, with nearly 20% working more than 50. In short, 10-hour days are expected, and some weekend work usually comes with the job.

This is an intense, deadline-driven, highly competitive industry. If you have a family with whom you like to spend a lot of time or if weekends are precious and getting home early is a priority, you will probably find far more limited opportunity than if you are driven, hard-working, and willing to sacrifice. That said, almost 20% of the industry reports working fewer than 40 hours per week, so it can be done, albeit perhaps at a lower salary.

Vacations can make up for some lost time, and over half of the engineers participating in the *Software Development Magazine* survey said they receive three to four weeks of paid vacation a year. However, being eligible and taking it are two different things, and nearly 10% reported that they will take none of their vacation time at all this year due to deadline pressures.

What Will You Work On?

Experts estimate that about half of all developers are working on either client/server or Internet/intranet software, and this part of the industry is one of the fastest growing. Most of the rest of the industry works on database-management software, or manufacturing, network, communications, or systems software.

For some developers, the specific project is the most important determinant of job satisfaction. Some demand to work on interesting projects; others want projects that stretch their skills. Some developers want to work on projects that will better society; others want to work on projects that are in a field they care about. Many other programmers, however, don't care what they're working on as long as it is lucrative.

Whatever their interests, it is imperative that developers have a strong work ethic and sense of responsibility for their software. The industry suffers terribly from technological drive-by shootings in which a hotshot prima donna programmer whips together a quick-and-dirty solution to a problem, and then moves on to greener pastures, leaving behind a miserable maintenance nightmare. I'll talk in the programming section about writing good, solid, maintainable code, but it starts with a commitment to be responsible for your own work product.

Jobs, Euphemisms, and Fancy Titles

So, what exactly do computer programmers do? What is the difference between a programmer, a software engineer, a software analyst, and a systems analyst? Who makes the most money and what training and experience do they need?

The very first thing you need to know about this industry is that there is absolutely no standard for job titles. Some companies distinguish between programmer, analyst, architect, designer, and so forth. Others call all these people software engineers.

The second thing you need to know is this: Lighten up. Folks tend to get very worked up about their titles, but how important is it? I suppose it can matter a bit when you are looking for your next job, but my personal priority begins with how interesting the work is, goes on to consider how much money they'll pay me, and only toward the bottom of my list comes the question of my title. If they give me really interesting work, and they pay me boatloads of money, they can call me a junior apprentice programmer and I'll be quite happy. Of course, some companies try the other trick—like something out of a Dilbert cartoon, they try to fob off a fancy title in lieu of other compensation. I suppose there is some solace in being Chief Director of Information Technology, but I find that some satisfaction is lost when all you can afford is to take the bus to work.

It's in the Cards

In Japan, exchanging business cards is an important ritual among some business people. Interestingly, the higher the rank a person holds, the simpler the title associated with that position. The Emperor's card just has one word: his name.

Non-title Titles

In 1992, I went to work for a startup organization within a large publisher's electronic delivery group. We were tired of the false competition in job titles and set out with idealistic zeal to eschew these distractions. Everyone, from top to bottom, would have the title "member of the development team." Well, everyone, that is, except the Vice Presidents of Development and the Chief Technology Officer. And, oh yes, the Directors of each team. And, if we want to attract great people, we'll have to designate some members as "senior member of the development team" (after all, all animals are equal but some are more equal than others).

It didn't take long before we threw out our idealism and created a cornucopia of titles. We were awash in job descriptions; at one ecstatic moment, we each had our own individual title. For a while, mine was "iconoclast." Finally, when we were sold to AT&T, they found that iconoclast didn't map well to their internal "job levels," and I was awarded the coveted title of Distinguished Software Engineer. A few months later, I was an *Extinguished* Software Engineer, but that is another story.

What Do Systems Analysts Analyze?

The Free On-line Dictionary of Computing (http://www.instantweb.com/foldoc/) defines Systems Analysis as the "study of the design, specification, feasibility, cost, and implementation of a computer system for business."

A systems analyst, one assumes, performs systems analysis. In truth, this term is left over from the old days of big-iron computing (that is—mainframes) and today serves only to suggest a senior programmer who can look beyond the "code," to consider the design of the system as a whole.

Mainframes, Minis, and Micros

Back in the ancient mists of the history of computers (about 30 years ago), computers were huge, room-filling beasts that required air-conditioned environments, were touched only by white-coated highly trained technicians and were programmed only by a small number of mathematicians. In the early 1970s, however, a few companies, notably Data General and Digital Equipment, came out with smaller, refrigerator-sized computers which could be programmed by anyone with sufficient curiosity. These "minicomputers" were revolutionary. Later, in the early '80s a couple of kids built the first Apple Computers in their garage, and the rest, as they say, is history.

Today, microcomputers are networked together, and some have grown as large as refrigerators! Even the smallest sub-notebook, however, has more power than a room-filling IBM 360 did back in 1972.

What Does Architecture Have to Do with Software?

The overall design of a program is called its *architecture*. The person responsible for understanding and creating the architecture of a system is called (appropriately) the *system architect*. Typically, this is a title reserved for very senior programmers who bring at least a decade of experience to their craft, and who are working on the development of a large system. There is, typically, only one architect on any project, and the architect is responsible for the entire project from a technical standpoint.

Geek Speak

Source Code

Source code is the set of instructions, created by a programmer, that teach a computer how to do its work.

Is Software Engineer a Contradiction in Terms?

When I was young and microcomputers were new, companies I worked for never hired programmers who had degrees in computer science, because they were all trained for mainframes and we were microcomputer hackers. These days, even the most hidebound universities are teaching Computer Science students in C++ and Java, and it is no longer a black mark to have a masters in computer science from MIT.

These hotshots are trained in a strict engineering discipline, and they think of themselves as *software engineers*. I can't quite bring myself to use that term. Engineers build bridges and power plants. We're just writing code. But, I'm showing my age.

Engineering Ladders of Success

Many companies establish a management ladder that programmers are invited to climb. Each rung on the ladder represents recognition of greater experience and skill. An example of such a ladder might include

- ➤ Apprentice Software Engineer
- ➤ Software Engineer
- ➤ Senior Software Engineer
- ➤ Master Software Engineer
- ➤ Software Scientist
- ➤ Senior Software Scientist
- ➤ Software Architect
- ➤ Distinguished Software Engineer

Note that there is a somewhat desperate attempt to differentiate titles and to recognize seniority of experience or expertise. Also, "Architect" is used here as a title rather

9

than a job description; this is a significant failing in many technical ladders. Other problems include the fact that no one can remember which title is "better" than the others, and finally that "title creep" dictates that each year you'll see more of the senior titles and fewer of the junior titles awarded.

Remember, in most companies, titles ratchet their way up—no one is ever kicked down a level. To make headroom for advancement, companies are called on to create ever more impressive titles for their programmers to grow into.

Also note that none of these terms suggest any level of management. It is not uncommon for engineers to undertake some level of managerial responsibility as they climb the ladder of achievement; however, many firms attempt to keep these two ladders (technical and management) separate. Thus, a managerial ladder might include

➤ Member of team
➤ Team leader
➤ Manager
➤ Director
➤ Vice President
➤ Chief Technology Officer

Others on the Team

Programmers, whatever their title, don't work in a vacuum. Once on a development team, you'll work with user interface designers, marketing specialists, managers, quality-assurance engineers, and others. This section briefly describes these jobs.

UI designers are responsible for creating the look and feel of software. I've never met a programmer who didn't think he could do this just fine by himself. I've never met one who actually can. The user interface was a much-neglected aspect of programming until recently, but as an industry, we've learned that the UI can make the difference between usable software and software that no one will want or buy.

Marketing is the subject of endless Dilbert jokes. These are the guys who promise their customers delivery of software you've not yet even designed. The only thing worse than having marketing on your team is not having them. Programmers, left to themselves, write wicked-cool technology-driven products in search of a problem to solve. Marketing ensures that when you are done, someone might actually want what you've created.

Quality Assurance is the art of testing your software sufficiently to ensure that the bugs, which inevitably hide in your program, are found before you ship the code to your customers, not afterward. Teaching the skills of quality assurance is a book in itself. Once again, programmers think they can do this themselves, and once again they are wrong. No one tests his own code as well as an expert can; the value of QA cannot be overstated.

Managers are a different question altogether. A great manager is invisible. Without the programmer being aware, the manager is clearing the path in front of him; ensuring that the programmer has the specifications, tools, and environment he needs to be as productive as possible.

Is It Too Late for Me?

When I learned to program, back in the early '70s, there was much less to learn. We worked on punch cards, programming in Fortran—a simple-symbol based language for creating scientific formulas (FORTRAN stood for FORmula TRANslation) or we punched holes in tape to make a desktop computer spit out the Fibonacci series (1,1,2,3,5,8,13,21...).

By the 1980s, microcomputers were new, and we had control over the entire machine but operating systems were much simpler and it took only a few months to reach a reasonable level of proficiency in programming languages such as Basic and C.

Today, operating systems are far more complex, and user expectations are far higher. The days of obscure commands entered at the command line are relegated to a distant and little-lamented past. Microsoft Windows and the Internet have raised our expectations of how software should behave, and along the way they've made the job of professional programmers far more difficult, and far more rewarding.

That said, it is not too late. While it will take you a few years to learn everything you might need to know, it will take you only a few months to learn enough to get started. The trick is learning the right set of skills and then leveraging these skills to get a job and learn more.

Geek Speak

Bugs, Mr. Rico! Millions of them!

Bugs—In the 1940s, engineers working on the Mark I military computer were confounded by an unexpected error in calculation. They took the machine apart and found a moth stuck between the points of an electromechanical relay. Since that time, any failure in the working of a program is known as a *bug*.

Geek Speak

The Fibonacci Series Is Not on TV

The Fibonacci series is a common assignment to computer science students. The first two numbers are 1; all subsequent numbers are the sum of the two before it in the list. Thus, 8 is the sum of 5 and 3, 13 the sum of 8 and 5, and so forth. We'll see more about this in Chapter 8.

I'm Not Good at Math

In the early days of computer science, proficiency in mathematics was a requirement. While a logical mind is helpful in every aspect of life, and perhaps especially so among programmers, skill in math is almost irrelevant today. What is needed is the ability to think clearly and rationally. Given that, everything else is just technique.

There is no magic to programming, although judgment is required. The single most important attribute is the willingness to stay with it and struggle through the intellectual challenges you'll face until you not only master the skills, but develop a deep intuitive sense of how programs "hang together" and accomplish their aims. This takes experience and perseverance more than native talent.

When I set out to hire programmers, I look for intellectual spark far more than a specific set of skills. I'm interested in curiosity, intellect, insight and, perhaps most easily overlooked, a sense of business priorities. I'm looking for people who are sensitive to and interested in the needs and requirements of the end user, and I'm looking for passion; that unswerving and unrelenting commitment to building a great product and getting it out the door.

Dropout Rate

I've worked with a number of friends and acquaintances who wanted to learn C++ (a powerful programming language), and here is what I've learned: The race goes not to the swiftest but to the most dedicated.

I have done no scientific study, but my sense is that only a small percentage of the hundreds of thousands of people who set out to learn to program each year actually finish their first course of study. My guess is that the vast majority drop out and give up before they finish half of their first book.

This is not because they can't do it, or that it is intrinsically too difficult. My theory is that life intrudes. Few who come to programming after college have the luxury to work at it full time; typically, they must continue to support themselves in their real job. They learn programming "on the side," and that means that every hour spent with a book and a compiler is an hour not spent with family, relaxing, or working on something else.

I estimate that a bright person can start from scratch and learn enough C++ to get a first job in about 300 hours. That means 12 hours a week for six months. If you are working full time, this means spending all day Saturday and half of Sunday, or a couple hours every night for six months. Either way, it is a tremendous commitment. (For those of you who bought my book *Sams Teach Yourself C++ in 24 Hours*, let me explain. That is 24 hours of lessons and 276 hours of practice, working through exercises, and writing your own programs!)

At the end of that 300 hours, you'll know enough to get a first job as a junior programmer. Six months of full-time work is usually required to achieve reasonable proficiency. Add another six months if you want to learn to program Windows (using, for example the Microsoft Foundation Classes) and perhaps another year to achieve expertise in an advanced field such as database programming or COM (all of which is introduced later in this book).

Going Beyond Skills

In addition to learning the necessary programming skills, languages and techniques, it is imperative that you take the time to learn about analysis and design. It is one thing to hack together a quick-and-dirty program for your own purposes, but if you are working on commercial software, then it is very important you understand what makes for good robust and reliable software. I will discuss these issues in detail in Chapter 9.

Don't Despair

About now I'm sure you're thinking of racing back to the store to see whether you can return this book and pick up that new Tom Clancy novel. Don't give up just yet. Getting started is the hardest part. Learning to program is possible; people with no prior experience do it every day.

I'll teach you everything you need to know to get started, and then it is just up to you. It does require a bit of discipline, but there are few fields that you can choose which are more rewarding or lucrative, or which are growing as quickly.

The Least You Need to Know

➤ There are tremendous opportunities in software.

➤ You don't have to be a mathematician to take advantage of them.

➤ The primary requirements for great programmers are to be bright, energetic, and perseverant.

Chapter 2

How Do I Learn?

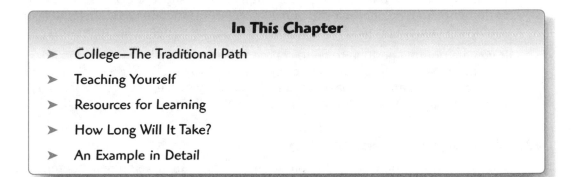

In This Chapter

➤ College—The Traditional Path

➤ Teaching Yourself

➤ Resources for Learning

➤ How Long Will It Take?

➤ An Example in Detail

By now you're convinced that programming offers a lucrative and interesting career, but how do you go about achieving the skills you need? Should you study in college? Set off on your own? Learn as you go? This chapter attempts to answer these questions and get you started on your career path.

College—The Traditional Path

In our culture, most advanced skills are learned in college. Programming has, until recently, been an interesting exception. While colleges have offered programming for the past 30 years, it has also been possible to bypass college, and many of the many successful programmers, including Bill Gates and me, either dropped out of college or never took a programming course there.

Computer Science

In the early days of computing, computer science courses were taught in the mathematics departments of technical universities. By the 1970s, however, computer science was considered a discipline in its own right.

In the 1980s, I shied away from hiring computer science majors, as I was developing for microcomputers, and the universities were teaching skills more appropriate to mainframe computers. By the late '80s, however, this dichotomy had turned around, and today computer science majors are well grounded not only in modern 32-bit microcomputer operating systems, but also in the finer points of object-oriented programming and software development.

One of the finest programmers I've ever hired came right out of a master's degree programming in computer science from MIT. What he lacked in practical work experience, he made up for in knowledge, interest, and the ability to work hard and solve problems.

If you are in a position to learn to program in a university, there are great advantages to doing so. You are offered a structured system of instruction, and what you learn about programming is placed in the context of a larger intellectual framework.

If you are not in a position to go to college to learn this skill, however, don't despair. It is still possible to teach yourself to program, and to get a very good job by doing so. More important, after you have just a few years' experience, your educational background becomes far less relevant to prospective employers.

Do You Want a Doctorate?

This book focuses on careers in applications and software development. Commercial programming is only part of the industry; another major part not discussed here is academic programming. Great work on computer science is being done at our universities, but that is outside the scope of this book.

Similarly, many thousands of programmers are hard at work developing artificial intelligence systems and expert systems, and this, too, is outside the scope of this book. It isn't that this work is unimportant, but rather it is distinct from the kinds of applications development most available in the computer job market. Further, and honestly, it is beyond my own expertise: AI, expert systems, and the related technologies are academic disciplines that exist in their own relatively independent world.

If you are interested in academic computing, or want to do research, or are interested in AI, then a doctorate in computer science may well be required. If you want to develop software for commercial applications, however, not only is a doctorate not necessary, it may also be detrimental to your career.

There are two reasons for this possibility. First, pursuit of a doctorate is time-consuming, and therefore delays acquiring the real-world experience needed for your next job. More important, however, is this: Many project leaders are reluctant to hire programmers who have doctorates for fear that they will take an academic, rather than a real-world, approach to programming.

The concern is that highly academic programmers do everything right in theory, but have little experience or knowledge about shipping product and making money while you do so. This is not an entirely fair or reasonable position; like any prejudice, it misses the mark by treating all programmers with doctorates as members of a group rather than as individuals. That said, the training you receive on the way to a doctorate might well be at odds with the kinds of real-world decisions you need to make in commercial software development.

Teaching Yourself

There was a time you could "read the law" and become a lawyer, apprentice with a doctor and practice medicine, or teach yourself to fly. Today, all these fields are closed to those without certificates of training; but programming is not.

When I became serious about programming as a career, in 1984, it was not hard to learn all you needed to know about microcomputer programming. One good book on Assembler, another on UNIX shell programming, and a good book on C (such as *C Primer Plus*) and I was off and running.

In the years since, the advent of new technology was fast and furious, but by choosing carefully, it wasn't all that hard to stay current—windowing, C++, class libraries, databases, each skill learned when needed.

The truth is that today it is a bit more difficult because in the past 10 years or so, microcomputer programming has become more complex. To sell yourself as a serious software engineer, you certainly need to know either C++, Java, or Visual Basic and to have at least a fundamental understanding of a windowing library—either Swing, if you are a Java programmer, or MFC or another platform-specific library if you are a C++ programmer.

Visual Basic programmers have an easier language, but they must master many advanced programming tools with mysterious acronyms such as ADO, MTS, MSMQ, ASP, and so forth. VB isn't for wimps anymore; it is a serious professional programming environment. Unfortunately, VB jobs usually pay a bit less than C++ or Java jobs.

Internet technology is coming even faster than that, and with Microsoft spending (literally) billions of dollars a year in research and development, the pace of change is only increasing.

That said, educating yourself can still be done; there is no reason you can't teach yourself all you need to know.

A Course of Study

If you are going to teach yourself, I propose you set up a course of study. I'll consider five such courses in this chapter. Appendix B provides a suggested reading list of some of the books I've found most helpful. Amazon, Barnes & Noble, and other sources provide recommendations and reader reviews and can be good sources for finding the newest and best books on a topic.

Course 1: C++ Applications Programmer

1. Start with a primer on C++. Learn the fundamental skills; focus on writing clean code.

2. Go on to advanced topics in C++ (such as *C++ Unleashed* and *Effective C++*), focusing on using the language well. Consider topics such as templates, exceptions, the standard libraries, and memory management.

3. Study object-oriented analysis and design; focus on using C++ as an implementation tool for object-oriented designs.

4. Learn a good windowing library such as MFC. Achieve expertise in window-based applications.

5. Learn about COM and DCOM and build client/server-distributed applications.

6. Begin Internet applications programming; build COM modules for use in ASP pages.

7. Learn ActiveX Template Library (ATL) and build ATL objects for use in Internet applications.

8. Extend your skills into Java.

9. Extend your skills into ASP.

10. Consider writing front-end applications in VB with back-end applications in C++.

Course 2: Java Applications Programmer

1. Start with a primer on Java. Learn the fundamental skills; focus on writing clean code.

2. Go on to advanced topics including SWING and related windowing techniques.

3. Study object-oriented analysis and design; focus on using Java as an implementation tool for object-oriented designs.

4. Build Java applications and Java applets. Learn the limits of the language and explore client/server considerations.

5. Learn about COM and DCOM, CORBA, and Java Beans. Build client/server-distributed applications.

6. Extend your skills into C++. Learn the fundamentals and then advanced topics. Consider differences in memory management, templates, and operator overloading.

Course 3: Visual Basic Applications Programmer

1. Start with a primer on Visual Basic. Write Windows applications and concentrate on writing clean code that is easily understood and maintained.

2. Study advanced topics in VB. Learn about COM and DCOM and write COM-based applications in VB.

3. Learn ADO and related object-oriented COM-based technology including MTS and MSMQ.

4. Study object-oriented analysis and design; focus on using VB as an implementation tool for object-oriented designs. Consider using VB as a Rapid Applications Development and Prototyping language.

5. Learn VBScript and extend your skills into Web-based scripting.

6. Learn ASP and build Web-based applications, especially Web Classes.

7. Extend your skills into Java or C++ programming.

Course 4: Web Programmer

1. Learn HTML and build Web pages.

2. Learn ASP fundamentals and DHTML and build interactive Web pages.

3. Learn to program in ASP and consider learning another scripting language, such as Python.

4. Extend your skills into VBScript or JavaScript.

5. Extend your skills into Java programming.

6. Study object-oriented analysis and design. Consider applying formal analysis to Web applications development.

7. Build Java applications and Java applets. Learn the limits of the language and explore client/server considerations.

8. Learn about COM and DCOM, CORBA and Java Beans. Build client/server-distributed applications.

Course 5: Database Programmer

1. Learn to use a relational database; read about database fundamentals.

2. Learn SQL syntax and write SQL statements and stored procedures.

3. Read about database theory and database normalization.

4. Learn about transactions and transaction management. Study about the ACID (Atomic, Consistent, Isolated, and Durable) test for databases.

5. Extend your skills into ASP and build front-end Web applications using scripts.

6. Extend your skills into C++ or Java to write front-end applications for databases.

7. Learn about object databases and understand the differences from relational databases.

Tailoring Your Course of Study

The details of the courses offered in these lists may not be precisely right for you; you must tailor these courses to your skills and interests. To do this well, you need advice from experts you trust. Join a user's group or a newsgroup on the Internet and ask for recommendations. As you progress in your studies, don't be afraid to change course as you learn more.

Resources for Learning

Here's the good news—the information is out there for the taking. There are books, magazines, Internet newsgroups, Web sites, white papers, online universities, and a host of other resources.

Books: Getting Started with a Primer

There are literally hundreds of books from which you can learn to program. Finding the right one, of course, is the tricky part. Here are some guidelines to consider when deciding on your first *programming* primer.

Do you like the tone and approach?   Read a few pages from the first chapter. Ideally, spend some time with the book. Do you enjoy reading this book? Is the author making it interesting and accessible? If the book makes you feel stupid and inadequate, put it back on the shelf and try another. (If the problem is just the title, figure it is the Marketing Department's fault, and keep reading!)

For this test to work, you must start at the beginning of the book. No matter how gifted the author, if you start reading in the middle of the book, you'll be lost. Try a few pages from the first chapter, and then a few from the second. Now, you can split the book open and read a page from the middle of the book.

Are there enough examples?   The key word here is enough examples. I like a lot of examples. If you teach me something, I like to see it in action. For me, one example is worth a thousand words. Other people hate lots of little examples, and feel that they bloat out the book. The point is to see whether this book matches your needs. That said, when in doubt, get a book with lots of examples; you can always skip over them.

Are they explained in detail?   If the book does have examples, are they explained in sufficient detail? There is little point in providing an example if you don't explain what is happening in that example.

Are the code lines numbered?   If the lines are not numbered, how does the author tell you what is happening in the code? Can you find the code he's explaining? Line numbers (or callouts) are a wonderful thing in a programming book.

Are there exercises at the end of the chapter?   This question is just like the one on examples. Many people like to test their skills as they go; others find them annoying and wasteful of space. If you like exercises, be sure this book has enough of them.

Does the book supply the answers to the exercises?   If the book does have exercises, does it also give you the answers?

What do they assume you already know?   Many books assume you are already a programmer. Does this book start where *you* are, or does it assume you know things you've not yet learned?

Is it comprehensive?   This is tough to figure out if you are a new programmer, but try to get a sense of what topics are covered and what topics are skipped. You may find it useful to compare the table of contents among a few different primers to see whether the book you're interested in teaches most of the same topics as the others.

Can you find the author?   If you have questions or issues, can you find the author? Does he provide an email address? What support can you expect from the author; does he have a Web site? (My email address is `jliberty@libertyassoci-ates.com`, and I do have a Web site on which I fully support all my books: `http://www.libertyassociates.com`).

Magazines

There is a huge publishing industry dedicated to special-interest magazines. There are magazines dedicated to programming in C++, Java, Visual Basic, Web programming, object-oriented programming, database programming, programming the Macintosh, programming for Windows, programming COM, programming CORBA, and so forth.

Taking a look at these magazines can be an inexpensive investment. Jump in your car and drive to the nearest bookstore with a large computer section and peruse their selection of special-interest computer magazines.

Internet Newsgroups

If you have an Internet service provider that supplies email and other Internet services for you, ask them whether they can set you up to read newsgroups. Newsgroups are unstructured discussion groups on specific topics. Take a look at `comp.lang.` Under this designation, my ISP provides

```
comp.lang.ada, comp.lang.api comp.lang.asm.x86, comp.lang.asm370,
comp.lang.awk, comp.lang.basic.misc, comp.lang.basic.powerbasic,
comp.lang.basic.realbasic, comp.lang.basic.visual.34d party,
comp.lang.basic.visual.announce, comp.lang.basic.visual.database,
comp.lang.basic.misc, comp.lang.beta, comp.lang.c comp.lang.c.moderated,
comp.lang.c++, comp.lang.c++.leda, comp.lang.c++.moderated, comp.lang.clarion,
comp.lang.clarion, comp.lang.clipper, comp.lang.clibber.visual-objects,
```

```
comp.lang.clos, comp.lang.clu, comp.lang.cobol, comp.lang.crass,
comp.lang.dylan, comp.lang.eiffel, comp.lang.forth, comp.lang.forth.mac,
comp.lang.fortran, comp.lang.functional, comp.lang.hermes, comp.lang.icon,
comp.lang.idl, comp.lang.idl-pvwave, comp.lang.java.advocacy,
comp.lang.announce, comp.lang.java.beans, comp.lang.java.corba,
comp.lang.database, comp.lang.gui, comp.lang.help, comp.lang.java.machine,
comp.lang.java.programmer, comp.lang.java.security, comp.lang.java.
➥softwaretools, comp.lang.javascript, comp.lang.labview, comp.lang.limbo,
comp.lang.lisp, comp.lang.lisp.franz, comp.lang.lisp.franz,
comp.lang.lisp.mcl, comp.lang.lgo, comp.lang.misc, comp.lang.modula2,
comp.lang.modula3, comp.lang.mumps, comp.lang.oberon, comp.lang.objective-c,
comp.lang.pascal.ansi-c, comp.lang.pascal.ansi-iso, comp.lang.pascal.borland,
comp.lang.pascal.delphi.advocacy, comp.lang.pascal.delphi.announce,
comp.lang.pascal.delphi.components.misc, comp.lang.pascal.misc,
comp.lang.perl.misc, comp.lang.perl.moderated, comp.lang.perl.modules,
comp.lang.perl.tk, comp.lang.pl1, comp.lang.pop, comp.lang.postscript,
comp.lang.prograph, comp.lang.prolog, comp.lang.python,
comp.lang.python.announce, comp.lang.rexx, comp.lang.rexx, comp.lang.sather,
comp.lang.scheme, comp.lang.scheme.c, comp.lang.scheme.scsh, comp.lang.
➥sigplan, comp.lang.smalltalk, comp.lang.tcl, comp.lang.tcl.announce,
comp.lang.vhdl, comp.lang.visual, comp.lang.vrml
```

Web Sites

In addition to the newsgroups, there is a wealth of Web sites on programming and programming-related issues. Here is an example of a single Web site that offers more than 14,000 links on programming.

The Cetus Links Web site (http://www.cetus-links.org) provides links to thousands of articles on computer programming topics.

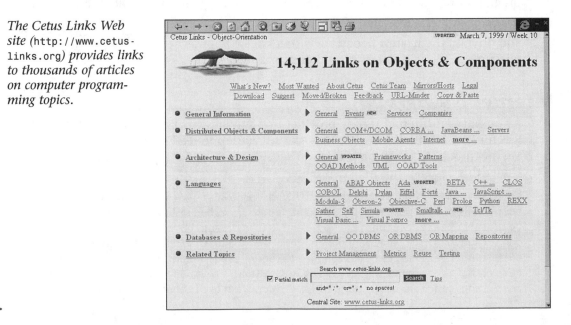

Online Universities

One of the more powerful resources to spring up on the World Wide Web is online universities. I'm affiliated with Ziff-Davis University, which I'm proud to say was inspired by an online course I taught back in 1993. ZDU now offers over 100 instructor-led courses on a variety of subjects, including Java, C++, Visual Basic, object-oriented analysis and design, Web programming, Web design, Perl, and so forth.

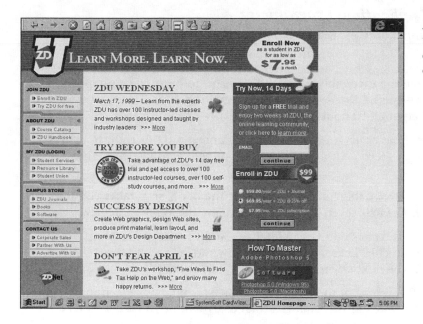

Ziff-Davis University provides Web-based courses on programming and other computer topics.

In addition, many accredited colleges now offer courses entirely over the Internet, and there are literally thousands of Web sites dedicated to providing online instruction of programming topics.

How Long Will It Take?

This, of course, is the $64,000 question: How long before you can go look for a job? The answer, you won't be surprised to learn, is that it depends on many factors.

How quickly can you learn technical material? Some folks read through a primer on a computer language and it all makes sense to them; they absorb it like a sponge. Others find that every bit of it is a struggle. My personal approach is always to read two books on the same technical material, from two different authors, and then to triangulate the information.

Let's work our way through one course of study, assigning particular books and guesstimating the time it would take.

An Example in Detail

You have decided, wisely, that C++ is the most promising starting point for a lucrative job in programming. Your goal is to keep working while you learn, and then to try to get a starting job, perhaps as an apprentice, working on C++; eventually planning to extend your skills as suggested previously.

Course 1: C++ Applications Programmer

1. Start with a primer on C++. Learn the fundamental skills; focus on writing clean code.

Once again, you make the incredibly insightful decision to begin with my primer *Sams Teach Yourself C++ in 21 Days*—but you know that these are 21 virtual days, each consisting of about eight to 10 hours of study.

You set aside two or three hours every evening, plus another six or eight hours on weekends, for a total of 16 to 20 hours per week. Your goal is to get through two chapters a week.

This schedule is quite reasonable for the first half of the book, so it takes you four weeks to get through the first seven chapters and review the Week in Review.

The next set of chapters covers pointers, references, and advanced functions, and is generally a bit more difficult. Let's say your pace slows down and it takes you six weeks to get through the next seven chapters and Week in Review.

Now you are in the final third of the book and you're studying advanced material. Allot another eight weeks to finish. That is a total of 8+6+4, or 18 weeks, to read through this book and cover the fundamentals.

If you are like me, you'll quickly read through another primer, probably from another author. That might take you an additional week or two; let's call that 20 weeks altogether.

You're not quite ready for your first job, so let's assume you continue your course of study a bit longer.

2. Go on to advanced topics in C++ (such as *C++ Unleashed* and *Effective C++*) focusing on using the language well. Consider topics such as templates, exceptions, the standard libraries, and memory management.

To achieve this goal, you read through *Effective C++* by Scott Meyers. Let's allow you four more weeks to work through this book and then it is on to *C++ Unleashed* (also my book, coincidentally).

C++ Unleashed covers many of the advanced topics you need in order to have credibility as a professional programmer, and we'll allow you one week per chapter, on average. Because you don't need every topic in this book, let's assume you'll spend about 12 weeks on these advanced topics.

At this point, you've spent 36 weeks and you know a good deal of C++. You may be ready to look for work, but you won't be very employable if you know nothing about Windows programming and object-oriented Analysis and design.

To be perfectly honest, it will take you between three and six months to get started in Windows applications and an additional six to 12 months to achieve expertise.

Now it is time to supplement what you've learned about object-oriented analysis and design in *C++ Unleashed* either by reading my book *Beginning Object-Oriented Analysis and Design* or by reading another book on the subject. Let's allow four to six weeks for this work before you can call yourself fully versed in the topic.

Summing It Up

So, are you stuck with a two-year course of study before you can apply for a job? Not necessarily. After 20 weeks, you knew the fundamentals of C++ and you might have looked for a job as an intern. After 36 weeks, you knew a great deal of C++ and were probably ready for a first job. At the end of a year, you knew the fundamentals of writing Windows applications in C++ and the MFC, and at the end of 18 months you were on your way to expertise.

Realistically, if you want to keep working while you study, you need to allow a full year before you'll have a marketable skill. But there is another way…

The apprentice system is not dead. If you can get a job in quality assurance or technical support on a project in C++, you may be able to supplement your self-study with working with programmers and studying their code, and then you may find that you can come up the learning curve much more quickly.

The Least You Need to Know

➤ Achieving the skills you need to become a successful programmer can be acquired through college, or by teaching yourself.

➤ If you're in a position to learn to program in a university, you're offered a structured system of instruction that places what you learn about programming into a larger intellectual framework.

➤ If you're not in a position to go to college to learn to program, you can teach yourself by setting up a course of study following the outline in this chapter.

➤ Resources are available and are there for the taking to assist you with learning to program.

Chapter 3

Getting Ready to Program

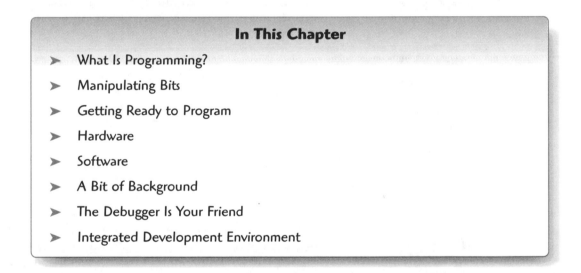

In This Chapter

- ➤ What Is Programming?
- ➤ Manipulating Bits
- ➤ Getting Ready to Program
- ➤ Hardware
- ➤ Software
- ➤ A Bit of Background
- ➤ The Debugger Is Your Friend
- ➤ Integrated Development Environment

All right, you're convinced there is high-paying work in programming, and that it is possible to learn it, but what, exactly is programming and what is it like to be a programmer?

There are some jobs for which we have an intuitive feel. We know (or at least we think we know) what it is teachers do because we started out as students. We think we know what it is like to be a lawyer, doctor, or police officer, because we've watched them work, if only on TV.

Programmers have had a tremendous impact on our society, but most folks have never seen a programmer work. It isn't really quite clear what it is they actually do.

This chapter describes the act of programming and tells you what tools you need to get started.

What Is Programming?

Programming is nothing more (and nothing less!) than writing out the series of steps the computer must perform to accomplish a specific task. These steps are written out using a special syntax called a programming "language," and the written steps themselves are called "source code" or "code."

Get with the Program

Programming—writing a series of instructions in a programming language.

The thing you need to know about computers is that, at bottom, they are really (really!) dumb. They don't know anything about letters, sentences, commands, numbers, buttons, windows, or the Internet. All computers know, at their deepest level, is electricity.

Picture two wires crossing. Either there is a lot of electricity at that junction, or there is very little. At some point, a computer considers the amount of electricity sufficient to call it "on"; otherwise, it is "off." These are the only possibilities: on or off.

Electricity can be on or off.

Binary, Take Two

Binary—a system with only two choices. Binary math consists of only 1s and 0s.

As humans, we can associate any other binary, or two-possibility, choice with on and off, such as "yes" or "no," or, more commonly, 1 or 0. (You may have noticed that some appliances such as coffeemakers have a 1 and 0 printed on their on-off switches.)

Imagine, now, two such junctions. We can now represent four "states" or conditions.

1. off, off
2. off, on
3. on, off
4. on, on

Or, we might write those as 0,0; 0,1; 1,0; 1,1. Two junctions, four possibilities.

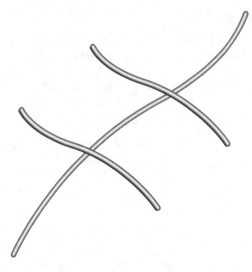

Two junctions increase the number of possibilities.

If we add a third junction, we double the possibilities to eight: 0,0,0; 0,0,1; 0,1,0; 0,1,1; 1,0,0; 1,0,1; 1,1,0; 1,1,1.

Each time a junction is added, it doubles the possibilities. Those of you old enough to have taken the "new math" in fifth grade (or young enough to have had a computer in fifth grade) know each of these 1s and 0s are called *binary digits*.

Binary is a numbering system that uses nothing but 1s and zeros. A **bi**nary digi**t** (or *bit*) is one of these ones or zeros. With eight binary digits, we can represent 256 possibilities. We call 8 binary digits a *byte*. (By the way, half a byte—4 bits—is called a *nybble*!)

With 2 bytes (or 16 bits) we can represent 65,536 different values, and with 4 bytes (or 32 bits) we can represent more than four billion different values!

Geek Speak

Byte Down on the Bit

Bit—a Binary Digit (1 or 0).

Byte—8 bits.

Now, four billion is a lot. If we spend, say, 128 values representing the letters of the alphabet (26 letters, plus 26 capitalized letters, plus punctuation and some other special characters), we still have just about four billion values left to work with!

With the ability to manipulate so many disparate values, quite a lot can be accomplished. Users can draw on the screen, create buttons, fill windows, create spreadsheets, launch the space shuttle, and control the exposure on your camera.

It's all just bits. Programmers do nothing but manipulate bits. But these days, most working programmers never notice.

Manipulating Bits

There was a time when programmers did notice. In the dark primitive days of computing (say, 20 years ago), programmers manipulated the bits directly. The first computer I ever programmed had lights on the front. Each light represented one bit. When the light was lit, the bit was set to 1. When the light was off, the bit was *cleared* to 0. I literally watched the bits set and clear (turn on and turn off) as I manipulated my program.

Geek Speak

blah blah
blah bla
h bl
b

In the Lingo

Programmers say that a bit is *set* when it is given the value 1 and *cleared* when given the value 0.

Those days are over. Thank goodness and Bill Gates. Today, programmers deal with much higher "abstractions" than bits and bytes. Now, programmers think about values, variables, windows, buttons, and text.

Programming has gotten easier, the tools have improved, more and more of the "grunt work" is done for you; and the result is that we can now build more complicated, more powerful software that is easier to use and easier to maintain. But I miss the lights.

Getting Ready to Program

This book does not teach you to program, but it does tell you what you need after you decide to learn. This book describes what hardware and software you need, and it explains all the tools and what they are for.

Hardware

It goes without saying, if you are going to make your living as a programmer, you need a computer. That said, what kind of computer you buy depends on what kind of programming you want to do.

You have quite a few choices, but the big three are Wintel, Macintosh, and UNIX.

Wintel

Don't try to look Wintel up on the stock market; it doesn't exist. Wintel is a word created from Windows and Intel and indicates a machine with an Intel microprocessor (for example, a Pentium) and a version of Microsoft Windows as the operating system.

There are a number of different Intel processors with a bewildering array of options and features, but they all share a common "instruction set."

An *instruction set* is the set of commands a particular microprocessor understands. A microprocessor is the heart of a computer; at the moment the most popular microprocessor is the Intel Pentium. Sharing a common instruction set means that software able to run on one can run on the other, and all Windows software runs on all Intel chips.

If you want to program for Windows, you need a computer with a chip from Intel or one that is 100% compatible. These are the boxes that used to be called "IBM compatible," and popular examples are made by Dell, Compaq, IBM, Gateway, Micron, and literally hundreds of others.

Macintosh

The Macintosh continues to be a wonderful, fascinating machine with a devoted following and the best commercials on Superbowl Sunday. Programming for the Mac and for Windows shares much in common, but they are not the same. Although you can learn to program on the Mac and then shift your skills over to Windows, the path is not direct and most programmers specialize in one or the other.

The Mac has a devoted following, many of whom *despise* Windows machines, but the simple market reality is that the Mac represents a very small percentage of the business computing world.

If you are looking to write *educational* software, for use by schools, the Mac might be a serious alternative. If the company you work for is heavily invested in Macs or you otherwise have a strong commitment to the Mac, then fine, it makes sense to put your efforts there. If not, and if you want to maximize your earnings potential, it makes no sense to lock yourself into a corner of the market.

Geek Speak

Wintel Is Not a Phone Company

Wintel—the combination of Windows and Intel. Used as shorthand for a Windows operating system running on a computer using an Intel microprocessor.

Cross-Platform Concerns

Windows has gone through a number of evolutions, and whereas programming for Windows 98 may be a bit different from programming for Windows NT or Windows 2000, the differences are minor and won't concern you until much later in your programming career.

UNIX

Not so long ago, UNIX was an obscure operating system relegated to use by geeks in universities. In the 1980s, there were the "operating-system wars" in which UNIX, the Mac, and Windows contended for the hearts and minds of business users, but by the early '90s the battle appeared to be over, and Microsoft had vanquished all opposition.

Along came the World Wide Web, however, and once again, everything changed. UNIX is the operating system of choice for many of the largest contenders for Web dominance, including Sun Microsystems. The advent of Linux, a free, easily installed and highly successful variant of UNIX, has again changed the equation, and WINE (WINdows Emulator) is a Linux add-on which will, in theory, enable you to run any program written for Windows on Linux.

How to Pronounce It

Linux—The first syllable is pronounced like Lynn. The second syllable rhymes with sticks.

The wheel is still in spin, and UNIX is certainly a contender, but for now the dominance of Windows seems overwhelming.

Which Operating System Is for You?

If you have no particular reason to choose one operating system over another, I strongly recommend you focus your energies on Microsoft development platforms, while keeping a keen eye on the alternatives.

Which Computer to Buy?

Now it has been determined you will be writing for Windows, the question becomes, which computer do you buy? I dare not recommend any specifics because by the time this book hits the shelves everything is obsolete. Instead, the following sections offer some guidelines.

Bigger, Faster, Better

Programming is one of the most demanding activities for a computer. No matter how fast your computer is, you want it to be faster. No matter how big your monitor is, you want it to be bigger. No matter how much room you have on your hard drive, you fill it up.

Just to give you an idea, my personal programming environment, consisting of all the programming languages, tools, and related files, fill over two gigabytes of hard disk. This would be even more, but I keep a lot of things off my drive and on CD.

Here are the factors to consider:

Memory.   You want a lot. The more memory you have the faster your computer can compile your programs, and waiting for your compiler is the bane of programming. I recommend at least 128MB; 256MB is better. The more the merrier.

Hard Drive.   This is less of an issue; it is hard to buy a computer today with less than a couple gigabytes of storage. I recommend you invest in a big, fast disk. Fast is more important than big, as long as you have a few gigabytes to play with.

Monitor.   Programmers tend to have a lot of windows open on their machine at one time. I'm a big believer in 21-inch displays, but they are expensive. 17 inches is fine, but smaller than that can feel cramped. Get a good monitor, one with no flicker at all, noninterlaced.

Internet Access.   You don't work in a vacuum, you need information from your compiler vendor and you need to exchange ideas with other programmers. The Internet is a magnificent resource. The faster your connection, the better. Developing for the Internet is discussed in greater detail in Chapter 5, "Internet Programming."

You can get started with a computer that costs no more than $1,000. If that is more than you expected, then start smaller. After all, you may want to see whether programming is going to work out before you invest too much.

If this becomes your career, you want to move up to the biggest, baddest, fastest, most powerful computer you can get your hands on. It doesn't matter, though; in 12 months whatever you buy will be a sorry, obsolete has-been. That is the nature of the business.

Software

What software you need is decided by what programming language you decide upon, which is discussed in Chapter 4, "Programming Languages."

For now, it is important to be familiar with the various *kinds* of tools used by programmers.

Editor

If a carpenter's most important tool is a hammer, then a programmer's most important tool is an editor. An editor is to programming what a word processor is to writing, but they are not the same.

33

Geek Speak

Letter to the Editor

Editor—a program for writing source code and saving it to a file.

A word processor is great at formatting text and laying it out for print or publication. An editor is great at creating, manipulating, and saving code in plain text ready for use as a program.

Modern programming editors know quite a bit about the language in which you are programming, and can be of assistance in organizing your code.

You can see a modern editor as follows. Ignore the details of the code; it is obscure C++ taken from my book *C++ from Scratch*. The point here is less what is written than the assistance I receive from the editor itself.

An editor is a tool for writing program code.

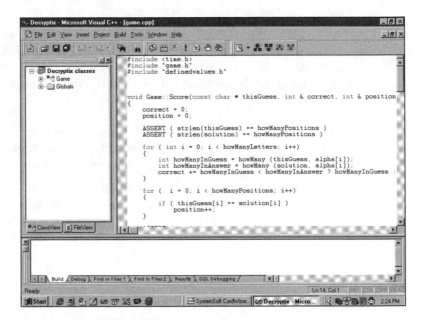

Unfortunately, this illustration is in black and white. On a color monitor, however, all of the *keywords* (that is, words that are special to the programming language) appear in blue. Comments (words written to the programmer and not part of the program itself) are in light gray. Numbers, printable strings, and so forth, can each have their own color.

In addition, modern editors can even help you program! The Visual Studio editor from Microsoft prompts you when writing code. While writing, it suggests the syntax needed at any given point, and also reminds you of the details of how to accomplish the current task.

It is possible to program with any text editor. Many programmers use Notepad or even a simple word processor. Modern programming editors, however, can make life a lot easier.

A Bit of Background

Computers, as stated previously, understand only binary digits. The instructions that computers respond to are actually a series of 1s and 0s, such as

1110001101001100011110000000001111001010001100110011001010100101010100001
➥1010001100101010101011001101010001100101010...

and so forth. These 1s and 0s are known as *machine language*. This is not exactly easy to read or work with for humans, although computers eat them up like popcorn. No one actually programs in machine language.

Assembler is a human-usable language that is *isomorphic* to machine language. Isomorphic means that it is one to one—that is, for every machine language command there is an Assembler command and vice versa.

In short, Assembler is a human equivalent of machine language. For example, rather than entering 10010001 11001101, you might enter the command MOV.

The details of what Assembler does are unimportant; what is important is that computers can interpret Assembler instructions very quickly. Assembler was the language of choice for many years because it was so efficient. When programmers say efficient, they mean two things: fast and small.

Efficient programs run quickly and take little memory. When memory was expensive and computers were slow, efficiency was very important and Assembler was king. Are you old enough to remember the original version of Lotus 1-2-3? It was written in Assembler. So were VisiCalc and Word Star.

Compilers and Linkers

Working with Assembler is very difficult, and it is hard to write and maintain large programs. Modern programming languages such as C++ attempt to maintain much of the efficiency of Assembler while providing an easier, more manageable language. Each C++ instruction might translate into a series of Assembler commands. This saves time and effort for the programmer, but at the cost of slightly slower and bigger programs.

C++ programs must ultimately be translated into Assembler and then fed to the computer in native machine language. The job of the *compiler* is to turn C++ into object code, which is on the way toward machine language.

C++ programs are often written with many different files of code working together. The job of the *linker* is to stitch these files together into a single program (to link together the links on the chain). A linker is fed the various object files created by the compiler and creates an executable program.

Compilers and Interpreters

Some languages don't work with compilers and linkers; they are interpreted by a program each time they are run. Microcomputer BASIC used to work like this.

Interpreted languages tend to be easier to program but they don't run as quickly; they are not as efficient. The code is slower and larger, and interpreted languages are not used very often for large, complex programs.

These days programmers don't talk much about interpreters, and instead distinguish between compiled languages (such as C++ and the more modern compiled Basic) on one hand and *scripted* languages on the other. Scripted languages, however, really are just interpreted languages.

Geek Speak

Compiling Facts

Compiler—a program that takes source code and turns it into a format closer to machine language.

Geek Speak

Two New Terms

Linker—a program that stitches together object files into a program.

Executable—a file that can be "run" as a program on your computer.

Get the Basics on BASIC

BASIC is the language on which Visual Basic is based. BASIC is an acronym that stands for **B**eginner's **A**ll-purpose **S**ymbolic **I**nstruction **C**ode.

BASIC was invented by John G. Kemeny and Thomas E. Kurtz at Dartmouth College in 1963. Many versions of BASIC have been popular over the years, including gwBasic, an early version of Microsoft Basic that stood for "Gee Whiz Basic."

In some ways, your Internet browser acts as an interpreter of HTML and JavaScript.

Java is a bit of a hybrid between compiled and interpreted languages. Rather than producing object code that can be run on your computer (as a compiler would), Java produces an intermediate format: p-code. The p-code is interpreted by the Java Virtual Machine on your computer (often built in to an Internet browser). P-code is faster than a script but slower than native machine language.

These details are not important except to understand that these differences determine which language will create programs that are faster, easier to use, or smaller.

The Debugger Is Your Friend

The most significant tool you'll need, after your editor (and possibly your compiler and linker), is a debugger. Debuggers help you find *bugs* or mistakes in your program.

With a good debugger, you can walk through your program one instruction at a time, watching the effect each instruction has on the values stored in your program. A good debugger can save hours, days, even weeks, of work hunting for obscure bugs.

Geek Speak

Bugs—You Just Want to Smash 'em

Bug—a programming error.

Integrated Development Environment

Okay, relax. There was a time when you had to search for an editor, a compiler, a linker and a debugger, each from different vendors. You then had to struggle to get them all to work together, but those days are over. Today you can just buy one single package: an integrated development environment, or IDE.

An IDE offers everything you need to get going, and a good bit more. A modern IDE has not only an editor, a compiler, and a linker—all of which work together smoothly—but also a number of other useful tools.

Visual Studio is Microsoft's Integrated Development Environment for C++, Java, Visual Basic, FoxPro, and Visual InterDev. That is, the same environment, look and feel is used for all these languages, although the specific tools vary as needed. You can buy each language package individually, so if you decide to learn C++, you can buy Visual C++ and you get the Visual Studio environment as part of that package.

The Visual Studio environment for Visual C++ is pictured as follows. There is a complete toolbar, an integrated editor, debugger, and compiler. The details of what is going on in this program are less important than the idea that many tools can be brought to bear at once, all working together with a common user interface.

The Visual Studio environment lets you develop C++ programs.

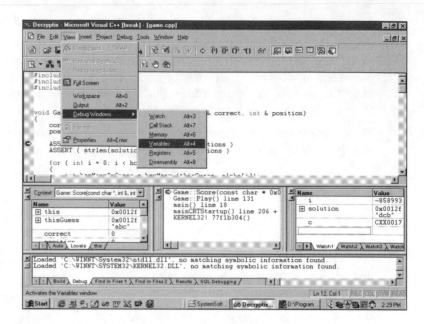

After you know what language you will be programming in, you can usually buy the tools quite inexpensively. There are free tools on the Internet, but I strongly recommend you resist the temptation to download them to your computer. These tools are typically not for the faint of heart; they are difficult to install and they typically are provided with little direct support. If you are going to learn to program, I advise you to buy the tools that are well supported by the vendor. You can buy a programming language in any large software store, and there are mail order sources dedicated to programming tools.

What Does All This Cost?

Depending on what language you choose, you should be able to buy all the software you need to develop in that language for around $100. Some books include free compilers or development environments. Typically, these are older versions of the development software; great for getting started but you'll want to upgrade to the latest and greatest pretty quickly if you are serious about this as a career choice.

The Least You Need to Know

➤ Programming is creating lists of instructions computers can understand and execute.

➤ Without a big investment (typically under $100), you can buy all the software you need; and if you are adventurous, you can even obtain it all for free on the Internet.

➤ Although there is a great deal to learn, there are many books available to help you, and hundreds of thousands of people have taught themselves to program with no formal instruction.

Part 2
Software Development

Is programming for you? What is the job of programmer really like? In this section, I'll intro-duce the fundamentals of programming. Although this is not a primer in any particular lan-guage, I will explore the key elements common to all modern programming languages, with a strong focus on those languages most in demand: C++, Java, and Internet scripting.

Programming Languages

Chapter 4

In This Chapter

➤ What Is a Programming Language?

➤ How Many Languages Should You Learn?

➤ Which Language?

➤ A Quick History of the Evolution of Programming Languages

➤ Working with Specific Languages

➤ How to Choose

If you ask my mother what I do for a living, she'll tell you I'm a programmer. To her, it is all one big thing: programming. To a programmer, however, that is like saying someone's a lawyer. Yes? What kind of law? Divorce lawyers have a very different job from defense attorneys.

Programmers tend to identify themselves, at least as a first approximation, by the kinds of programs they write. I write desktop and Internet applications. I have friends who write systems level software. Different jobs.

What Is a Programming Language?

As discussed in the previous chapter, a programming language is a specific set of words and syntax used to create programs—executable files that can be run on your computer. Word, Excel, and Internet Explorer are three examples of programs written by teams of programmers at Microsoft. Eudora, Netscape, and Lotus Notes are examples of programs written by other companies. It's getting harder and harder to come up with examples of well-known programs written by other companies, but that is a story for another book.

While several languages have been mentioned so far, such as Assembler, Visual Basic, and C++, this chapter covers a number of different languages, and reviews their advantages and disadvantages.

How Many Languages Should You Learn?

About 10 years ago, I had a discussion with a programmer who asserted that a good software engineer ought to know a half dozen languages. Programming languages were, in his opinion, like tools. You don't use a hammer to tighten a nut, and you don't use C++ to write a program best written in Pascal.

This is a logical argument, an excellent analogy, and in my mind it is at least somewhat misleading. I might argue that a better analogy is to spoken language.

Most people become fluent in only one language, and are stronger in that native language than in any other. There are exceptions to this rule, but if I want to say something quickly and with maximum expressiveness, I'm going to do a much better job in my native language than in any other. Yes, French may be more romantic, but if I tell my wife I love her in French I might inadvertently say that I want an egg salad sandwich.

If this is true, you might ask, why is it that I know how to program in C, C++, Pascal, Basic, HTML, SQL, Java, JScript, ASP, COBOL, Dibol, and half a dozen other obscure languages. It was an accident—honest.

In the course of a career in programming, you are often asked to take on projects that require, for one reason or another, learning a new language. Often this is because the new language is one to which the team has already committed. This has some benefit, however, because, just as in spoken languages, the lessons learned in one language can help you better to understand the syntax of another. Learning Portuguese is a lot easier if you already know Spanish, and learning Assembler will certainly help you understand C++.

In addition, times change and languages evolve. It is your job to keep current, just as a doctor must keep current with the latest techniques in medicine.

In 1992, I moved from C to C++ because C++ is better and my skills were in danger of becoming obsolete. In recent years, I've learned ASP, JScript, Java, and so forth, because each offered new career-growth opportunities.

After all, if you moved for business reasons to a country where they speak a different language, you might find yourself using that language more often than your native tongue.

Here's my advice: Recognize that in time you'll probably learn quite a few languages, but start with only one. John Paul Getty is reported to have said, "Do put all your eggs in one basket, but make sure you watch that basket." I suggest you start out by putting all your programming eggs in the basket of a single language. After you master that language, you can branch out to other languages, broadening your marketability. And take heart; the first language is the hardest, whichever you start with!

Which Language?

That advice, of course, begs the question, "Which language should I start with?" This chapter reviews the options, but to cut to the chase, there are only five languages I'd advise you to consider seriously. And which one you choose will be determined more by what you want to do—that is, what kind of work you want to pursue, than by anything intrinsic to the capabilities of the language itself.

The contending languages for a first-time programmer looking for a career are, in my opinion:

➤ C++

➤ Java

➤ Visual Basic

➤ Internet Scripting (HTML, DHTML, JavaScript, and so on)

➤ Assembler

C++ is the language of choice for commercial software development. The overwhelming majority of large commercial software is written in C++, and C++ programmers tend to be among the most highly paid in the industry. I illustrate many of the programming concepts in this book in C++ because I suspect this will be the language you'll want to learn.

Java is clearly a strong alternative for commercial software development, and many organizations are turning their attention to Java, although some that have made that change have shifted back to C++. Fortunately, C++ and Java are so similar that 90% of what you learn about one applies to the other. If you don't set out to learn C++ first, Java is a great alternative.

Visual Basic (VB) is a terrific environment for creating prototypes quickly and for rapid application development. On the other hand, many programmers are reluctant to use Visual Basic for enterprise-level applications (that is, big, complex robust software) because VB applications tend to be very large and very slow.

The advantage of learning VB first is that it is very easy to learn and you receive almost immediate gratification: You'll turn out snazzy Windows programs far faster than you might with C++ or Java. In the past few years, VB has become the development language of choice for serious Internet applications. Although C++ and Java may be more powerful, VB is so easy to work with, and so ideally suited to Internet technology, that many C++ programmers find themselves learning VB just to keep up. That said, compensation for VB programming still lags behind that for C++ and Java.

Internet Scripting encompasses all the tools used for building Web sites, including JavaScript (also known ECMAScript), VBScript, ASP, HTML, DHTML, and so forth. Becoming an Internet programmer can be a very lucrative path if you already have credentials as a C++ or Java programmer. Without that, you will be in the same pay category as VB programmers.

Learning Assembler is not in any way a realistic choice, unless you really want to learn, in great detail, how computers (and for that matter, programming languages) really work. The simple fact is that Assembler is no longer a viable language for most software development. In other words, learning Assembler is like learning Latin: You may never use the language directly, but you'll learn a lot about how all the other languages are put together.

The bulk of the rest of this chapter reviews these languages in more detail, with an eye toward understanding the strengths and weaknesses of each. Before we do that, however, let's take a moment to put these languages in context.

A Quick History of the Evolution of Programming Languages

For many years, the principal goal of computer programmers was to write programs that were both small and fast. A program needed to be small, because memory was expensive, and it needed to be fast, because processing power was also expensive.

As computers have become smaller, cheaper, and faster, and as the cost of memory has fallen, these priorities have changed. Today the cost of a programmer's time far outweighs the cost of memory or processing speed. Well-written, easy-to-maintain code is at a premium.

Take It Easy

Easy-to-maintain means that as business requirements change, the program can be extended and enhanced without great expense.

Solving problems

The problems programmers are asked to solve have also been changing. Twenty years ago, programs were created to manage large amounts of raw data. The people writing the code and the people using the program were all computer professionals. Today, computers are in use by far more people, and most know very little about how computers and programs work. Computers are tools used by people who are more interested in solving their business problems than struggling with the computer.

Interestingly, for these programs to become easier to use, they became more sophisticated and thus far harder to create.

The days when users were willing to enter cryptic commands at esoteric prompts, only to see a stream of raw data, are long behind us. Today's programs use sophisticated "user-friendly" interfaces, involving multiple windows, menus, dialog boxes, and the myriad of metaphors with which we've all become familiar. The programs written to support this new approach are far more complex than those written just 10 years ago.

Warp Speed, Mr. Data

Data—the information and values in your program.

Procedural, Structured, and Object-Oriented Programming

Until recently, programs were thought of as a series of procedures that acted upon data. A procedure, or function, is a set of specific instructions executed one after the other. Procedures have names, and are self-contained units of code.

Procedures can call one another. When a procedure calls another procedure, execution stops in the first and begins in the second. When the second ends, control returns to the first, but, of course, that second procedure could, in the interim, have called a *third* procedure. You can see this process illustrated here.

Functions and Procedures

Procedure or function—an identified block of instructions, executed one after another.

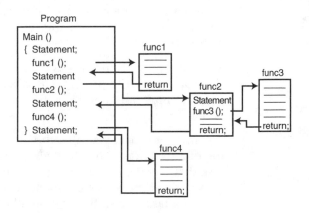

Program procedures can call one another.

In procedural programming, data (that is, the values manipulated) were kept separate from procedures, and the trick in programming was to keep track of which functions called which other functions, and what data was changed. Over time, as programs became more complex, following the thread of a program became nearly impossible, as you can see from this example.

Procedural programs could grow so complex they would be impossible to figure out.

Spaghetti Code

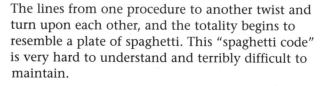

Procedure 1

Procedure 2

Procedure 3

Geek Speak
blah blah blah bl blah bl b

Structural Integrity

Structured programming—a technique of dividing a program into short procedures and controlling the flow of the program among these procedures.

The lines from one procedure to another twist and turn upon each other, and the totality begins to resemble a plate of spaghetti. This "spaghetti code" is very hard to understand and terribly difficult to maintain.

Structured programming was created to cut through this confusion. The principal idea behind structured programming is as simple as the concept of divide and conquer.

A computer program can be thought of as consisting of a set of tasks. In a structured program, any task that is too complex to be described is simply broken down into a set of smaller component tasks, until the tasks are sufficiently small and self-contained so that they are easily understood.

As an example, computing the average salary of every employee of a company is a rather complex task. You can, however, break it down into these subtasks:

1. Find out what each person earns.
2. Count how many people you have.
3. Total all the salaries.
4. Divide the total by the number of people you have.

Totaling the salaries can be broken down into

1. Get each employee's record.
2. Access the salary.
3. Add the salary to the running total.
4. Get the next employee's record.

In turn, obtaining each employee's record can be broken down into

1. Open the file of employees.
2. Go to the correct record.
3. Read the data from disk.

Structured programming remains an enormously successful approach for dealing with complex problems. By the late 1980s, however, some of the deficiencies of structured programming had become all too clear.

First, it is natural to think of your data (employee records, for example) and what you can do with your data (sort, edit, and so on) as related ideas. But structured programming does not accommodate this idea.

Second, programmers found themselves repeatedly devising new solutions to old problems. This is often called "reinventing the wheel," and is the opposite of reusability.

The idea behind reusability is to build components that have known properties, and then to be able to plug them into your program as you need them.

The way we are now using computers—with menus and buttons and windows—fosters a more interactive, event-driven approach to computer programming. Event-driven means that an event happens—for example, the user presses a button or chooses from a menu—and the program must respond. Programs are becoming increasingly interactive, and it has become important to design for that kind of functionality.

Old-fashioned programs forced the user to proceed step-by-step through a series of screens. Modern event-driven programs present all the choices at once and respond to the user's actions.

Object-Oriented Programming

Object-oriented programming provides techniques for managing enormous complexity, achieving reuse of software components, and coupling data with the tasks that manipulate that data.

The essence of object-oriented programming is to treat data and the procedures that act upon the data as a single "object"—a self-contained entity with an identity and certain characteristics of its own.

Encapsulation and Data Hiding

When an engineer needs to add a resistor to the device she is creating, she doesn't typically build a new one from scratch. She walks over to a bin of resistors, examines the colored bands that indicate the properties, and picks the one she needs. The resistor is a "black box" as far as the engineer is concerned—she doesn't much care how it does its work as long as it conforms to her specifications; she doesn't need to look inside the box to use it in her design.

The property of being a self-contained unit is called *encapsulation*. With encapsulation, programmers can accomplish *data hiding*. Data hiding is the highly valued characteristic that an object can be used without the user knowing or caring how it works internally. Just as you can use a refrigerator without knowing how the compressor works, you can use a well-designed object without knowing about its internal data members.

Similarly, when the engineer uses the resistor, she need not know anything about the internal state of the resistor. All the properties of the resistor are encapsulated in the resistor object; they are not spread out through the circuitry. It is not necessary to understand how the resistor works in order to use it effectively. Its data is hidden inside the resistor's casing.

The Big Event

Event driven—programs that respond to events such as the user clicking on a button, choosing from a menu, or otherwise spontaneously interacting with the program.

Object of My Affection

Object—An object is a *thing*. To a programmer, an object is an instance of a *type* the programmer has created. Objects have characteristics and behavior.

Inheritance and Reuse

When the engineers at Acme Motors want to build a new car, they have two choices: They can start from scratch, or they can modify an existing model. Perhaps their Star model is nearly perfect, but they'd like to add a turbocharger and a six-speed transmission. The chief engineer would prefer not to start from the ground up, but rather to say, "Let's build another Star, but let's add these additional capabilities. We'll call the new model a Quasar." A Quasar is a kind of Star, but one with new features.

Object-oriented languages support the idea of reuse through *inheritance*. A new type, which is an extension of an existing type, can be declared. This new subclass is said to derive from the existing type and is sometimes called a *derived type*. The Quasar is derived from the Star and therefore inherits all its qualities, but can add to them as needed.

Polymorphism

The new Quasar might respond differently than a Star does when you press down on the accelerator. The Quasar might engage fuel injection and a turbocharger, while the Star would simply let gasoline into its carburetor. A user, however, does not have to know about these differences. He can just "floor it," and the right thing happens, depending on which car he's driving.

Object-oriented languages support the idea that different objects do "the right thing" through polymorphism. *Poly* means many, and *morph* means form. Polymorphism refers to the same name taking many forms.

The Goals of Object-Oriented Programming

The goal of object-oriented programming is to create code that is correct, reliable, robust, extensible, maintainable, efficient, and portable. The goal is also to create software that can be delivered on time and within budget.

Geek Speak

A Message for You

Message—different parts of an object-oriented program send messages to one another requesting work or information.

Polymorphism—the ability for many related objects each to respond to the same message differently yet appropriately.

Correct

Correct code meets the requirements as specified by the person who asked you to write the program. That is, you've built the right thing, and it does what it is supposed to do.

The hidden difficulty in this simple concept is creating a specification that is sufficiently detailed, so you can build a design and implement a system that does what the customer envisioned. In some ways, creating the specification is the hardest part of programming.

Object-oriented analysis is the process of nailing down this specification. Object-oriented design is the process of planning how you will achieve the specified requirements in your program. Object-oriented programming is the technique of implementing the design that rises out of analysis.

Reliable

There are two ways in which a program can be reliable. First, it must not crash unexpectedly. Second, it must perform as expected over a long period of time with little need for maintenance.

Reliability can be measured in many ways. One common industry standard is "minutes of unplanned downtime per year." For example, "no more than 30 minutes of unplanned downtime per year" would be a measure of quite high reliability.

This measure can be reformulated as a percentage—what percent of the time is the system operating properly? The AT&T standard for reliability in the long-distance network has been described as seven nines of reliability, that is 99.99999% reliability.

Object-oriented techniques help build more reliable systems by fostering the creation of smaller interacting components that can be tested independently of the entire system.

It is worth noting, however, that reliability, as everything else, comes at a cost. You can buy 99.99999% reliability, but it isn't cheap. Typically, this kind of reliability requires complete redundancy among systems and very expensive hardware and software solutions; but it can be accomplished if that is your priority.

This prioritizing is typical of the kinds of problems you confront as a software engineer. You will often be in the position of trading off among cost, efficiency, reliability, time to market, and a host of other factors to find the optimal solution to a particular business problem.

Robust

A system is robust when it is reliable even in the face of unexpected circumstances. Customers may enter bogus or unanticipated data, they may shut off the machine in the middle of an operation, and the Internet may become suddenly unavailable. The job of your software is to respond to these predictable if unexpected exigencies without crashing.

In the book *The Mythical Man Month*, Fred Brooks states that the goal of building a robust program is not that there is some way in which your program will run successfully, but that there is no way in which it will fail.

Object-oriented development assists in building robust systems because each object is responsible for its own state.

By allowing each object to manage its own state, a single object may fail, but the entire system does not become corrupted.

Extensible and Maintainable

The biggest problem in software is that requirements change more quickly than software can be written. By the time your program is completed, there are a new set of requirements; the goal is to build software that can evolve without breaking. Software that can evolve is called *extensible*—you can extend its functionality without breaking your existing code.

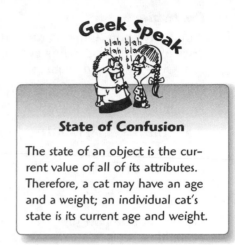

Geek Speak

State of Confusion

The state of an object is the current value of all of its attributes. Therefore, a cat may have an age and a weight; an individual cat's state is its current age and weight.

Maintainability is closely related to extensibility. Extensibility describes a system's capability to add new features. A maintainable product is one that can be understood by developers who must keep it working, and that is easily repaired and adjusted.

Code that cannot be read cannot be maintained. Clever, cute tricks become traps for the benighted programmer who must maintain the code long after you've gone on to the next contract. The customer, of course, is left holding the bag.

Object-oriented programming encourages encapsulation, and this prevents changes in one section of the code from rippling through the entire design. This makes code much more maintainable. Polymorphism enables programmers to extend the behavior of the system, without breaking and rebuilding the existing, working, and tested parts.

Efficient

The goal of efficient software is to use as little memory and require as little disk space as possible, all other things being equal.

As the cost of memory and disk space decreases and the cost of developer time increases, building efficient code is less important than building code that is extensible and maintainable. Compilers and other tools can greatly enhance the efficiency of code; today programmers spend more time on building for the future than investing heavily in extracting the last iota of efficiency.

This is typical of the kinds of tradeoffs you will make every day as you design and implement software. Efficiency is a factor, but often it is not the driving factor in the success of applications development.

Portable

Portability is the ability to run, or at least rebuild, your software on a different hardware platform or operating system. Some languages facilitate portability; others do not. Object-oriented languages are not necessarily more portable than procedural languages were.

Portability comes in the following "flavors":

➤ **Runtime portability.** You can run this program on any platform.

➤ **Compile-time portability.** You must recompile but you can use the same source code.

➤ **Design time.** You must recode but the design works on any platform.

Java tries to support runtime portability; C and C++ strongly support compile-time portability. Scripting languages are less portable, but easier to rewrite.

Working with Specific Languages

With this background knowledge about the history of programming languages, you are ready to make a choice about where you want to start. The following sections review four of the five language choices mentioned previously: C++, Java, Visual Basic, and Assembler. I'll cover Internet Scripting in Chapter 5: "Internet Programming."

Working with C++

C++ is a complex language that offers tremendous flexibility and power. It is not easy to learn, but it is not terribly difficult, either.

The Advantages of C++

C++ is a powerful, efficient, and flexible language.

"Powerful" means that the language has advanced features enabling programmers full control over the development of their program. This power includes the ability to examine and adjust values in memory directly. In short, C++ is like a power-tool—you can work very effectively, but you can also hurt yourself very badly if you don't know what you are doing. Programmers say that C++ gives you all the rope you need to hang yourself.

"Efficient" means that the programs created in C++ run quickly and take up very little room in memory. That is, they use the resources of the computer very efficiently with very little waste.

"Flexibility" means that there are many ways to accomplish the same task in C++ and that the simple elements of the language can be assembled together in many ways.

C++ inherits all of these characteristics from C, but adds to that venerable programming language the attributes of object-oriented programming. This makes for a language that creates programs that are easier to maintain and more robust and reliable than the programs written in C and that meet the objectives of being correct, extensible, maintainable, reusable, portable, and delivered on time and within budget.

C++ has been in use as a commercial software development language for more than a decade and is supported by mature industry-tested tools such as editors for writing programs and debuggers for testing your work.

Integrated development environments make programming easier, and application frameworks take the drudgery out of programming for modern operating systems such as Windows NT.

The Disadvantages of C++

C++ is a complex language, with many key words and many features. Because it is built on C, and C was designed as a middle step between Assembler and higher-level languages such as Basic and Cobol, C++ forces you to understand a bit more about the computer chip and bits and bytes than, for example, Visual Basic does. This is either a bug or a feature, depending on your perspective.

The biggest problem with C++ is that it is very easy to write programs with subtle bugs. For example, because in C++ you must manage memory directly (that is, you must allocate memory and then delete it when you are finished), it is possible to write a program with a memory "leak." A memory leak occurs when you allocate memory and then fail to delete it; that memory is lost to your program from then on—as if it "leaked" out of the program.

With a large, complex program, small leaks can add up to a real problem. Your program appears to run fine for a while, but then it runs out of memory and crashes. This bug can be particularly hard to find.

The process of automatically cleaning up lost memory is called "garbage collection." Java supports garbage collection but C++ does not. Garbage collection is not free, it slows down your application, and C++ assumes you can do a better job yourself so it doesn't perform that service.

In a related problem, because C++ gives you direct control over memory, it is possible to "overwrite" memory inadvertently. In C++, unlike in most other languages, you can place a value directly into a location in memory. That's great—it gives you terrific control—but if you write to the wrong place, you can create bugs that are miserably difficult to locate.

The classic symptom of that problem is that you think you find a bug, you change the code, and the bug "moves." The program no longer fails as it did before—it fails in a different location! Few C++ programmers have avoided the purgatory of spending day after day chasing this kind of bug.

What C++ Is Like

C++ is an object-oriented language, and when you program well in C++, you are thinking about objects and their responsibilities. Tiny programs in C++ look very much like programs in C, but larger C++ programs are completely different. Later in the book, I'll walk you through a complete, rather complex C++ program so that you can get a sense of what they are like.

Java

Java was, for a short while, the hottest programming language in computer history. Starting in about 1996 and lasting about two years, there was so much talk about Java I couldn't go to a cocktail party without being asked by friends and acquaintances when I was going to be writing about Java.

I looked at Java a number of times and what I saw was a language with a lot of potential, but serious limitations for commercial software development. While everyone was writing in Java, or at least so it seemed, the only thing being produced were jiggling letters and bouncing images. No commercial software was being released, and having looked at the tools, that absence was no surprise.

Now that the hype has settled down, and Java and its related tools have matured, it is a more serious programming language. I'm pleased that my *Programming from Scratch* series will include a book on Java because I now believe it is a realistic alternative to C++ for commercial software development.

How Is Java Different?

Java is based on C++ and shares many characteristics of that language. The authors of Java made two critical changes, however.

First, they set out to simplify the language. They intentionally left out of Java the capabilities they felt get most programmers into trouble. Of these, the most important is the direct manipulation of memory. In Java, unlike in C++, you do not directly allocate memory, and you don't have to clean up after your objects. All of this is taken care of for you.

The second significant change is that Java does not typically produce compiled code. Instead, it produces an intermediate form called *byte-code*. This code enables programs written in Java to run on any platform that supports the Java Virtual Machine (JVM). There is a JVM for every significant platform, which means you can write a program one time in Java and have it run on either a Wintel machine, a Macintosh, or a UNIX system—a significant time-saving feature.

The Advantages of Java

Java code is easier to write than C++, but provides nearly all the flexibility and power of C++. Further, just about any Java program can be implemented as an applet, so that it can be embedded into an HTML page and "run" inside a browser.

Java also provides powerful memory management not available in C++, and it provides built-in support for the ability to write programs that do more than one thing at a time (multithreading). Although you can write multithreaded memory-safe programs in C++, it is far easier to do so in Java.

The Disadvantages of Java

Although it is true that there are some esoteric things that are harder to do in Java than in C++, this is not a problem for the overwhelming majority of programmers. It turns out that the things that are harder to do, you very rarely want to do, anyway.

There are only two significant disadvantages to Java when compared to C++. The first is that the code it produces tends to be slower, but this can be mitigated somewhat by the creation of compiled Java code. The second is that the tools—that is, the editors and debuggers—are not nearly as robust and well written, yet.

All of this is a direct result of Java being a very new language. It is my guess that the boundaries between these two languages will become less sharp over time, and many programmers will move freely and easily between them.

What Java Is Like

Programming in Java is much like programming in C++—you are focused on the creation of interacting objects. One decision in Java, however, is whether you are creating an application—that is, a standalone program—or you are writing an applet. Applets run within a browser and tend to be smaller and more limited than full-blown applications.

Visual Basic

C++ programmers tend to sneer at Visual Basic, for some good reasons and for some very bad reasons. The worst of these reasons is a "macho" devotion to obscure and arcane programming languages, coupled with a morbid fear that if programming becomes easy enough, they'll all be out of work.

The Advantages of Visual Basic

VB is far easier to program than C++ and thus it is possible to create a working Windows program in a very short time. In fact, for many simple programs, you never really have to write much code; you can just use a visual interface to drag buttons and list boxes onto a form and then run the resulting program.

The Disadvantages of Visual Basic

Because VB shields you from many of the details of programming, there are some tasks that are very hard or nearly impossible with VB but are straightforward with a language such as C++. In addition, the code produced by Visual Basic tends to be

57

slower than that produced by more efficient languages, and for the same reasons, the executable files tend to be much larger and therefore take up more disk space.

Of course, one tremendous limitation of Visual Basic is that it can produce programs only for the Windows environment. For many projects, this is not at all a significant limitation; for other projects, VB can't be used.

What Visual Basic Is Like

Programming in VB is very different from programming in lower-level languages such as C++ and Java. When you start Visual Basic, you are presented with a form, which you can populate with the standard Windows interface objects such as buttons, list boxes, and so forth.

You'll find a toolkit along the left side of the window; simply click on the widget you want and then draw it right onto the form. This is a wonderfully simple programming environment in which you can quickly become very productive.

In Visual Basic, you can design simple programs by dragging items from a toolbar onto a form.

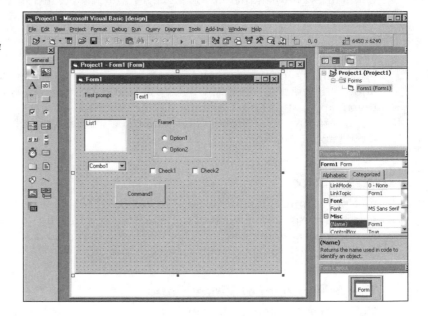

Assembler

Ultimately, it all comes down to machine code, whatever language you use. C++, Java, VB, and so forth all create machine code in the end, because this is the only language understood by the microprocessor (the chip).

Assembler was created to provide a form of machine code usable by humans (poor, limited, stupid creatures that we are). Assembler is isomorphic with machine code: Every assembler command translates directly into a machine code command. There is an absolute 1:1 correspondence between Assembler instructions and machine code instructions.

In Assembler, nothing is hidden. You must move bytes of data among the registers in the microprocessor and you must manipulate the computer's memory directly.

This is the language to learn if your goal is really to understand programming in all its details. Assembler hides nothing—to work in Assembler, you must understand how the chip itself manages its data.

Learning Assembler first is like learning to drive by starting with a course in automotive mechanics. I'd wager that you'd learn an awful lot about cars by learning to strip down an engine and transmission and build it up again. When it came time for you to learn how to shift into first gear, you'd have a fundamental understanding of what you were trying to accomplish and how to go about it. The interaction between clutch, gear, shift lever, accelerator, and transmission would be no mystery.

That said, lots of folks learn to drive without ever learning to tear down their transmission. If you told me you wanted to make your living as a professional driver, and you were going to spend six months first learning how engines work, I wouldn't say you were crazy; just unusually patient and thorough.

This, by the way, is exactly how I learned C. I already knew how to tinker with some higher-level programming languages, but I wanted to be a real programmer. My buddy, Skip Gilbrech, who was a commercial software developer, suggested I start with Assembler.

I read engineering manuals on the 8086 chip and studied Assembler. My programs manipulated memory directly, moving values in and out of registers and tracking flags and memory allocation as I went. Later, when it came time to learn C, it was a piece of cake.

The Disadvantages of Learning Assembler

So why not learn Assembler as your first language? The answer is that the world has become a lot more complicated than it was back in 1985 when I learned Assembler. The applications we are building today are larger and more complex, and we simply can't afford to build them one molecule at a time.

Higher-level languages such as C++ have become more efficient, narrowing the differences between C++ and Assembler. Finally, and most important, computers and memory have become faster and cheaper, and so minimal improvements in efficiency no longer matter much except in unusual circumstances.

Thus, virtually no commercial software is written in Assembler today, and unless you have a lot of time, the effort of learning Assembler will not translate into paid work; it serves only to provide an underlying base of knowledge as you move forward. If you have the discipline and time, great, but most folks really want to get on with learning the language they'll use for work.

What Assembler Is Like

Assembler programming is not unlike C++ or Java programming, except that the tools are more limited, and the actual code is more arcane.

Other Programming Languages

There are thousands of other programming languages in use worldwide. Some are specialized to scientific or other esoteric uses; others are in use principally in certain industries or in academia.

If your goal is to be a commercial software developer, however, your realistic choices are limited to C++, Java, and Visual Basic, or to writing for the Internet.

For the overwhelming majority of aspiring software engineers, these are the right choices.

How to Choose

I propose you choose according to your priorities.

If your goal is to get up and running as quickly as possible, and maximizing your profit is less important than quickly becoming productive, I recommend Visual Basic.

If you are serious about a career in programming, and want a skill that will be lucrative and in high demand, then I recommend C++ and/or Java; this book emphasizes these two languages above all others.

In any case, what you learn here about these languages applies, in large measure, to whatever you end up doing. As we go, I'll point out differences among the various languages and programming options.

If you are less interested in programming and more interested in working on the Internet, then focus your skills on the scripting languages, and after you feel comfortable with these, then go on to Java or C++.

If your priority is to learn programming inside out and to be a highly respected programmer who lives and breathes bits and bytes and understands the chip in detail, start with Assembler. For 98% of you, this is not the right choice, but for that remaining 2%, the die-hard bit-heads, accept no alternative.

The Least You Need to Know

➤ Whichever path you choose to follow, the first language is always the most difficult.

➤ After you get over the initial learning curve, you may find that it is a very rewarding and exciting experience to make the computer dance to the music you write.

Internet Programming

In 1990, the Internet was a commerce-free zone of information used principally by hackers, academics, and developers. The majority of transactions were email or newsgroups, and there was little general public interest. Today, it is a powerful, commercial, anarchic medium that shows every sign of having the kind of impact on our culture that few technologies other than the telephone, automobile, and television have had.

The World Wide Web

I first saw the Web in 1993. At the time I was hard at work developing a proprietary online service that offered email, rich text, graphics, and hyperlinks. When I saw the Web, I knew our product was in serious trouble; but I underestimated how quickly the Web would become ubiquitous. Today, just six years later, you can't find a major American corporation without a Web site, and I support my books at `http://www.libertyassociates.com`.

Programming the Web

The underlying technology of the Web is fairly simple, but the increasingly dynamic, interactive, multimedia aspects of the Web have added layer upon layer of technology. When you strip it all down, it begins with a transport layer called *H*yper*T*ext *T*ransport *P*rotocol (HTTP).

HTTP "*HyperText* Transport Protocol"

Protocol—an agreed-upon convention. In this case, a protocol describes the order in which information is sent, the parts of the header, and so forth.

Server—a computer whose job is to provide information to client machines. In this case, a Web server's job is to "serve" pages to client machines.

Tag! You're It

Tag—a special word or symbol set in text indicating how the text that follows should be displayed.

The transport layer describes the details of how data moves through the Internet—the byte order, header information, and so forth. The job of HTTP is to move a Web page from a server (a centralized computer) to your browser. That's it. You ask for a page, and the server sends it to you: HTTP defines the *protocol* for how that is done.

HTTP is a connectionless system. That is, each time you make a request, the system fulfills that request and then moves on to the next person. There is no connection; no way to keep track of whether the person who asked for one page is the same person who asks for the next page.

Of course, on top of HTTP, you can build all sorts of connections by writing additional software. I'll cover some examples later in this chapter when I talk about ASP and other advanced Web technology.

HTML

The principal technology of the Web, for most developers, is not HTTP—which is fairly invisible to most of us—but rather HTML: the *HyperText Markup Language*. HTML is a very simple set of *tags* designed to mark up text and describe how that text should be displayed.

Here's how it works. When you enter a URL into your browser, your browser works with your Internet service provider to access that site and read the page you've asked for.

The browser reads through the page, letter by letter, picking out the tags and using the tags to determine how to display the text and other items sent along with the page.

If the page has nothing but text, the browser just displays it *as is*. Typically, however, tags will change the display of the text, providing information about font, size, images, links, and so forth. Actually, HTML itself doesn't say *anything* about display: That is up to the browser. HTML just designates some text as a heading, or a title, or as emphasized; how this information is translated into larger fonts, or different colors, is up to the browser.

Everything but the URL

URL: **U**niform **R**esource **L**ocator— The address of an item on the World Wide Web.

There are, now, additions to HTML which *do* provide more explicit display information, but those additions involve advanced forms of HTML that need not concern you right from the start. HTML itself, however, is not a display language, it is a markup language: That is, it marks text as to its meaning, and the browser decides what to do with that information.

In short, then, an HTML page is text plus tags. The best way to get a sense of this convention is to look at a real Web page.

Fire up your browser, and navigate to www.libertyassociates.com. That will bring you to the default page on my site, www.libertyassociates.com/index.htm. From here, we can examine some of the pages on my site to get a sense of what HTML is about. As you can see, the home page offers a number of navigation choices.

Click on **Our Philosophy** (the last entry under "About Us") to go to that page.

Default Pages

Most often, you don't ask for a page explicitly; when you enter, for example, www.cnn.com, you implicitly ask for the default page at that site. The page is sent to your browser (using HTTP) and your browser is responsible for reading that page and displaying its contents.

It's easy to look behind the scenes of a Web page such as this one to see the code that makes it work.

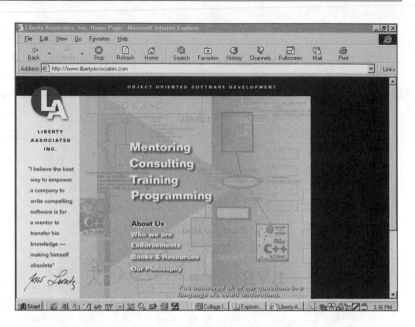

Because this page is simple, it will be easy to interpret its code.

This page is fairly simple, and opening its source will give a good sense of what HTML is about. Right click on the page and choose **View Source**.

```
0:  <!DOCTYPE HTML PUBLIC "-//IETF//DTD HTML//EN">
1:  <html>
2:
```

```
 3:   <head>
 4:   <meta http-equiv="Content-Type"
 5:   content="text/html; charset=iso-8859-1">
 6:   <meta name="GENERATOR" content="Microsoft FrontPage 2.0">
 7:   <title>Our Philosophy</title>
 8:   </head>
 9:
10:   <body bgcolor="#FFFFFF" vlink="#808080" alink="#800000"
11:   topmargin="0" leftmargin="0">
12:   <div align="left">
13:
14:   <table border="0" cellpadding="0" cellspacing="0" width="454"
15:   bgcolor="#FFFFFF">
16:       <tr>
17:           <td valign="top" width="22" bgcolor="#FFFFFF"><img
18:           src="images/black_spacer.gif" width="22"
➥height="40"></td>
19:           <td><div align="left"><table border="0" cellpadding="0"
20:           cellspacing="0" width="454" bgcolor="#FFFFFF">
21:               <tr>
22:                   <td valign="top" width="432"
➥bgcolor="#FFFFFF"><img
23:                   src="images/tagline_sub.gif" width="454"
24:                   height="40"><p><br>
25:                   <font size="3"><img src="images/phil_tl.gif"
26:                   alt="Our Philosophy" width="350"
➥height="18"></font></p>
27:                   <p><font size="3">Liberty Associates has a single
28:                   guiding business principle: The highest quality
29:                   of service in the industry. Period.</font></p>
30:                   <p><font size="3">It goes beyond a commitment to
31:                   doing it right; my name is on every contract; my
32:                   reputation is on every line of code. Nothing
33:                   ships without my express approval. <em>Nothing.
➥</em></font></p>
34:                   <p><font size="3">I personally guarantee it.<br>
35:                   </font><img src="images/jessesig.gif" width="125"
36:                   height="57"></p>
37:                   </td>
38:               </tr>
39:           </table>
40:           </div></td>
41:       </tr>
42:   </table>
43:   </div>
44:   </body>
45:   </html>
```

I've numbered the lines to make this discussion easier. The tool in which this program was created adds the text shown on line 0, so we'll ignore it. Line 1 is the first tag we want to examine

```
<html>
```

This tag begins the page, followed on line 3 by the <head> tag—indicating that what is to follow is the header for the page. Lines 4-6 include technical details we can skip. Line 7 begins with the <title> tag, followed by the title of the page: "Our Philosophy" and ending with the </title> tag. This pairing is typical of HTML, a set of text is bracketed by a begin tag and an end tag. In this case, <title> is the begin tag indicating that what follows is the title, and </title> is the end tag indicating that we're finished now with the title. This title will be shown in the browser's window.

The next line, line 8, has the end-head title </head>, indicating the end of the header information.

As you can see, an end tag is exactly like the begin tag except that a forward slash (/) precedes it. You would expect, then, that there will be an end html tag, and if you peek down to line 45, you will find it.

Much of the rest of this is fairly advanced, but you get the general idea; text is bracketed by tags that indicate how the browser is to deal with the text itself. Take a look at line 27. The <p> tag forces a new *p*aragraph. This paragraph break is followed by a request for font size 3. Again, HTML indicates relative size, but the browser interprets this into a specific font size. The rest of this line, through the beginning of line 29, is just text that appears according to the settings that have already been processed. The font and paragraph end tags are at the end of line 29.

Take a look at line 35. It begins with an end tag for the font which began on line 34, but is then followed by a new tag: img. This is an image—a picture. The source (src) for this picture is a file images/jessesig.gif, and that information is followed by instructions on how wide and high to render the picture. Image tags take no end tag; they are self-contained. The </p> tag that follows is the end of the paragraph that began on line 34.

The tags on lines 37-43 all refer to tables and divisions, advanced topics beyond the scope of this discussion, but within the rather simple world of markup tags for HTML. Any good primer on HTML will teach you how to make all of this work, with little effort. If you're interested, check out *The Complete Idiot's Guide to Creating an HTML 4 Web Page*, by Paul McFedries (Que, 1997, ISBN: 0-7897-1490-6).

Creating HTML Pages

There are two ways to go about creating a page in HTML: with a simple text editor or with a Web-development tool. The easiest is to open a text-editor such as Notepad and just write out the HTML by hand.

You can create Web pages in a text editor such as Notepad—just save your page with the extension HTM.

After you've saved the file, choose the File menu in your browser, select the command to open a local file, and browse to the file on your disk. When you open it, it should look like this:

Here's your Notepad file opened in a Web browser.

There are a few things to notice, comparing the output with the code you've written. Here's the code from the example again, this time with line numbers so we can examine it:

```
0:  <HTML>1:  <HEAD>2:  <Title> A Test Page, hand-written </title>
➥</head>3:  <body>4:  <h1>This is a level 1 heading </h1>5:  This is
➥just text.
6:  I might want to <em>emphasize</em> some text
7:  <h2>This is a level 2 headng </h2>
8:  </body>
9:  </html>
```

It begins, as we expect, with the <HTML> tag, balanced by the closing tag on line 9. Notice that you do *not* have to match case—upper or lower or any combination is fine. You might consider making your tags uppercase so they'll stand out from the body text, but it's just a matter of style.

On line 1, we provide the <HEAD> tag, then the <Title> tag on line 2. Notice also that the title end-tag and the head end-tag are both on line 2—each tag does not need its own line.

Look at lines 5 and 6 and then at the output. We put the text on different lines, but the new line was converted to a space in the output. HTML does not respect new line breaks you create by pressing **Enter**; you must make your line break explicit using <br>.

Also on line 6, notice that we used the <em> tag. <em> indicates *emphasis*, but it is up to the browser to decide whether this means italic, bold, or any other effect. In our case, it made the text italic.

Similarly, the <h1> and <h2> tags indicate heading 1 and heading 2, but don't tell the browser what this style means: The size and effects are up to the browser.

Finally, notice the typo on line 7. In a typical word processor, this error would be caught, but Notepad doesn't notice, and if you aren't careful, you'll publish this typo and tens of thousands of Web browsers *will* notice!

Using a Web Development Environment

I said there were two ways to create your page. You just looked at writing HTML code. The second is to use an HTML editor or development environment such as FrontPage or HotDog. Actually, there are dozens of alternatives, from programs that provide simple, almost incidental support for HTML, to highly sophisticated Web development tools such as Visual InterDev.

You can use a visual Web page editor to create your pages.

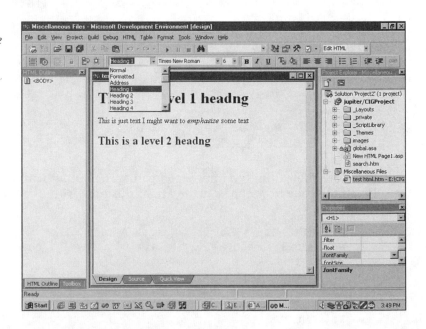

As you can see, this tool offers a WYSIWYG development environment which makes setting the display much easier; much more like working in a modern word processor.

These integrated development environments for the Web make creating Web pages much easier, but they hide so much of HTML from you that it's easy to become lost and confused when you need to adjust your code by hand. Most integrated development environments for Web development also offer a view of the page that reveals the HTML source code.

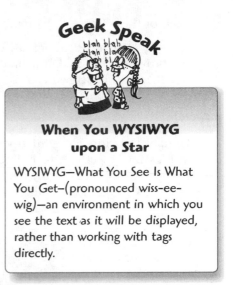

When You WYSIWYG upon a Star

WYSIWYG—What You See Is What You Get—(pronounced wiss-ee-wig)—an environment in which you see the text as it will be displayed, rather than working with tags directly.

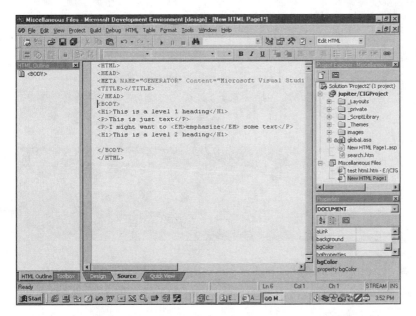

Even though you're using an editor, it's easy to peek at the code you're creating.

Be sure to read through the source code frequently, and be sure you understand what the tool is doing for you. For example, examining this source code reveals that at the end of the file I've managed to make a heading of nothing more than a space

```
<H1> </H1>
```

  is a nonbreaking—or mandatory—space. On the next line, I've created a paragraph around a space.

```
<P> </P>
```

69

Both of these lines can be removed.

Only by looking at the actual HTML code can you figure out what is really going to the browser. That said, it is hard to go back to tightening screws by hand after you've bought a power screwdriver.

Links

Perhaps the most powerful aspect of HTML is the ability to support hypertext (the HT in HTML!). Hypertext is a link from within your text to other pages on the Web. Here, I've created a link from the words support products to my own Web site; the browser displays this link as an underlined phrase, but when I click on the phrase, a new browser is opened on my home page.

Clicking a link transports the viewer to a new page, on the current site or anywhere on the Web.

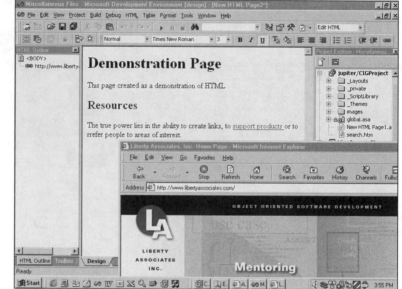

Opening the source code shows that this magic is accomplished by a single tag:

```
<A href="http://www.libertyassociates.com"> support products</A>
```

This tag is somewhat more complex than others. It begins with A, indicating an anchor tag. An anchor tag *anchors* a link. The anchor tag can have up to three attributes—NAME, HREF, and TITLE. Here we show only one attribute, HREF.

The HREF is a Hypertext REFerence, and creates the link to another page on the Web. The use of Name and Title is an advanced topic, and we won't cover it here. The anchor tag ends, as you'd expect with the </A> tag, but before it ends, it includes the text to display. This allows us to put in the words "support products" and have these words link to our page, rather than having to explicitly display the page to which we are linking. You can supply an image within the anchor tag instead. For example, you could use a small picture of a house as a button to return to your home, or main, page.

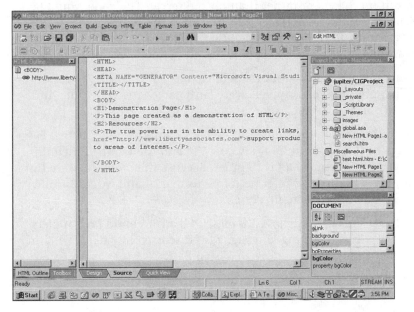

Here's the code that creates the hyperlink.

It May Be Dynamic, but It Ain't Interactive

HTML is a powerful tool for displaying text and graphics over the Web. The text can be updated far more quickly than, for example, can a book or newspaper. For a while, this was enough; but Web developers quickly decided they'd like to be able to solicit information from their subscribers, and the form was born.

CGI

Forms solicit feedback or other information, and then process that information on the server, responding to the user's input and displaying new information dynamically. In the early days of the Web, this process was managed by CGI—the Common Gateway Interface. CGI was a protocol; the actual implementation of CGI was through scripting languages such as PERL.

The problem with CGI is that each script runs in its own process. This is a fancy systems analyst way of saying each was like its own program and each used a lot of systems resources. This setup did not scale well; after the server was handling many CGI requests, it began to slow down noticeably.

Programmers began to search for solutions to this dilemma. There were two fundamental approaches to resolving this problem: client-side execution and server-side applications.

Java and ActiveX

Java's initial promise was not as a better programming language, but as a language in which you could write client-side programs. The idea was that you'd write a small "applet" that would run on the client rather than on the server. The code would be piped down to the client as part of the HTML file, and then the browser would interpret the code, passing it in to a Java Virtual Machine (JVM) which was built into the browser. Netscape was the first browser to support this idea, and it lit up the industry.

The potential for Java applets was huge, but the reality that set in within a year or two was somewhat disappointing. Java applets were fairly large, and it became difficult to find applets that supported much more than animation.

Microsoft responded to the challenge by creating ActiveX components. The idea here was that you'd develop small objects in C++, Java, or VB, and then embed them in Web pages, much as you might embed a Java Applet. Because these objects were tiny and compiled, the idea was that they'd offer better performance and would fit into Microsoft's overall component-based architecture.

Both of these technologies are fairly advanced topics. To learn to build Java applets, you need to learn Java as a programming language (as I discussed in Chapter 4) and to learn ActiveX, you need proficiency in C++ or Visual Basic.

JavaScript, JScript, and VBScript

The industry needed a simpler client-side solution, and Netscape worked with Sun to develop JavaScript. Actually, this language was originally called LiveScript, but at the time Netscape was going to release it, Java was the rage. The association between JavaScript and Java is only in the minds of the marketing department; they have virtually nothing in common except that they are both client-side development languages.

JavaScript has mutated into various work-alike forms, including Microsoft's JScript and the industry was in some danger of having a cornucopia of similar but different dialects of this language. Fortunately, both Microsoft and Netscape have now agreed on a standard, given the unattractive name ECMAScript.

VBScript is an alternative client-side scripting language offered only by Microsoft, which allows scripts to be written in a language very similar to Visual Basic.

Let's add a very simple script to the demonstration page. We'll ask our script to tell us the current date and time by displaying it on the screen. Using VB, our source code now looks like this:

```
<HTML>
<HEAD>
<META NAME="GENERATOR" Content="Microsoft Visual Studio 6.0">
<TITLE></TITLE>
```

```
</HEAD>
<BODY>
<H1>Demonstration Page </H1>
<P>This page created as a demonstration of HTML</P>
<H2>Resources</H2>
<P>The true power lies in the ability to create links, to <A
href="http://www.libertyassociates.com">support
products</A> or to refer people to areas of interest.</P>

Here is some VB Script to tell you what time it is:
<Script language=VBScript> Document.Write(Now)</script>.

</BODY>
</HTML>
```

The line we're interested in has the <Script> tag. This tag is followed by a language attribute; in this case, setting the language to VBScript. This is followed by a call to the Write() method of the Document object (Document.Write()), which is passed the value Now. Now is a VBScript construct for the current date and time. The job of the Write method is to write the value passed in, and so the net of this statement is that the current date and time are fetched from the system and printed to the document. Simple.

Script, of course, can be far more complex than this. It is possible to create functions and advanced programming constructs in a script, and to invoke these scripted functions as needed.

Advantages and Disadvantages

The advantage of scripting languages is that they are easy to write; the disadvantage is that they typically have poor performance and do not scale well. As important, for many purposes, the script is sent to the client browser, and so the business logic (the rules of how to process data) is exposed to the user. This is a serious drawback for many applications.

Active Server Pages (ASPs)

One solution to all these problems is to run the script not on the client, but rather on the server. Microsoft developed Active Server Pages, which manage server-side scripting but present simple HTML to the browser. Here's how it works: When a request comes to the server for an ASP page, that page is read at the server. An ASP page consists of simple HTML mixed together with ASP scripting instructions. The output of both the HTML and the ASP is just more HTML. It is this output that is sent down to the browser. By the time it gets to the client, it is nothing but HTML.

To turn our previous example into ASP code, rename the file from New HTML Project 1.htm to New HTML Project 1.asp. That's all there is to it. Now, to add server script, you add the attribute "Runat = Server" to the <Script> tag. Here's the new source file:

```
<HTML>
<HEAD>
<META NAME="GENERATOR" Content="Microsoft Visual Studio 6.0">
<TITLE></TITLE>
</HEAD>
<BODY>
<H1>Demonstration Page </H1>
<P>This page created as a demonstration of HTML</P>
<H2>Resources</H2>
<P>The true power lies in the ability to create links, to <A
href="http://www.libertyassociates.com">support
products</A> or to refer people to areas of interest.</P>

Here is some VB Script to tell you what time it is:
<Script language=VBScript> Document.Write(Now)</script>.
<Script language=VBScript Runat = Server>
Response.Write(Date)
</script>.

</BODY>
</HTML>
```

You will notice that ASP does not have a Document object. The objects in ASP include Request and Response. As you might guess, Request is the object sent from the browser *to* the server, asking for information and Response is the object sent back to the browser. Here we are telling the Response object to write to the browser, passing in the Date.

Note that this is server script, and so you can no longer just run this file from your local machine. This ASP file must be added to a server project, running on a machine properly set up to support ASP. The task of setting up Microsoft Internet Information Server (or another ASP-compatible server) is not difficult, but it is, sadly, also beyond the scope of this book. If you don't already have this up and running, take my word for it that this code will work, and that it will run at the server, just as it is supposed to.

ASP and Databases

Web applications become particularly powerful when you put your data up on the Web. The issues surrounding database access on the Web are complex, but ASP and other technologies do simplify things greatly. In Chapter 12, I'll consider databases in some detail, so I'll delay this discussion until then.

ASP and Connections

Earlier I said that HTML is connectionless. That statement is true, but ASP adds a Session object, which provides a virtual connection and allows us to keep track of a user's session over time. In addition, modern HTML and ASP both use *cookies*, small client-side files that can help a Web server keep vital information about who has visited the site.

This cookie allows a Web site you've previously visited to welcome you back and to know what information you've seen already and what is new for you. Therefore, on top of the connectionless HTML, ASP and cookies provide many of the benefits of a connection-based system.

No-Bake Cookies

Cookie—a small file stored on the client machine.

The Least You Need to Know

➤ Programming for the Web can be accomplished in HTML, ASP, VB, JavaScript, and VBScript, among other languages.

➤ To add power and flexibility, you can add scripted code.

➤ Scripts can run either at the server or the client.

➤ The Web is growing and expanding rapidly, and the associated technology is getting more complex and powerful every day.

Chapter 6

Parts of a Language

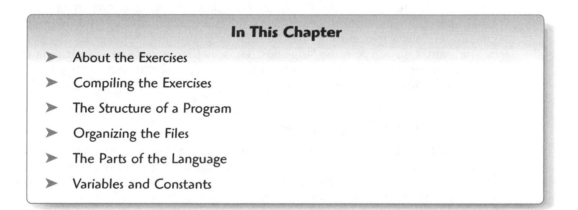

In This Chapter

➤ About the Exercises

➤ Compiling the Exercises

➤ The Structure of a Program

➤ Organizing the Files

➤ The Parts of the Language

➤ Variables and Constants

The next few chapters cover the fundamentals of programming. While I will show examples from specific programming languages, with an emphasis on C++ and Java, the general principles apply to virtually any programming you might do.

About the Exercises

I don't intend that you use this book as a primer in programming, but rather as a general introduction to these topics. Please see Appendix A for a list of recommended books for learning each programming language.

Because I don't focus on any one language, the examples are drawn from C++, Java, Visual Basic, HTML, JavaScript, and many other sources.

The majority of the programming examples, however, are in C++, for several reasons:

1. C++ is the No. 1 programming language for commercial software development. If you are going to become a professional programmer, C++ is an overwhelming favorite as the right language to learn.

2. Java is probably the best alternative as a first language. Because C++ is very close to Java, and the path from C++ to Java is fairly straightforward, the lessons learned by using C++ in this book will not be wasted or off-point.

3. C++ is cross-platform (you can run C++ programs on Windows, Macintosh, UNIX, and so forth) and therefore you should be able to try these exercises no matter what platform you are using.

4. C++ illustrates virtually every aspect of programming.

5. C++ is object-oriented, and therefore you can focus on high levels of abstractions—that is, you can model complex problems without worrying about bits and bytes when you don't want to.

6. There are inexpensive (or free!) C++ compilers available.

7. I know C++ well, and thus can illustrate these examples most clearly in C++.

This last point is not a joke and in fact is a powerful lesson in professional programming. People tend to use the tools with which they are most comfortable. Taken to an extreme, this tendency can be problematic. The old expression "when all you have is a hammer, the whole world looks like a nail" is a warning against unduly limiting your tool set. It is important you use the right programming language for the specific job. That said, C++ is a versatile language that does the job needed—illustrating the fundamentals of programming—and all things being equal, I'll turn to C++ first when I need to get a job done right.

Compiling the Exercises

As stated in the previous numbered list, there are any number of inexpensive compilers available with which you can learn C++. This book is not a primer (I've written quite a few C++ primers and you can find them listed in Appendix A), but if you do want to try the exercises shown here, you'll need a compiler.

There are free compilers available on the Internet, but in my experience these are very difficult for novice programmers. They come with no product support and the documentation is not always easy to understand.

Any number of commercial compilers are available, the most notable are from Microsoft, Borland, Symantec, and Watcom, but there are others as well. When pressed, I recommend the Microsoft Visual C++ compilers. The least expensive commercial version of this compiler costs well under $100, and a stripped-down and limited-use version actually comes free with the latest edition of my book *Sams Teach Yourself C++ in 21 Days, Complete Compiler Edition*.

I have used Microsoft compilers since 1987 and have been very happy with the level of support and the feature set and reliability. Others disagree, and Microsoft is not known for being at the very bleeding edge of compliance with the ISO standard, so you may be happier with another compiler. In any case, all the C++ code in this book and all my other books on C++ does compile with the Microsoft Visual C++ compiler.

Appendix B has some short notes on setting up and using the Visual C++ compiler and debugger, which at least gets you started if you decide you do want to try these exercises. Let me emphasize, however, these exercises are provided to illustrate the fundamentals of programming, and not to teach you C++. You do not miss much if you just read the exercises without compiling and running them.

If you want to try the Java code, you need only obtain the Java Developer Kit for Java 2.0. This is available free on the Internet, and also is included with a number of books—see Appendix A for a list of books on Java.

The Structure of a Program

Every programming language requires some form of structure in the files you create. In Visual Basic, this structure is provided for you by the development environment. You just open a form, drag in controls, and double-click on the controls to access the associated code snippets. The VB development environment packages it all together and manages the files for you.

With most other programming languages, the syntax of the language dictates the organization of the files. For example, C++ programs always include a function named main(). Here is a very simple C++ program as an example:

Listing 6.1   A Simple C++ Program

```
#include <iostream.h>

int main()
{
    cout << "Hello world\n";
    return 0;
}

Output
Hello world
Analysis:
```

This simple program is filled with obscure *syntax*. The syntax of a language is the set of rules about which words have meaning and how statements are assembled.

The first line

```
#include <iostream.h>
```

is a special directive telling the precompiler (which runs before the compiler) to include a needed file into the program (that file is called iostream.h). We don't care about the particulars here except to note that this line is needed to manage printing to the screen in standard C++.

In other languages, this task might be accomplished by including other needed files. For example, in Java you might fulfill a similar requirement with the line

```
import java.awt.*
```

As stated previously, every C++ program has a main function:

```
int main()
{
```

In C++, functions are designated by their name (in this case, `main`) and a pair of parentheses. The `int` at the beginning of the definition of main indicates that this function "returns" a value. When a function is *called* (or invoked), it runs some code and then returns to whichever procedure called it. When it returns, it can bring along a value.

`Main` is called by the operating system, so it returns an integer value to the system when the program concludes. In DOS or UNIX, this value can be examined by a batch file, so that you can invoke a program and then take an action depending on what value you get back. This feature is not used very much in modern Windows programming.

In C++, all functions are bracketed by braces({}). You'll note an opening brace at the beginning of the function ({) and a closing brace at the end (}).

Between the braces is this line:

```
cout << "Hello world\n";
```

This is the line that actually prints the words "Hello world" to the screen. The slash-n (\n) combination at the end of that line indicates a new line—that is, there is a "carriage return" at the end of the printed line.

Geek Speak

A Carriage Return Is Not Bringing a Baby Buggy Back

For those of you under 30, a carriage return refers to an antiquated device known as a typewriter. These mechanical machines struck a piece of paper with a metal bar on which was etched a letter. The bar struck the paper through an inked ribbon, and hence printed the letter onto the paper. The paper sat in a carriage, which jogged to the left after each letter was struck. When the carriage came to the margin at the end of the line, a bell sounded and the human operator pushed a lever that both returned the carriage to the start of the line and jogged the paper up a line ready for the operator to type some more. This was a very primitive form of word processing—don't even get me started on correction fluid.

Typewriters were once all the rage in creating office documents.

The point here is not the details of C++ syntax, but rather that there is a very rigid structure to which you must adhere.

Organizing the Files

In C++, Java, Assembler, and most other languages, you must manage these files yourself. You must keep track of your files, add them to your project and ensure they are properly compiled and linked.

When I was a boy, this process was far more difficult. We were responsible for creating "make files" that managed a project and told the tools (that is, the compiler and linker) what files to compile and when to do so. Today's integrated development environments create projects and manage the interdependencies among the files for you.

The Parts of the Language

The remainder of this chapter reviews the fundamentals of various programming languages, including variables, constants, expressions, operators, and comments. If you've never programmed at all, this discussion will give you a feel for the building blocks of programming languages. If you already program, even as a hobby, you may want to skim this quickly as it should be simple review.

Comments

When you are writing a program, you can look at the code, and it is always clear and self-evident what you are trying to do. Funny thing, though—a month later, when you return to the program, it can be quite confusing and unclear. I'm not sure how that confusion creeps into your program, but it always does.

To fight the onset of confusion, and to help others understand your code, you want to use comments. Comments are simply text that is ignored by the compiler, but that may inform the reader what you are doing at any particular point in your program.

Types of Comments

C++ comments come in two types: the double-slash (//) comment, and the slash-star (/*) comment. The double-slash comment, which I refer to as a *C++-style comment,* indicates to the compiler to ignore everything that follows this comment until the end of the line.

The slash-star (/*) comment mark indicates that the compiler should ignore everything that follows until it finds a star-slash (*/) comment mark. I'll call these *C-style comments*. Every /* must be matched with a closing */.

As you might guess, C-style comments are used in the C language as well, but C++-style comments are not part of the official definition of C.

Many C++ programmers use the C++-style comment most of the time, and reserve C-style comments for blocking out large blocks of a program. You can include C++-style comments within a block "commented out" by C-style comments; everything, including the C++-style comments, is ignored between the C-style comment marks.

Using Comments

As a general rule, the overall program should have comments at the beginning, telling you what the program does. Each function should also have comments explaining what the function does and what values it returns. Finally, any statement in your program that is obscure or less than obvious should be commented as well.

Comment Out Code

One useful feature of comments is that, because they aren't executed, you can "comment out" troublesome lines of code to see how the program works without them. Doing so is an essential part of the debugging process.

Listing 6.2 demonstrates the use of comments, showing that they do not affect the processing of the program or its output.

Listing 6.2   Using Comments

```
1: #include <iostream.h>
2:
3: int main()
4: {
5:  /* this is a comment
6:  and it extends until the closing
7:  star-slash comment mark */
8:    cout << "Hello World!\n";
9:    // this comment ends at the end of the line
10:   cout << "That comment ended!\n";
11:
12:  // double slash comments can be alone on a line
13: /* as can slash-star comments */
14:     return 0;
15: }
```

```
Output
Hello World!
That comment ended!
```

```
Analysis:
```

The comments on lines 5 through 7 are completely ignored by the compiler, as are the comments on lines 9, 12, and 13. The comments on lines 9 and 12 ended with the end of the line, however, whereas the comments on lines 5 and 13 required a closing comment mark.

Comments at the Top of Each File

Many programmers like to put a comment block at the top of every file. The exact style of this block of comments is a matter of individual taste or team policy, but typically these headers include the following:

➤ The name of the function or program.

➤ The name of the file.

➤ A description of how the program works.

➤ The author's name.

➤ A revision history (notes on each change made).

➤ What compilers, linkers, and other tools were used to make the program.

➤ Additional notes as needed.

For example, this block of comments might appear at the top of the Hello World program.

```
/*************************************************************

Program:       Hello World

File:          Hello.cpp

Contents:      Main (complete program listing in this file)

Description:   Prints the words "Hello world" to the screen

Author:        Jesse Liberty (jl)

Environment:   Microsoft Visual C++ 6
               Win NT Workstation

Notes:         This is an introductory, sample program.

Revisions:     1.00  1/1/00 (jl) First release
               1.01  2/4/01 (jl) Capitalized "World"


*************************************************************/
```

If you *do* include this kind of header, it is imperative that you keep the notes and descriptions up-to-date. A common problem with headers such as these is that they are neglected after their initial creation, and over time they become increasingly misleading. When properly maintained, however, they can be an invaluable guide to the overall program.

A Final Word of Caution About Comments

Comments that state the obvious are less than useful. In fact, they can be counterproductive, because the code may change and the programmer may neglect to update the comment. What is obvious to one person may be obscure to another, however, so judgment is required.

Writing comments well is a skill few programmers master. Some programmers use comments sparingly, striving for readable code. These programmers see comments as a cheat: If the code is obscure, rewrite it. Others comment every line, adding little value to the source code and cluttering up their code.

So, how do you use comments well? Here's a good rule of thumb: Assume your audience can read the programming language, but can't read your mind. Let the source code tell what you are doing, and use comments to explain why you are doing it.

Variables and Constants

Programs need a way to store the data they use. Variables and constants offer various ways to work with numbers and other values.

You may remember *variables* from high school (let the Interest Rate=x where x is the variable for interest rate).

From a programmer's point of view, a variable is a location in your computer's memory in which you can store a value and from which you can later retrieve that value.

To understand this, you must first understand a bit about how computer memory works. Your computer's memory can be thought of as a series of cubbyholes, all lined up in a long row. Each cubbyhole—or memory location—is numbered sequentially. These numbers are known as *memory addresses*.

Various Variables

Variable—a named location in memory in which you can store a value.

Variables not only have addresses, they have names. For example, you might create a variable named myAge. Your variable is a label on one of these cubbyholes so that you can find it easily, without knowing its actual memory address.

Represented here is a schematic representation of this idea. As you can see from the figure, we've declared a variable named myVariable. myVariable starts at memory address 103.

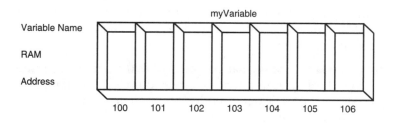

A schematic representation of memory.

85

A RAM Without Horns

RAM is Random Access Memory. When you run your program, it is loaded into RAM from the disk file. All variables are created in RAM as well. When programmers talk of memory, it is usually RAM to which they are referring.

Setting Aside Memory

When you define a variable in C++, you must tell the compiler not only what its name is, but also what kind of information it will hold: integer, character, and so forth. We call this information the variable's *type*.

C++, like Java, is strongly typed—every variable is of a specific type, and that type must be declared. BASIC is loosely typed; when you declare a variable, its type is implicit and understood by the values you store in it.

In loosely typed languages such as BASIC, the type of a variable is relatively unimportant; in strongly typed languages, it is critical.

Why Bother with Strong Typing?

The advantage of programming in a loosely typed language is that you don't have to be bothered with explicit control of the type of each variable, and you don't have to declare variables in advance of using them.

The advantage of strongly typed languages is that you can enlist the compiler in finding bugs. By predeclaring everything, you in essence tell the compiler, "I'm going to use this variable to hold integers. If I try to put anything else in here, remind me." The compiler reminds you with a compile error.

Compile errors are good. They happen reliably when you are creating your code and so your customer never sees them. You fix them before you ship your code.

Runtime errors are bad. They often happen only intermittently and only when you run the code. These errors are the ones that sneak into your program, undetected by your Quality Assurance team until a hundred thousand users write in demanding a refund.

Types and memory

Each memory location (cubbyhole) is one byte. If the type of variable you create is four bytes in size, it needs four bytes of memory, or four cubbies. The type of the variable (for example, int) tells the compiler how much memory (how many cubbyholes) to set aside for the variable.

Because computers use bits and bytes to represent values, and because memory is measured in bytes, it is important that you eventually understand and are comfortable with these concepts.

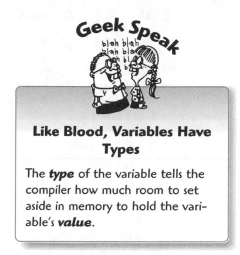

Like Blood, Variables Have Types

The *type* of the variable tells the compiler how much room to set aside in memory to hold the variable's *value*.

Size of Integers

On any one computer, each variable type takes up a single unchanging amount of room. That is, an int might be two bytes on one machine, and four on another, but on either computer it is always the same, day in and day out.

Actually, the size of an integer (or any other type) is a function not only of the computer you are using, but also the programming language and the specific compiler or interpreter. Thus, on a Pentium, using C++ with a 32-bit compiler such as Visual C++ 6.0, an integer is four bytes.

You can almost certainly ignore all of this detail, however, until you are much further along in your programming. I mention it here only to give you a sense of the kinds of issues that might arise as you move among different languages and different platforms.

If you are curious about the size of objects on your machine, fire up your C++ compiler and run this code:

Listing 6.3   Determining Size of Objects

```
1:    #include <iostream.h>
2:
3:    int main()
4:    {
5:      cout << "The size of an int is:\t\t"    << sizeof(int)    << "
➥bytes.\n";
6:      cout << "The size of a short int is:\t" << sizeof(short)  << "
➥bytes.\n";
7:      cout << "The size of a long int is:\t"  << sizeof(long)   << "
➥bytes.\n";
```

continues

Listing 6.3   Continued

```
8:      cout << "The size of a char is:\t\t"    << sizeof(char)    << "
➡bytes.\n";
9:      cout << "The size of a float is:\t\t"   << sizeof(float)   << "
➡bytes.\n";
10:     cout << "The size of a double is:\t"    << sizeof(double)  << "
➡bytes.\n";
11:
12:         return 0;
13: }
```

```
The size of an int is        4 bytes.
The size of a short int is   2 bytes.
The size of a long int is    4 bytes.
The size of a char is        1 bytes.
The size of a float is       4 bytes.
The size of a double is      8 bytes.
```

Signed and Unsigned

Some languages differentiate between signed integers and unsigned. A signed integer may be negative or positive; an unsigned integer is always positive. Because both types use the same number of bits, an unsigned integer can hold a larger positive value. For example, using a 32-bit C++ compiler, an unsigned integer ranges from 0 to 4,294,967,295, but a signed integer ranges from –2,147,483,648 to 2,147,483,647. For more on why these numbers make sense, take a look at Appendix C, "Binary Math."

Different Bytes for Different Sites

On your computer, the number of bytes presented might be different!

Fundamental Variable Types

Most programming languages offer a variety of built-in types, including integers and characters. Many offer support for floating decimal numbers (for example, numbers with fractional parts) and some offer support for more complex types.

As a general rule, the programming languages that aim to be easier to use (such as Visual Basic) offer more complex types. The more powerful programming languages, such as C++ and Java, tend to provide simpler types that act as building block primitives from which you build your own more complex types.

Defining a Variable

In C++, you create, or *define*, a variable by stating its type, followed by one or more spaces, followed by the variable name and a semicolon. The variable name can be virtually any combination of letters, but cannot contain spaces. Legal variable names include x, J23qrsnf, and myAge. The following statement defines an integer variable called myAge:

```
int myAge;
```

As a general programming practice, try to use names that tell you what the variable is for. Names such as myAge or howMany are much easier to understand and remember than names such as xJ4 or theInt. If you use good variable names, you'll need fewer comments to make sense of your code.

Try this experiment: Guess what these pieces of programs do, based on the first few lines of code:

Example 1

```
int main()
{
     int x;
     int y;
     int z;
     z = x * y;
}
```

Example 2

```
int main ()
{
     int Width;
     int Length;
     int Area;
     Area = Width * Length;
     return 0;
}
```

As you probably noticed, these code fragments do essentially the same thing: Declare three integer values and then determine the product of the first two. However, the second group is much more intuitive—because you declare variables called Length, Width, and Area, it's easy to manipulate them with just a basic knowledge of geometry.

Keywords

Some words are reserved by the programming language, and you may not use them as variable names. These are *keywords* used by the language to control your program. Keywords typically include if, while, for, and main. Your language manual should provide a complete list, but generally, any reasonable name for a variable is almost certainly not a keyword.

Case Sensitivity

Some languages are case sensitive. That means that they recognize a difference between lowercase and UPPERCASE letters. If your language is case sensitive, it distinguishes between "if" (a keyword) and "IF" (not a keyword).

Geek Speak

A Case of Sensitivity

Case Sensitive—If a language is case sensitive, then words are differentiated by the case of the letters. In other words, UPPERCASE and lowercase letters are considered to be different. A variable named age is different from Age, which is different from AGE.

Check This Out

Assign, Not Declare

Note that this does not say "width is equal to five" as it would in mathematics. That statement in C++ would be

```
Width == 5
```

Rather, it says "assign 5 to width." Assignment uses a single equal sign (=) whereas equates uses a double equal sign (==). The syntax is arbitrary, confusing, and error-prone.

C++ and Java are case sensitive; BASIC is not. In all these languages, many programmers prefer to use all lowercase letters for their variable names. If the name requires two words (for example, my car)—remember, spaces are not allowed—there are two popular conventions: my_car or myCar. The latter form is called *camel notation*, because the capitalization looks something like a hump.

Creating More Than One Variable at a Time

In C++, Java, and many other languages, you can create more than one variable of the same type in one statement by writing the type and then the variable names, separated by commas. For example:

```
unsigned int myAge, myWeight;   // two
➥unsigned int variables
int area, width, length;        // three ints
```

As you can see, myAge and myWeight are each declared as unsigned integer variables. The second line declares three individual int variables named area, width, and length. The type (int) is assigned to all the variables, so you cannot mix types in one definition statement.

Assigning Values to Your Variables

You assign a value to a variable by using the assignment operator (=). Therefore, you would assign 5 to Width by writing

```
int Width;
Width = 5;
```

You can combine these steps and initialize Width when you define it by writing

```
int Width = 5;
```

Initialization looks very much like assignment, and with integer variables, the difference is minor.

Listing 6.4 shows a complete program, ready to compile, that computes the area of a rectangle and writes the answer to the screen.

Listing 6.4 A Program Ready to Compile

```
1:    // Demonstration of variables
2:    #include <iostream.h>
3:
4:    int main()
5:    {
6:       int Width = 5, Length;
7:      Length = 10;
8:
9:      // create  an int Width and initialize with
10:        // result of multiplying Width by Length
11:       int Area  = Width * Length;
12:
13:      cout << "Width:" << Width << "\n";
14:      cout << "Length: "  << Length << endl;
15:      cout << "Area: " << Area << endl;
16:    return 0;
17:  }

Width: 5
Length: 10
Area: 50
```

Line 2 includes the required include statement for the iostream's library so that cout will work. Line 4 begins the program.

On line 6, Width is defined as an integer, and its value is initialized to 5. Another integer, Length, is also defined, but it's not initialized. On line 7 the value 10 is assigned to Length.

On line 11 an integer, Area, is defined, and it is initialized with the value obtained by multiplying Width times Length. On lines 13 through 15, the values of the variables are printed to the screen. Note that the key word endl creates a new line.

Advanced Topic: Wrapping Around in Unsigned Integers

The fact that unsigned integers have a limit to the values they can hold is only rarely a problem, but what happens if you do run out of room?

When an unsigned integer reaches its maximum value, it wraps around and starts over, much as a car odometer might. Listing 6.5 shows what happens if you try to put too large a value into a short integer.

Listing 6.5 Entering Too Large a Value

```
1: #include <iostream.h>
2: int main()
3: {
4:     unsigned short int smallNumber;
5:     smallNumber = 65535;
6:     cout << "small number:" << smallNumber << endl;
7:     smallNumber++;
8:     cout << "small number:" << smallNumber << endl;
9:     smallNumber++;
10:    cout << "small number:" << smallNumber << endl;
11:    return 0;
12: }

small number: 65535
small number: 0
small number: 1
```

On line 4, smallNumber is declared to be an unsigned short int, which on my computer is a two-byte variable able to hold a value between 0 and 65,535. On line 5, the maximum value is assigned to smallNumber, and it is printed on line 6.

On line 7, smallNumber is incremented; that is, 1 is added to it. The symbol for incrementing is ++ (as in the name C++—an incremental increase from C). Therefore, the value in smallNumber would be 65,536. But unsigned short integers can't hold a number larger than 65,535, so the value is wrapped around to 0, which is printed on line 8.

On line 9 smallNumber is incremented again, and its new value, 1, is printed on line 10.

Wrapping Around a *Signed Integer*

A signed integer is different from an unsigned integer, in that half of its values are negative. Instead of picturing a traditional car odometer, you might picture one that rotates up for positive numbers and down for negative numbers. One mile from zero is either 1 or –1. When you run out of positive numbers, you run right into the largest negative numbers and then count back down to zero. Listing 6.6 shows what happens when you add 1 to the maximum positive number in an unsigned short integer.

Listing 6.6 Adding 1 to the Maximum Positive Number

```
1: #include <iostream.h>
2: int main()
3: {
```

```
4:      short int smallNumber;
5:      smallNumber = 32767;
6:      cout << "small number:" << smallNumber << endl;
7:      smallNumber++;
8:      cout << "small number:" << smallNumber << endl;
9:      smallNumber++;
10:     cout << "small number:" << smallNumber << endl;
11:   return 0;
12:   }
```

```
small number: 32767
small number: -32768
small number: -32767
```

On line 4, `smallNumber` is declared this time to be a `signed` short integer (if you don't explicitly say that it is `unsigned`, it is assumed to be `signed`). The program proceeds much as the preceding one, but the output is quite different. To fully understand this output, you must be comfortable with how `signed` numbers are represented as bits in a two-byte integer. For details, check Appendix C.

The bottom line, however, is that just like an `unsigned` integer, the `signed` integer wraps around from its highest positive value to its highest negative value.

Constants

Like variables, constants are data storage locations. But variables vary; constants on the other hand, and as you may have guessed, do not vary.

C++ has strict rules about constants. For example, you must initialize a constant when you create it, and you cannot assign a new value later; after a constant is initialized, its value is, in a word, constant.

Literal Constants

There are two types of constants: *literal* and *symbolic*.

A literal constant is a value typed directly into your program wherever it is needed. For example:

```
int myAge = 39;
```

Geek Speak

Constant Craving

Constant—a data storage location that contains an unchanging value.

Literally Speaking

Literal—a numeric value used as a constant.

Star Light, Star Bright

The asterisk or star (*) indicates multiplication. The + and - signs obviously mean addition and subtraction, respectively; whereas you use a slash (/) to indicate division.

myAge is a variable, of type int; 39 is a literal constant. You can't assign a value to 39, and its value can't be changed.

Symbolic Constants

A symbolic constant is a constant that is represented by a name, just as a variable is. Unlike a variable, however, after a constant is initialized, its value can't be changed.

If your program has one integer variable named students and another named classes, you could compute how many students you have, given a known number of classes, if you knew there were 15 students per class:

```
students = classes * 15;
```

In this example, 15 is a literal constant. Your code would be easier to read, and easier to maintain, if you substituted a symbolic constant for this value:

```
students = classes * studentsPerClass
```

If you later decided to change the number of students in each class, you could do so where you define the constant studentsPerClass without having to make a change every place you used that value.

The Least You Need to Know

➤ A compiler transforms the program code into an executable program file the computer can run.

➤ Programs are organized using a formal structure that keeps like sections of code well organized.

➤ Languages consist of a variety of statements that describe and manipulate data.

Statements

The analogy between programming languages and human languages such as English or Russian is so strong that we talk about programming language as having a syntax and consisting of statements. In most languages, a *statement* refers to a single step in a program.

Statements are the building blocks of a programming language. In C++ and Java, each statement ends with a semicolon. In some other languages, statements end with a new line (that is, each line is a statement). Many languages support the idea of compound statements—a group of statements that can be used where you might otherwise use a single statement, analogous to a paragraph.

The analogy can be taken only so far. The syntax for any given programming language is, by its nature, arbitrary and precise. Novice programmers spend a lot of time worrying about getting the syntax exactly correct because if they fail to do so, their programs won't compile or run properly. It is imperative to think beyond the syntax of a language, however, and to consider the *semantics* of the language. The semantics of a language describe what you are trying to accomplish—that is, what the program *does*.

This chapter and the next few describe some of the syntax of C++ and other languages, and along the way I try to convey some of the semantics of programming. While there is a fair amount of detail about C++ and Java, the principles transcend these languages and are applicable to all programming.

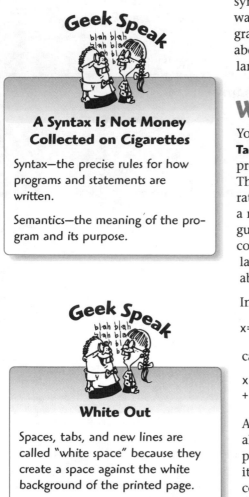

Geek Speak

A Syntax Is Not Money Collected on Cigarettes

Syntax—the precise rules for how programs and statements are written.

Semantics—the meaning of the program and its purpose.

Geek Speak

White Out

Spaces, tabs, and new lines are called "white space" because they create a space against the white background of the printed page.

White Space

You create white space by pressing the **spacebar**, the **Tab** key or the **Enter** button (for a new line). Most programming languages ignore extra white space. That is, in most languages, if two words can be separated by a single space, two or more spaces, a tab, or a new line can also separate them. Of course, languages that use a new line to indicate the end of a command cannot ignore the new line, and some languages are an exception and care very much about extra spaces.

In C++ or Java, the statement

x=a+b;

can just as correctly be written as

x   =a
+   b   ;

Although this last variation is perfectly legal, it is also foolish. White space can be used to make your programs more readable and easier to maintain, or it can be used to create horrific and indecipherable code. The difference is the critical element in programming: human judgment.

Blocks and Compound Statements

In most modern languages, any place you can put a single statement, you can put a compound statement, also called a *block*. In C++ and Java, a block begins with an opening brace (`{`) and ends with a closing brace (`}`). For example,

```
{
    temp = a;
    a = b;
    b = temp;
}
```

This block of code acts as one statement and swaps the values in the variables a and b. Other languages use slightly different syntax, but most modern languages support the idea of a block of code.

Expressions

Any legal statement that equates to a value of some kind is called an *expression*.

All expressions are statements, but, of course, not all statements are expressions.

The myriad pieces of code that qualify as expressions might surprise you. Here are three examples:

```
3.2                     //
➥returns the value 3.2

PI                      // float
➥const that returns the value 3.14

SecondsPerMinute        // int const that returns 60
```

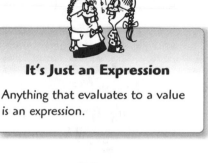

Geek Speak

It's Just an Expression

Anything that evaluates to a value is an expression.

Geek Speak

Returns Desk

An expression is said to return a value. Therefore, 3+2; returns the value 5 and so is an expression.

Assuming that `PI` is a constant equal to 3.14 and `SecondsPerMinute` is a constant equal to 60, all three of these statements are expressions.

In C++ and Java, even assignment statements are expressions. For example, the complicated expression

```
x = a + b;
```

not only adds a and b and assigns the result to x, but returns the value of that assignment (the value of x) as well.

Therefore, this statement is also an expression. Because it is an expression, it can be on the right side of an assignment operator:

```
y = x = a + b;
```

This line is evaluated in the following order:

Add a to b.

Assign the result of the expression a + b to x.

Assign the result of the assignment expression x = a + b to y.

If a, b, x, and y are all integers, and if a has the value 2 and b has the value 5, both x and y will be assigned the value 7.

Operators

An operator is a symbol that causes the program to take an action. Operators act on operands, and in many languages all operands are expressions.

Assignment Operator

As discussed in the previous chapter, the assignment operator (=) causes the operand on the left side of the assignment operator to have its value changed to the value on the right side of the assignment operator. The expression

```
x = a + b;
```

assigns the value that is the result of adding a and b to the operand x.

An operand that legally can be on the left side of an assignment operator is called an *l-value*. That which can be on the right side is called (you guessed it) an *r-value*.

Constants are r-values. They cannot be l-values. Therefore, you can write

```
x = 35;          // ok
```

but you cannot legally write

```
35 = x;          // error, not an l-value!
```

Mathematical Operators

There are five mathematical operators: addition (+), subtraction (−), multiplication (*), division (/), and modulus (%).

Addition and subtraction work as you would expect, although subtraction with unsigned integers can lead to surprising results, if the result is a negative number. Remember, *unsigned* integers have no negative values. You saw something much like this yesterday, when variable overflow was described. Listing 7.1 shows what happens when you subtract a large unsigned number from a small unsigned number in C++.

Not All Languages Follow This Convention

The syntax I just described apply to C++ and Java. Other languages may differ slightly.

Listing 7.1   Subtracting a Large Unsigned Number

```
1: // Demonstrates subtraction and
2: // integer overflow
3: #include <iostream.h>
4:
5: int main()
6: {
7:    unsigned int difference;
8:    unsigned int bigNumber = 100;
9:    unsigned int smallNumber = 50;
10:   difference = bigNumber - smallNumber;
11:   cout << "Difference is: " << difference;
12:   difference = smallNumber - bigNumber;
13:   cout << "\nNow difference is: " << difference <<endl;
14:       return 0;
15: }

Difference is: 50
Now difference is: 4294967246
```

The subtraction operator is invoked on line 10, and the result is printed on line 11, much as we might expect. The subtraction operator is called again on line 12, but this time a large unsigned number is subtracted from a small unsigned number. The result would be negative, but because it is evaluated (and printed) as an unsigned number, the result is an overflow, as I described in the previous chapter.

Integer Division and Modulus

Integer division is somewhat different from everyday division. In fact, it is exactly like the division you originally learned in fourth grade. "Class, how much is 21 divided by four?" The answer, to a fourth grader, is, "5, remainder 1."

When an adult divides 21 by 4, the result is a real number (a number with a fraction). Integers don't have fractions, and so when you ask a programming language to divide two integers, it responds like a fourth grader, giving you the whole number value without the "remainder."

The answer to 21 divided by 4, to a programming language or a fourth grader, is 5. Just as you can ask the fourth grader to then tell you the remainder, you can use the modulus operator (%) to ask your programming language for the remainder. To get the remainder, you take 21 modulus 4 (21 % 4) and the result is 1. The modulus operator tells you the remainder after an integer division.

Finding the modulus turns out to be very useful in certain circumstances. For example, you might want to print a statement on every 5th action. How can you tell when you have a multiple of 5?

To do this, you take advantage of the observation that any number whose modulus 5 value is 0 is an exact multiple of 5. Thus 1 % 5 is 1, 2 % 5 is 2, and so forth, until 5 % 5, whose result is 0. 6 % 5 is back to 1, and this pattern continues until the next multiple of 5, which is 10.

Therefore, you create a counter and increment that counter each time you take an action, and then test that counter modulus with 5. If the result is 0, you have done this action a multiple of 5 times and you can print your statement. Listing 7.2 illustrates how this task might be done. There is code here that is quite advanced, but if you read through the code ignoring what you don't understand, you still get an idea for what is going on.

Listing 7.2   A Counter and Increment That Counter Each Action

```
#include <iostream.h>

int main()
{
 for ( int i = 1; i <= 20; i++)
  {
     cout << "Action taken!" << endl;
     if ( i % 5 == 0 )               // test for every 5th
        cout << ">>>>>>>>>>>> Five accomplished!" << endl;
  }
 return 0;
}

Action taken!
Action taken!
Action taken!
Action taken!
Action taken!
>>>>>>>>>>>> Five accomplished!
Action taken!
```

```
Action taken!
Action taken!
Action taken!
Action taken!
>>>>>>>>>>> Five accomplished!
Action taken!
Action taken!
Action taken!
Action taken!
Action taken!
>>>>>>>>>>> Five accomplished!
Action taken!
Action taken!
Action taken!
Action taken!
Action taken!
>>>>>>>>>>> Five accomplished!
```

This code works by creating a variable (i), which I initialize to the value 1. It then loops 20 times, printing Action taken! on each loop. This modest operation stands in for whatever work you want to do 20 times. The program tests i by using modulus 5

```
if ( i % 5 == 0 )
```

and when that value is 0 (every fifth time) it prints Five accomplished!

Combining the Assignment and Mathematical Operators

It is not uncommon to want to add a value to a variable, and then to assign the result back into the variable. If you have a variable myAge and you want to increase the value by two, you can write

```
int myAge = 5;
int temp;
temp = myAge + 2;  // add 5 + 2 and
put it in temp
myAge = temp;          // put it
back in myAge
```

Throw Me for a Loop

This code uses a for loop, which is a programming device explained later in this chapter. The essence of this for loop is that we take the action of printing a message once for each value of I, 0 through 19.

This method, however, is terribly convoluted and wasteful. In C++ and Java, you can put the same variable on both sides of the assignment operator, and therefore the preceding becomes

```
myAge = myAge + 2;
```

101

which is much better. In algebra, this expression would be meaningless, but in a modern programming language it reads as "add two to the value in myAge and assign the result to myAge."

Even simpler to write, but perhaps a bit harder to read is

```
myAge += 2;
```

The self-assigned addition operator (+=) adds the r-value to the l-value and then reassigns the result into the l-value. This operator is pronounced "plus-equals." The statement would be read "myAge plus-equals two." If myAge had the value 4 to start, it would have 6 after this statement.

There are self-assigned subtraction (–=), division (/=), multiplication (*=), and modulus (%=) operators as well.

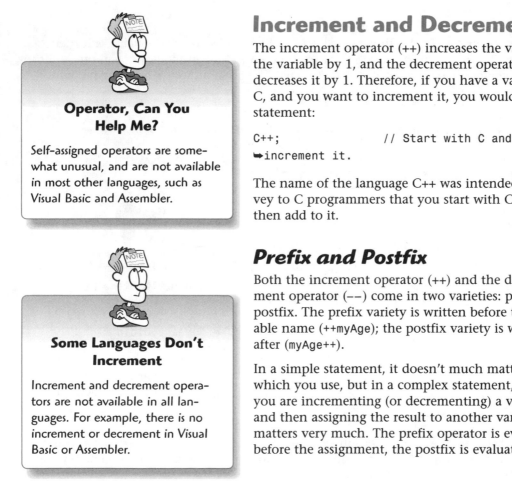

Operator, Can You Help Me?

Self-assigned operators are somewhat unusual, and are not available in most other languages, such as Visual Basic and Assembler.

Some Languages Don't Increment

Increment and decrement operators are not available in all languages. For example, there is no increment or decrement in Visual Basic or Assembler.

Increment and Decrement

The increment operator (++) increases the value of the variable by 1, and the decrement operator (––) decreases it by 1. Therefore, if you have a variable, C, and you want to increment it, you would use this statement:

```
C++;              // Start with C and
➥increment it.
```

The name of the language C++ was intended to convey to C programmers that you start with C and then add to it.

Prefix and Postfix

Both the increment operator (++) and the decrement operator (––) come in two varieties: prefix and postfix. The prefix variety is written before the variable name (++myAge); the postfix variety is written after (myAge++).

In a simple statement, it doesn't much matter which you use, but in a complex statement, when you are incrementing (or decrementing) a variable and then assigning the result to another variable, it matters very much. The prefix operator is evaluated before the assignment, the postfix is evaluated after.

The semantics of prefix is this: Increment the value and then fetch it. The semantics of postfix is different: Fetch the value and then increment the original.

This can be confusing at first, but if x is an integer whose value is 5 and you write

```
int a = ++x;
```

you have told the compiler to increment x (making it 6) and then fetch that value and assign it to a. Therefore a is now 6 and x is now 6.

If, after doing this, you write

```
int b = x++;
```

you have now told the compiler to fetch the value in x (6) and assign it to b, and then go back and increment x. Therefore, b is now 6, but x is now 7. Listing 7.3 shows the use and implications of both types.

Listing 7.3 Using Prefix and Postfix

```
1:  //Demonstration of the
2:  // prefix and postfix increment and
3:  // decrement operators
4:  #include <iostream.h>
5:  int main()
6:  {
7:      int myAge = 39;        // initialize two integers
8:      int yourAge = 39;
9:      cout << "I am: " << myAge << " years old.\n";
10:     cout << "You are: " << yourAge << " years old\n";
11:     myAge++;               // postfix increment
12:     ++yourAge;             // prefix increment
13:     cout << "One year passes...\n";
14:     cout << "I am: " << myAge << " years old.\n";
15:     cout << "You are: " << yourAge << " years old\n";
16:     cout << "Another year passes\n";
17:     cout << "I am: " << myAge++ << " years old.\n";
18:     cout << "You are: " << ++yourAge << " years old\n";
19:     cout << "Let's print it again.\n";
20:     cout << "I am: " << myAge << " years old.\n";
21:     cout << "You are: " << yourAge << " years old\n";
22:         return 0;
23: }
```

```
I am       39 years old
You are    39 years old
```

continues

Listing 7.3   Continued

```
One year passes
I am        40 years old
You are     40 years old
Another year passes
I am        40 years old
You are     41 years old
Let's print it again
I am        41 years old
You are     41 years old
```

On lines 7 and 8, two integer variables are declared, and each is initialized with the value 39. Their values are printed on lines 9 and 10.

On line 11, myAge is incremented using the postfix increment operator, and on line 12, yourAge is incremented using the prefix increment operator. The results are printed on lines 14 and 15, and they are identical (both 40).

On line 17, myAge is incremented as part of the printing statement, using the postfix increment operator. Because it is postfix, the increment happens after the print, and so the value 40 is printed again. In contrast, on line 18, yourAge is incremented using the prefix increment operator. Thus, it is incremented before being printed, and the value displays as 41.

Finally, on lines 20 and 21, the values are printed again. Because the increment statement has completed, the value in myAge is now 41, as is the value in yourAge.

Precedence

In the complex statement

```
x = 5 + 3 * 8;
```

which is performed first, the addition or the multiplication? Depending on which you perform first, the resulting value will vary. If the addition is performed first, the answer is 8 * 8, or 64. If the multiplication is performed first, the answer is 5 + 24, or 29.

Every operator has a precedence value. Multiplication has higher precedence than addition, and therefore the value of the expression is 29.

When two mathematical operators have the same precedence, they are performed in left-to-right order. Therefore,

```
x = 5 + 3 + 8 * 9 + 6 * 4;
```

is evaluated multiplication first, left to right. Therefore, 8*9 = 72, and 6*4 = 24. Now the expression is essentially

```
x = 5 + 3 + 72 + 24;
```

Now the addition, left to right, is 5 + 3 = 8; 8 + 72 = 80; 80 + 24 = 104.

Be careful with this. Some operators, such as assignment, are evaluated in right-to-left order! In any case, what if the precedence order doesn't meet your needs? Consider the expression

```
TotalSeconds = NumMinutesToThink + NumMinutesToType * 60
```

In this expression, you do not want to multiply the `NumMinutesToType` variable by 60 and then add it to `NumMinutesToThink`. You want to add the two variables to get the total number of minutes, and then you want to multiply that number by the literal constant 60 to get the total seconds.

In this case, you use parentheses to change the precedence order. Items in parentheses are evaluated at a higher precedence than any of the mathematical operators. Thus

```
TotalSeconds = (NumMinutesToThink + NumMinutesToType) * 60
```

will accomplish what you want.

Nesting Parentheses

For complex expressions, you might need to nest parentheses one within another. For example, you might need to compute the total seconds and then compute the total number of people who are involved before multiplying seconds times people:

```
TotalPersonSeconds = ( ( (NumMinutesToThink + NumMinutesToType) * 60) *
(PeopleInTheOffice + PeopleOnVacation) )
```

This complicated expression is read from the inside out. First, `NumMinutesToThink` is added to `NumMinutesToType`, because these are in the innermost parentheses. Then this sum is multiplied by 60. Next, `PeopleInTheOffice` is added to `PeopleOnVacation`. Finally, the total number of people found is multiplied by the total number of seconds.

This example raises an important related issue. This expression is easy for a computer to understand, but very difficult for a human to read, understand, or modify. Here is the same expression rewritten, using some temporary integer variables:

```
TotalMinutes = NumMinutesToThink + NumMinutesToType;
TotalSeconds = TotalMinutes * 60;
TotalPeople = PeopleInTheOffice + PeopleOnVacation;
TotalPersonSeconds = TotalPeople * TotalSeconds;
```

This example takes longer to write and uses more temporary variables than the preceding example, but it is far easier to understand. Add a comment at the top to explain what this code does, and change the 60 to a symbolic constant. You then have code that is easy to understand and maintain.

```
// compute total number of seconds people spend thinking and typing
TotalMinutes = NumMinutesToThink + NumMinutesToType;
TotalSeconds = TotalMinutes * SECONDS_In_A_MINUTE;
TotalPeople = PeopleInTheOffice + PeopleOnVacation;
TotalPersonSeconds = TotalPeople * TotalSeconds;
```

The Nature of Truth

Many languages, such as C++ and Java, have a boolean type (often called bool). A boolean type is one that has only two values (boolean math works only with the values 1 and 0). These boolean values are typically called true and false.

Some older languages treat the value 0 as false and all other values as true. C++ inherits this from C, but unlike C, standard C++ now includes a bool type.

Relational Operators

The relational operators are used to determine whether two numbers are equal, or if one is greater or less than the other. Every relational statement evaluates to either true or false. If the integer variable myAge has the value 39, and the integer variable yourAge has the value 40, you can determine whether they are equal by using the relational "equals" operator:

```
myAge == yourAge;  // is the value in myAge the same as in yourAge?
```

This expression evaluates to the boolean value false, because the variables are not equal. The expression

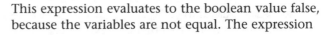

```
myAge > yourAge;  // is myAge greater than
                  yourAge?
```

evaluates to false.

There are six relational operators: equals (==), less than (<), greater than (>), less than or equal to (<=), greater than or equal to (>=), and not equals (!=). Table 7.1 shows each relational operator, its use, and a sample code use.

Not One but Two

Note that in C++ and Java the equals operator is two equal signs (==), because one equal sign is used for the assignment operator (=).

Table 7.1   The Relational Operators

Name	Operator	Sample	Evaluates
Equals	==	100 == 50; 50 == 50;	false true
Not Equals	!=	100 != 50; 50 != 50;	true false
Greater Than	>	100 > 50; 50 > 50;	true false
Greater Than or Equals	>=	100 >= 50; 50 >= 50;	true true
Less Than	<	100 < 50; 50 < 50;	false false
Less Than or Equals	<=	100 <= 50; 50 <= 50;	false true

Program Flow

Normally, your program flows along line by line in the order in which it appears in your source code. From time to time you want the flow of your program to branch. Perhaps you want to take one path if a particular condition is true; another path otherwise. For example, the program might be processing year-end salary reviews and it takes one path if the employee is in management; another path if the employee is in the union.

One way to accomplish this branching is with an *if statement*. The if statement enables you to test for a condition (such as whether two variables are equal) and branch to different parts of your code, depending on the result.

if Statements

The simplest form of an if statement is this:

```
if ( expression )
    statement;
```

The expression in the parentheses can be any expression, but it usually contains one of the relational expressions. If it evaluates true, the statement is executed; otherwise, it is skipped.

```
if ( bigNumber > smallNumber )
    bigNumber = smallNumber;
```

This code compares bigNumber and smallNumber. If bigNumber is larger, the second line sets its value to the value of smallNumber.

Because a block of statements surrounded by braces is exactly equivalent to a single statement, quite a bit of work can be done if the expression evaluates true:

```
if ( expression )
{
     statement1;
     statement2;
     statement3;
}
```

Here's a simple example of this usage:

```
if ( bigNumber > smallNumber )
{
     bigNumber = smallNumber;
     cout << "bigNumber: " << bigNumber << "\n";
     cout << "smallNumber: " << smallNumber << "\n";
}
```

This time, if bigNumber is larger than smallNumber, not only is it set to the value of smallNumber, but also an informational message is printed. Listing 7.4 shows a more detailed example of branching based on relational operators.

Listing 7.4   Branching Based on Relational Operators

```
1:  // Demonstrating the if statement
2:  // used with relational operators
3:  #include <iostream.h>
4:  int main()
5:  {
6:       int RedSoxScore, YankeesScore;
7:       cout << "Enter the score for the Red Sox: ";
8:       cin >> RedSoxScore;
9:
10:      cout << "\nEnter the score for the Yankees: ";
11:      cin >> YankeesScore;
12:
13:      cout << "\n";
14:
15:      if ( RedSoxScore > YankeesScore )
16:          cout << "Go Sox!\n";
17:
18:      if ( RedSoxScore < YankeesScore )
19:      {
20:          cout << "Go Yankees!\n";
21:          cout << "Happy days in New York!\n";
22:      }
```

```
23:
24:        if ( RedSoxScore == YankeesScore )
25:        {
26:              cout << "A tie? Naah, can't be.\n";
27:              cout << "Give me the real score for the Yanks: ";
28:              cin >> YankeesScore;
29:
30:            if (RedSoxScore > YankeesScore)
31:                cout << "Knew it! Go Sox!";
32:
33:            if (YankeesScore > RedSoxScore)
34:                cout << "Knew it! Go Yanks!";
35:
36:            if (YankeesScore == RedSoxScore)
37:                cout << "Wow, it really was a tie!";
38:        }
39:
40:        cout << "\nThanks for telling me.\n";
41:         return 0;
42: }

Enter the score for the Red Sox: 10

Enter the score for the Yankees: 10

A tie? Naah, can't be
Give me the real score for the Yanks: 8
Knew it! Go Sox!
Thanks for telling me.
```

This program asks for user input of scores for two baseball teams, which are stored in integer variables. The variables are compared in the if statement on lines 15, 18, and 24.

If one score is higher than the other, an informational message is printed. If the scores are equal, the block of code that begins on line 24 and ends on line 38 is entered. The second score is requested again, and then the scores are compared again.

Note that if the initial Yankees score was higher than the Red Sox score, the if statement on line 15 would evaluate as false, and line 16 would not be invoked. The test on line 18 would evaluate as true, and the statements on lines 20 and 21 would be invoked. The if statement on line 24 would be tested, and this would be false (if line 18 was true). Thus, the program would skip the entire block, falling through to line 39.

In this example, getting a true result in one if statement does not stop other if statements from being tested.

else

Often your program wants to take one branch if your condition is true, another if it is false. In Listing 7.4, you wanted to print one message (Go Sox!) if the first test (RedSoxScore > Yankees) evaluated true, and another message (Go Yanks!) if it evaluated false.

The method shown so far, testing first one condition and then the other, works fine but is a bit cumbersome. The keyword else can make for far more readable code:

```
if (expression)
     statement;
else
     statement;
```

Listing 7.5 demonstrates the use of the keyword else.

Listing 7.5   Using the Keyword else

```
1:     // demonstrating the if statement
2:     // with else clause
3:     #include <iostream.h>
4:     int main()
5:     {
6:         int firstNumber, secondNumber;
7:         cout << "Please enter a big number: ";
8:         cin >> firstNumber;
9:         cout << "\nPlease enter a smaller number: ";
10:        cin >> secondNumber;
11:        if (firstNumber > secondNumber)
12:             cout << "\nThanks!\n";
13:        else
14:             cout << "\nOops. The second is bigger!";
15:
16:            return 0;
17:    }
```

```
Please enter a big number: 10

Please enter a smaller number: 12
Oops. The second is bigger!
```

The if statement on line 11 is evaluated. If the condition is true, the statement on line 12 is run; if it is false, the statement on line 14 is run. If the else clause on line 13 were removed, the statement on line 14 would run whether or not the if statement was true. Remember, the if statement ends after line 12. If the else was not there, line 14 would just be the next line in the program.

Remember that either or both of these statements could be replaced with a block of code in braces.

110

Advanced if *Statements*

It is worth noting that any statement can be used in an if or else clause, even another if or else statement. Therefore, you might see complex if statements in the following form:

```
if (expression1)
{
    if (expression2)
        statement1;
    else
    {
        if (expression3)
            statement2;
        else
            statement3;
    }
}
else
    statement4;
```

Logical Operators

Often you want to ask more than one relational question at a time. "Is it true that x is greater than y, and also true that y is greater than z?" A program might need to determine that both of these conditions are true, or that some other condition is true, in order to take an action.

Imagine a sophisticated alarm system that has this logic: "If the door alarm sounds AND it is after six p.m. AND it is NOT a holiday, OR if it is a weekend, then call the police." Three logical operators are used to make this kind of evaluation.

Logical AND

A logical AND statement evaluates two expressions, and if both expressions are true, the logical AND statement is true as well. If it is true that you are hungry, AND it is true that you have money, THEN it is true that you can buy lunch.

Logical OR

A logical OR statement evaluates two expressions. If either one is true, the expression is true. If you have money OR you have a credit card, you can pay the bill. You don't need both money and a credit card; you need only one, although having both would be fine as well.

111

Logical NOT

A logical NOT statement evaluates true if the expression being tested is false. This statement is tricky; here's how it works: If the expression being tested is false, the value of the test is true. Therefore

```
if ( !(amountDeposited  == 75) )
```

is true only if the amount deposited in the soda machine is not equal to the actual price of 75 cents. You read this "if it is not true that amountDeposited is equal to 75...."

Note that this test is exactly the same as

```
if ( amountDeposited != 75 )
```

`switch` **Statements**

Complex `if` statements can become quite confusing when nested too deeply, and many languages offer an alternative in statements—usually called *case*, or *choice*, or, as in C++ and Java, *switch*.

Unlike `if` statements, which evaluate one value, `switch` statements allow you to branch on any of a number of different values. The general form of the `switch` statement is

```
switch (expression)
{
case valueOne: statement;
                    break;
case valueTwo: statement;
                    break;
....
case valueN:    statement;
                    break;
default:        statement;
}
```

where `expression` is any legal expression, and the `statements` are any legal statements or block of statements which evaluate to an integer value.

If one of the case values matches the expression, execution jumps to those statements and continues to the end of the switch block, unless a break statement is encountered. If nothing matches, execution branches to the optional default statement. If there is no default and there is no matching value, execution falls through the switch statement and the statement ends. Listing 7.6 illustrates this concept.

112

Listing 7.6 Execution Falling Through the switch Statement

```
1:   //Demonstrating the use
2:   // of switch statement
3:
4:   #include <iostream.h>
5:
6:   int main()
7:   {
8:     unsigned short int number;
9:     cout << "Enter a number between 1 and 5: ";
10:    cin >> number;
11:    switch ( number )
12:    {
13:       case 0:   cout << "Too small, sorry!";
14:                 break;
15:       case 5:  cout << "Good job!\n";  // fall through
16:       case 4:  cout << "Nice Pick!\n"; // fall through
17:       case 3:  cout << "Excellent!\n"; // fall through
18:       case 2:  cout << "Masterful!\n"; // fall through
19:       case 1:  cout << "Incredible!\n";
20:                break;
21:       default: cout << "Too large!\n";
22:                break;
23:    }
24:    cout << "\n\n";
25:     return 0;
26:  }
```

```
Enter a number between 1 and 5: 3
Excellent!
Masterful!
Incredible!

Enter a number between 1 and 5: 8
Too large!
```

The user is prompted for a number. That number is given to the switch statement. If the number is 0, the case statement on line 13 matches, the message Too small, sorry! is printed, and the break statement ends the switch. If the value is 5, execution switches to line 15 where a message is printed, and then falls through to line 16, another message is printed, and so forth until hitting the break on line 20.

Twice Is Twice As Nice

This output is the result of running the program twice.

The net effect of these statements is that for a number between 1 and 5, that many messages are printed. If the value of number is not 0–5, it is assumed to be too large, and the default statement is invoked on line 21.

Loops

One significant interruption in the flow of a program is a loop. A loop is just a way of repeatedly doing the same thing again and again. Programmers call this repetition *iteration.*

It is often useful to loop in a program. You may be examining a series of values or taking the same action against every member of a collection.

The simplest loop is created with the dreaded goto statement.

Geek Speak

Are You Saying I'm Redundant, That I Repeat Myself?

Iteration—doing the same thing repeatedly.

The Roots of Looping Goto

In the primitive days of early computer science, programs were nasty, brutish, and short. Loops consisted of a label, some statements, and a jump.

In C++, a label is just a name followed by a colon (:). The label is placed to the left of a legal C++ statement, and a jump is accomplished by writing goto followed by the label name. Listing 7.7 illustrates this.

Listing 7.7   Demonstrating a Simple Goto

```
1:      // Demonstrates a simple goto
2:      // statement with a label
3:
4:      #include <iostream.h>
5:
6:      int main()
7:      {
8:          int counter = 0;        // initialize counter
9:      loop:   counter ++;             // top of the loop
10:             cout << "counter: " << counter << "\n";
11:          if (counter < 5)            // test the value
12:              goto loop;              // jump to the top
13:
14:          cout << "Complete. Counter: " << counter << ".\n";
15:       return 0;
16:      }
```

```
counter: 1
counter: 2
counter: 3
counter: 4
counter: 5
Complete. Counter: 5.
```

On line 8, counter is initialized to 0. The label loop is on line 9, marking the top of the loop. The variable counter is incremented and its new value is printed. The value of counter is tested on line 11. If it is less than 5, the if statement is true and the goto statement is executed. This causes program execution to jump back to line 9. The program continues looping until counter is equal to 5, at which time it "falls through" the loop and the final output is printed.

Why Goto *Is Shunned*

The goto statement has received some rotten press lately, and it's well deserved. These goto statements can cause a jump to any location in your source code, backward or forward. The indiscriminate use of goto statements has caused tangled, miserable, impossible-to-read programs known as "spaghetti code." Because of this, computer science teachers have spent the past 20 years drumming one lesson into the heads of their students: "Never, ever use goto!"

To avoid the use of goto, more sophisticated, tightly controlled looping commands have been introduced: for, while, and do...while. Using these commands makes programs that are more easily understood, and goto is generally avoided in languages such as C++ and Java, although it is still an integral part of Visual Basic.

While *Loops*

A while loop causes your program to repeat a sequence of statements as long as the starting condition remains true. In the example of goto, in Listing 7.7, the counter was incremented until it was equal to 5. Listing 7.8 shows the same program rewritten to take advantage of a while loop.

Listing 7.8   Demonstrating a While Loop

```
1:      // Demonstration of
2:      // Looping with while
3:
4:      #include <iostream.h>
5:
6:      int main()
7:      {
```

continues

115

Listing 7.8   Continued

```
8:      int counter = 0;                // initialize the condition
9:
10:     while( counter < 5 )     // test condition still true
11:       {
12:          counter++;                // body of the loop
13:          cout << "counter: " << counter << "\n";
14:       }
15:
16:     cout << "Complete. Counter: " << counter << ".\n";
17:       return 0;
18:    }
```

Output

```
counter: 1
counter: 2
counter: 3
counter: 4
counter: 5
Complete. Counter: 5.
```

Analysis

This simple program demonstrates the fundamentals of the while loop. A condition is tested, and if it is true, the body of the while loop is executed. In this case, the condition tested on line 10 is whether counter is less than 5. If the condition is true, the body of the loop is executed; on line 12 the counter is incremented, and on line 13 the value is printed. When the conditional statement on line 10 fails (when counter is no longer less than 5), the entire body of the while loop (lines 11–14) is skipped. Program execution falls through to line 15.

More Complicated While Statements

The condition tested by a while loop can be as complex as any legal C++ expression. This can include expressions produced using the logical && (AND), || (OR), and ! (NOT) operators.

At times you want to return to the top of a while loop before the entire set of statements in the while loop is executed. The continue statement jumps back to the top of the loop.

At other times, you may want to exit the loop before the exit conditions are met. The break statement immediately exits the while loop, and program execution resumes after the closing brace.

For example, you might write

```
0:   #include <iostream>
1:   #include <string>
2:   using namespace std;
3:
4:   int main()
5:   {
6:     int howManyExpected = 5;
7:     string buffer;
8:      int i = 0;
9:     while ( i < 5 )
10:           {
11:                   cout << "Enter 5 letters, press enter. (q to quit): ";
12:                   cin >> buffer;
13:
14:                   if ( buffer == "q" )
15:                           break;
16:
17:                   if ( buffer.length() != 5 )
18:                   {
19:                           cout << "Please enter exactly 5 ";
20:                           cout << "letters or q to quit.\n";
21:                           continue;
22:                   }
23:                   cout << "Excellent, your entry was: " << buffer <<
  ↪endl;
24:                   buffer = "";
25:                   i++;
26:           }
27:           return 0;
28:   }
```

On line 9, we enter a while loop, testing the counter value i which was initialized on line 8. In this while loop, we will prompt the user for five strings of letters, each of which must have exactly five letters.

On line 12, we capture the user's choice. Don't worry about how cout or cin work; they simply move text to and from the user interface.

On line 14, we examine the input and if it is q, we want to stop the loop, accomplished on line 15 by calling break. If we get past that test, on line 17 we check the length of the string entered and if it is not 5, we print a warning message and then we call continue, which causes us to loop to the top of the for statement without incrementing the counter i.

Finally, if we pass all these tests, we do the work of the for statement (in this case, printing the message), increment the counter, and go back to the top of the while loop.

Do...While

It is possible that the body of a while loop will never execute. The while statement checks its condition before executing any of its statements, and if the condition evaluates false, the entire body of the while loop is skipped.

The do...while loop solves this problem. It executes the body of the loop before its condition is tested and ensures that the body always executes at least one time.

When programming while loops, you'll often find yourself setting up a starting condition, testing to see whether the condition is true, and incrementing or otherwise changing a variable each time through the loop.

A for loop combines three steps into one statement. The three steps are initialization, test, and increment. A for statement consists of the keyword for followed by a pair of parentheses. Within the parentheses are three statements separated by semicolons.

The first statement is the initialization. Any legal statement can be put here, but typically this is used to create and initialize a counting variable. Statement 2 is the test, and any legal *expression* can be used here. This serves the same role as the condition in the while loop. Statement 3 is the action. Typically a value is incremented or decremented, although any legal statement can be put in the third position. Listing 7.9 illustrates this concept.

Listing 7.9 Demonstrating Looping with Do...While

```
1:      // Demonstration of
2:      // Looping with for
3:
4:      #include <iostream.h>
5:
6:      int main()
7:      {
8:        int counter;
9:        for (counter = 0; counter < 5; counter++)
10:          cout << "Looping! ";
11:
12:        cout << "\nCounter: " << counter << ".\n";
13:        return 0;
14:      }

Looping!  Looping!  Looping!  Looping!  Looping!
Counter: 5.
```

The for statement on line 9 combines the initialization of counter, the test that counter is less than 5, and the increment of counter all into one line. The body of the for statement is on line 10. Of course, a block could be used here as well.

118

The Least You Need to Know

➤ Programming languages are strongly analogous to human languages: They contain syntax and statements.

➤ Expressions are statements that provide a value.

➤ Incrementing and decrementing increases or decreases a value by one, respectively.

➤ Certain mathematical operations take precedence over others.

➤ Loops let you perform an operation numerous times.

WOW!

Functions

A function is, in effect, a subprogram that can act on data and return a value. In some programming languages, functions are called subroutines. Each function has its own name, and when that name is encountered, the execution of the program branches to the body of that function. This is *calling* the function. When the function returns, execution resumes on the next line of the calling function. This flow is illustrated here.

A function is a subprogram that is called, executes, and returns.

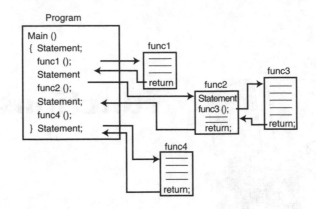

Well-designed functions perform a specific and easily understood task. Complicated tasks should be broken down into multiple functions, and then each can be called in turn.

Functions come in two varieties: user-defined and built-in. Built-in functions are part of your development language—they are supplied by the manufacturer for your use.

Return Values, Parameters, and Arguments

When you call a function, it can do work and then provide a value as a result of that work. This is called its *return value*.

Some languages distinguish between functions that return a value and those that do not (often called *procedures*). Other languages, such as C++ and Java, lump both of these together as simply "functions."

You can also send values into the function. The description of the values you send is called a parameter list.

```
int myFunction(int someValue, float someFloat);
```

This declaration indicates that myFunction will return an integer and it will take two parameters: an integer value and a float.

A parameter describes the *type* of the value which will be passed into the function when the function is called. The actual values you pass into the function are called the *arguments*.

```
int theValueReturned = myFunction(5,6.7);
```

Programming Terminology

Function—a subprogram that can act upon data and then return to the calling program, often with a value.

Procedure—a term for functions that do not return a value.

Parameter—describes the type of value you'll pass into a function.

Argument—a value you pass into a function.

122

Here we see that an integer variable *theValueReturned* is initialized with the value returned by myFunction, and that the values 5 and 6.7 are passed in as arguments. The type of the arguments must match the declared parameter types. Listing 8.1 illustrates the use of a function.

Listing 8.1   Illustrating a Function

```
1:   // illustrating a function
2:   // note the return type is integer
3:   // and this function takes two parameters
4:   #include <iostream.h>
5:   int Area(int length, int width);
6:
7:   int main()
8:   {
9:     int lengthOfYard;
10:    int widthOfYard;
11:    int areaOfYard;
12:
13:    cout << "\nHow wide is your yard? ";
14:    cin >> widthOfYard;
15:    cout << "\nHow long is your yard? ";
16:    cin >> lengthOfYard;
17:
18:    areaOfYard= Area(lengthOfYard,widthOfYard);
19:
20:    cout << "\nYour yard is ";
21:    cout << areaOfYard;
22:    cout << " square feet\n\n";
23:    return 0;
24:  }
25:
26:  int Area(int length, int width)
27:  {
28:      return length * width;
29:  }
```

Output

```
How wide is your yard? 100

How long is your yard? 200

Your yard is 20000 square feet
```

Analysis

On line 5, I declare the function in what is called a prototype. This section of code tells the compiler the return type, name, and parameters for the function.

Not a Working Model

Prototype—In C++, a prototype defines a function and tells the compiler its return type, name, and parameter list. Not all languages use prototypes, and some make them optional.

Compare the prototype with the definition of the function on line 26. Note that the name, the return type, and the parameter types are the same. If they were different, a compiler error would have occurred. In fact, the only required difference is that the function prototype ends with a semicolon and has no body.

You pass the arguments into the function in the order in which you declare and define the parameters, but there is no matching of the names. Had you passed in `widthOfYard`, followed by `lengthOfYard`, the `FindArea()` function would have used the value in `widthOfYard` for length and `lengthOfYard` for width. The body of the function is always enclosed in braces, even when it consists of only one statement, as in this case.

Execution of Functions

When you call a function, execution begins with the first statement after the opening brace ({). Functions can also call other functions and can even call themselves.

Local Variables

You can not only pass in variables to the function, but also declare variables within the body of the function. This is done using local variables, so named because they exist only locally within the function itself. When the function returns, the local variables are destroyed and they are no longer available.

Local variables are defined like any other variables. The parameters passed in to the function are also considered local variables and can be used exactly as if they had been defined within the body of the function. Listing 8.2 shows an example of using parameters and locally defined variables within a function.

Listing 8.2   Using Parameters Within a Function

```
1:      #include <iostream.h>
2:
3:      float Convert(float);
4:      int main()
```

```
5:      {
6:          float TempFer;
7:          float TempCel;
8:
9:          cout << "Please enter the temperature in Fahrenheit: ";
10:         cin >> TempFer;
11:         TempCel = Convert(TempFer);
12:         cout << "\nHere's the temperature in Celsius: ";
13:         cout << TempCel << endl;
14:             return 0;
15:     }
16:
17:     float Convert(float TempFer)
18:     {
19:         float TempCel;
20:         TempCel = ((TempFer - 32) * 5) / 9;
21:         return TempCel;
22:     }
```

Output

```
Please enter the temperature in Fahrenheit: 212

Here's the temperature in Celsius: 100

Please enter the temperature in Fahrenheit: 32

Here's the temperature in Celsius: 0

Please enter the temperature in Fahrenheit: 85

Here's the temperature in Celsius: 29.4444
```

Analysis

On lines 6 and 7, I declare two float variables, one to hold the temperature in Fahrenheit and one to hold the temperature in degrees Celsius. The user is prompted to enter a Fahrenheit temperature on line 9, and that value is passed to the function Convert().

Execution jumps to the first line of the function Convert() on line 19, where a local variable, also named TempCel, is declared. Note that this local variable is not the same as the variable TempCel on line 7. This variable exists only within the function Convert(). The value passed as a parameter, TempFer, is also just a local copy of the variable passed in by main() as an argument to the Convert() method.

125

This function could have named the parameter FerTemp and the local variable CelTemp, and the program would work equally well. You can enter these names again and recompile the program to see this work.

The local function variable TempCel is assigned the value that results from subtracting 32 from the parameter TempFer, multiplying by 5, and then dividing by 9. This value is then returned as the return value of the function, and on line 11 it is assigned to the variable TempCel in the main() function. The program prints the value on line 13.

The program is run three times. The first time, the value 212 is passed in to ensure that the boiling point of water in degrees Fahrenheit (212) generates the correct answer in degrees Celsius (100). The second test is the freezing point of water. The third test is a random number chosen to generate a fractional result.

Function Statements

There is virtually no limit to the number or types of statements that you can place in the body of a function. Although you can't define another function from within a function, you can *call* another function. Functions can even call themselves, which is discussed in the section on recursion.

Although there is no limit to the size of a function in C++, well-designed functions tend to be small. Many programmers advise keeping your functions short enough to fit on a single screen so that you can see the entire function at one time. This is a rule of thumb, often broken by very good programmers, but a smaller function is easier to understand and maintain.

Each function should carry out a single, easily understood task. If your functions start getting large, look for places where you can divide them into component tasks.

More About Return Values

Functions return a value or return void. Void is a signal to the compiler that no value will be returned. Many languages, such as Visual Basic, do not use this explicit designation.

To return a value from a function in C++ or Java, write the keyword **return** followed by the value you want to return. The value might itself be an expression that returns a value. For example:

```
return 5;
return (x > 5);
return (MyFunction());
```

These are all legal return statements, assuming that the function MyFunction() itself returns a value. The value in the second statement, return (x > 5), will be false if x is not greater than 5, or it will be true. What is returned is the value of the expression, false or true, not the value of x.

126

When the `return` keyword is encountered, the expression following `return` is returned as the value of the function. Program execution returns immediately to the calling function, and any statements following the `return` are not executed.

It is legal to have more than one `return` statement in a single function. Listing 8.3 illustrates this idea.

Listing 8.3   Demonstrating Multiple Return Statements

```
1:      // Demonstrating multiple return
2:      // statements
3:
4:      #include <iostream.h>
5:
6:      int Doubler(int AmountToDouble);
7:
8:      int main()
9:      {
10:
11:         int result = 0;
12:         int input;
13:
14:         cout << "Enter a number between 0 and 10,000 to double: ";
15:         cin >> input;
16:
17:         cout << "\nBefore doubler is called... ";
18:         cout << "\ninput: " << input << " doubled: " << result <<
➥"\n";
19:
20:         result = Doubler(input);
21:
22:         cout << "\nBack from Doubler...\n";
23:         cout << "\ninput: " << input << "    doubled: " << result
➥<< "\n";
24:
25:
26:         return 0;
27:      }
28:
29:      int Doubler(int original)
30:      {
31:         if (original <= 10000)
32:             return original * 2;
33:         else
34:             return -1;
35:         cout << "You can't get here!\n";
36:      }
```

Output

```
Enter a number between 0 and 10,000 to double: 9000

Before doubler is called...
input: 9000 doubled: 0

Back from doubler...

input: 9000    doubled: 18000

Enter a number between 0 and 10,000 to double: 11000

Before doubler is called...
input: 11000 doubled: 0

Back from doubler...
input: 11000   doubled: -1
```

Analysis

This program requests a number on lines 14 and 15, and printed on line 18, along with the local variable result. The function `Doubler()` is called on line 20, and the input value is passed as a parameter. The result will be assigned to the local variable result, and the values will be reprinted on line 23.

On line 31, in the function `Doubler()`, the parameter is tested to see whether it is greater than 10,000. If it is not, the function returns twice the original number. If it is greater than 10,000, the function returns –1 as an error value.

The vigilant reader will note that the statement on line 35 is never reached, because regardless of whether the value is greater than 10,000, the function returns before it gets to line 35, on either line 32 or line 34. This is a logical error in the program, and a really good compiler will point it out for you.

Overloading Functions

C++ enables you to create more than one function with the same name. Doing so is called *function overloading*. Visual Basic and Java do not support this capability. The functions must differ in their parameter list, with a different type of parameter, a different number of parameters, or both. Here's an example:

```
int myFunction (int, int);
int myFunction (long, long);
int myFunction (long);
```

`myFunction()` is overloaded with three different parameter lists. The first and second versions differ in the types of the parameters, and the third differs in the number of parameters.

The return types can be the same or different on overloaded functions. You should note that two functions with the same name and parameter list, but different return types, generate a compiler error.

Function overloading is also called *function polymorphism*. *Poly* means many, and *morph* means form: A polymorphic function is many-formed.

Function polymorphism refers to the ability to "overload" a function with more than one meaning. By changing the number or type of the parameters, you can give two or more functions the same function name, and the right one will be called by matching the parameters used. This allows you to create a function that can average integers, doubles, and other values without having to create individual names for each function, such as `AverageInts()`, `AverageDoubles()`, and so on.

Suppose you write a function that doubles whatever input you give it. You would like to be able to pass in an int, a long, a float, or a double. Without function overloading, you would have to create four function names:

```
int DoubleInt(int);
long DoubleLong(long);
float DoubleFloat(float);
double DoubleDouble(double);
```

With function overloading, you make this declaration:

```
int Double(int);
long Double(long);
float Double(float);
double Double(double);
```

This overloaded function is easier to read and easier to use. You don't have to worry about which one to call; you just pass in a variable, and the right function is called automatically.

Recursion

A function can call itself. This action is called *recursion*, and recursion can be direct or indirect. Recursion is direct when a function calls itself; it is indirect when a function calls another function that, in turn, calls the first function.

Don't Worry If This Seems Tough

Recursion is notoriously difficult to understand. If this section leaves your head spinning, don't panic! You may find you enjoy this concept, but if not, just set it aside and come back to it after six months of programming; it may make a lot more sense by then.

Some problems are most easily solved by recursion, usually those in which you act on data and then act in the same way on the result. Both types of recursion, direct and indirect, come in two varieties: those that eventually end and produce an answer, and those that never end and produce a runtime failure. Programmers think that the latter is quite funny (when it happens to someone else).

It is important to note that when a function calls itself, a new copy of that function is run. The local variables in the second version are independent of the local variables in the first, and they cannot affect one another directly, any more than the local variables in main() can affect the local variables in any function it calls, as was illustrated in Listing 8.4. To illustrate solving a problem using recursion, consider the Fibonacci series:

$$1,1,2,3,5,8,13,21,34\ldots$$

Each number, after the second, is the sum of the two numbers before it. A Fibonacci problem might be to determine what the 12th number in the series is.

One way to solve this problem is to examine the series carefully. The first two numbers are 1. Each subsequent number is the sum of the previous two numbers. Therefore, the seventh number is the sum of the sixth and fifth numbers. More generally, the *n*th number is the sum of *n*–2 and *n*–1, as long as *n* > 2.

Recursive functions need a stop condition. Something must happen to cause the program to stop recursing, or it will never end. In the Fibonacci series, n < 3 is a stop condition.

The algorithm to use is this:

1. Ask the user for a position in the series.
2. Call the fib() function with that position, passing in the value the user entered.
3. The fib() function examines the argument (*n*). If *n* < 3 it returns 1; otherwise, fib() calls itself (recursively) passing in *n*-2, calls itself again passing in *n*-1, and returns the sum.

If you call fib(1), it returns 1. If you call fib(2), it returns 1. If you call fib(3), it returns the sum of calling fib(2) and fib(1). Because fib(2) returns 1 and fib(1) returns 1, fib(3) will return 2.

If you call fib(4), it returns the sum of calling fib(3) and fib(2). We've established that fib(3) returns 2 (by calling fib(2) and fib(1)) and that fib(2) returns 1, so fib(4) will add these numbers and return 3, which is the fourth number in the series.

130

Taking this one more step, if you call fib(5), it will return the sum of fib(4) and fib(3). We've established that fib(4) returns 3 and fib(3) returns 2, so the sum returned will be 5.

This method is not the most efficient way to solve this problem (in fib(20) the fib() function is called 13,529 times!), but it does work. Be careful: If you feed in too large a number, you'll run out of memory. Every time the program calls fib(), memory is set aside. When it returns, memory is freed. With recursion, memory continues to be set aside before it is freed, and this system can eat memory very quickly. Listing 8.4 implements the fib() function.

Listing 8.4 Implementing the Fib Function

```
1: /* Demonstrates recursion
2: by implementing the Fibonacci
➥series:
3: 1,1,2,3,5,8,13,21,34...
4: Ask the user for a position in
➥the series.
5: Call the fib() function with
➥that position,
6: passing in the value the user
➥entered.
7: The fib() function examines the
➥argument (n). I
8: if n < 3 it returns 1;
➥otherwise, fib() calls itself
9: (recursively) passing in n-2,
➥calls itself again passing
10: in n-1, and returns the sum. */
11: #include <iostream.h>
12:
13: int fib (int n);
14:
15:    int main()
16:    {
17:
18:       int n, answer;
19:       cout << "Enter number to find: ";
20:       cin >> n;
21:
22:       cout << "\n\n";
23:
24:       answer = fib(n);
25:
26:       cout << answer << " is the " << n << "th Fibonacci number\n";
```

Keep the Number Small

When you run this listing, enter a small number (less than 15). Because this program uses recursion, it can consume a lot of memory.

continues

Listing 8.4   Continued

```
27:          return 0;
28:    }
29:
30:    int fib (int n)
31:    {
32:      cout << "Processing fib(" << n << ")... ";
33:
34:      if (n < 3 )
35:      {
36:         cout << "Return 1!\n";
37:         return (1);
38:      }
39:      else
40:      {
41:         cout << "Call fib(" << n-2 << ") and fib(" << n-1 <<
    ➥").\n";
42:         return( fib(n-2) + fib(n-1));
43:      }
44:    }
```

Output

```
Enter number to find: 6

Processing fib(6)... Call fib(4) and fib(5).
Processing fib(4)... Call fib(2) and fib(3).
Processing fib(2)... Return 1!
Processing fib(3)... Call fib(1) and fib(2).
Processing fib(1)... Return 1!
Processing fib(2)... Return 1!
Processing fib(5)... Call fib(3) and fib(4).
Processing fib(3)... Call fib(1) and fib(2).
Processing fib(1)... Return 1!
Processing fib(2)... Return 1!
Processing fib(4)... Call fib(2) and fib(3).
Processing fib(2)... Return 1!
Processing fib(3)... Call fib(1) and fib(2).
Processing fib(1)... Return 1!
Processing fib(2)... Return 1!
8 is the 6th Fibonacci number
```

Analysis

Lines 19 and 20 of the program ask for a number to find and assign that number to *n*. It then calls `fib()` with *n*. Execution branches to the `fib()` function, where, on line 32, it prints its argument.

The argument *n* is tested on line 34 to see whether it equals 1 or 2; if so, `fib()` returns. Otherwise, it returns the sums of the values returned by calling `fib()` on *n*–2 and *n*–1.

It cannot return these values until the call (to `fib()`) is resolved. Therefore, you can picture the program diving into fib repeatedly, until it hits a call to `fib()` that returns a value. The only calls that return a value immediately, are the calls to `fib(2)` and `fib(1)`. These are then passed up to the waiting callers, which in turn add the return value to their own and then return.

These two figures illustrate this recursion into `fib()`:

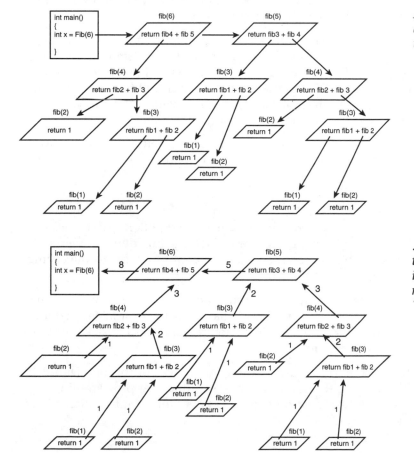

Here the program feeds data into various iterations of the `fib` routine...

...and here you can see the `fib` routine returning its data to the main routine.

In the example, *n* is 6 so fib(6) is called from main(). Execution jumps to the fib() function, and *n* is tested for a value less than 3 on line 34. The test fails, so fib(6) returns the sum of the values returned by fib(4) and fib(5).

```
42:            return( fib(n-2) + fib(n-1));
```

That means that a call is made to fib(4) [because *n* == 6, fib(*n*-2) is the same as fib(4)] and another call is made to fib(5) [fib(*n*-1)] and then the function you are in [fib(6)] waits until these calls return a value. When these return a value, then this function can return the result of summing those two values.

Because fib(5) passes in an argument that is not less than 3, fib() will be called again, this time with 4 and 3. fib(4) will in turn call fib(3) and fib(2).

The output traces these calls and the return values. Compile, link, and run this program, entering first 1, then 2, then 3, building up to 6, and watch the output carefully.

This would be a great time to start experimenting with your debugger. Read your debugger documentation to figure out how to put a break point on line 20 and then trace into each call to fib(), keeping track of the value of *n* as you work your way into each recursive call to fib().

Recursion is not used often, but it can be a powerful and elegant tool for certain needs.

This Is Hard, So Take It Easy

Don't worry if all this recursion is a little confusing. Even experienced programmers have a little trouble with it. Feel free to take a deep breath and come back to it a little later. For that matter, feel free to forget it, and go have a cookie.

How Functions Work—A Look Under the Hood

When you call a function, the code branches to the called function, parameters are passed in, and the body of the function executes. When the function completes, it returns a value (unless the function returns void), and control returns to the calling function.

How is this task accomplished? How does the code know where to branch to? Where are the variables kept when they are passed in? What happens to variables that are declared in the body of the function? How is the return value passed back out? How does the code know where to resume?

Most introductory books don't try to answer these questions, but this one will, because without understanding this information, you'll find that programming remains a fuzzy mystery. The explanation requires a brief tangent into a discussion of computer memory.

Levels of Abstraction

One of the principal hurdles for new programmers is grappling with the many layers of intellectual abstraction. Computers, of course, are just electronic machines. They don't know about windows and menus, they don't know about programs or instructions, and they don't even know about 1s and 0s. All that is really going on is that voltage is being measured at various places on an integrated circuit. Even this is an abstraction: Electricity itself is just an intellectual concept, representing the behavior of subatomic particles.

Few programmers bother much with any level of detail below the idea of values in RAM. After all, you don't need to understand particle physics to drive a car, make toast, or hit a baseball, and you don't need to understand the electronics of a computer to program one.

You do need to understand how memory is organized, however. Without a reasonably strong mental picture of where your variables are when they are created, and how values are passed among functions, it all remains an unmanageable mystery.

Partitioning RAM

When you begin your program, your operating system (such as DOS or Microsoft Windows) sets up various areas of memory based on the requirements of your compiler. As a C++ programmer, you'll often be concerned with the *global name space*, the *free store*, the *registers*, the *code space*, and the *stack*.

Global variables are in global name space. I'll talk more about global name space and the free store later, For now, I'll focus on the registers, code space, and stack.

Registers are a special area of memory built right into the Central Processing Unit (CPU). They take care of internal housekeeping. A lot of what goes on in the registers is beyond the scope of this book, but what programmers are concerned about the set of registers responsible for pointing, at any given moment, to the next line of code. These are called registers, together, the *instruction pointer*. It is the job of the instruction pointer to keep track of which line of code is to be executed next.

The code itself is in code space, which is that part of memory set aside to hold the binary form of the instructions you created in your program. Each line of source code is translated into a series of instructions, and each of these instructions is at a particular address in memory. The instruction pointer has the address of the next instruction to execute.

The program's binary instructions reside in the code space, and the instruction pointer holds the address of the next line to be executed.

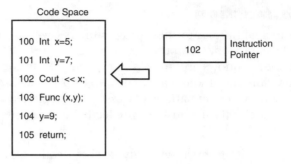

The stack is a special area of memory allocated for your program to hold the data required by each of the functions in your program. It is called a stack because it is a last-in, first-out queue, much like a stack of dishes at a cafeteria.

The last item placed on the stack is also the first item removed.

Last-in, first-out means that whatever is added to the stack last is the first thing taken off. Most queues are like a line at a theater: The first one in line is the first one out. A stack is more like a stack of coins: If you stack 10 pennies on a tabletop and then take some back, the last three you put on are the first three you take off.

When data is "pushed" onto the stack, the stack grows; as data is "popped" off the stack, the stack shrinks. It isn't possible to pop a dish off the stack without first popping off all the dishes placed on after that dish.

A stack of dishes is the common analogy. It is fine as far as it goes, but it is wrong in a fundamental way. A more accurate mental picture is of a series of cubbyholes aligned top to bottom. The top of the stack is whatever cubby the stack pointer (which is another register) happens to be pointing to.

Each of the cubbies has a sequential address, and one of those addresses is kept in the stack pointer register. Everything below that magic address, known as the top of the stack, is considered to be on the stack. Everything above the top of the stack is considered to be off the stack and invalid.

136

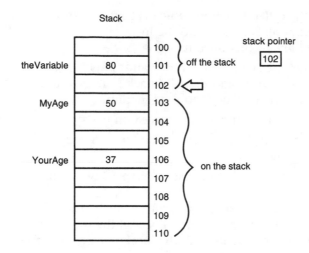

When data is put on the stack, it is placed into a cubby above the stack pointer, and then the stack pointer is moved to the new data. When data is popped off the stack, all that really happens is that the address of the stack pointer is changed by moving it down the stack.

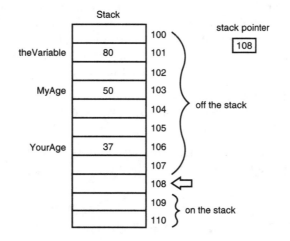

The Stack and Functions

Here's what happens when a program, running on a PC under DOS, branches to a function:

1. The address in the instruction pointer is incremented to the next instruction past the function call. That address is then placed on the stack, and it will be the return address when the function returns.

2. Room is made on the stack for the return type you've declared. On a system with two-byte integers, if the return type is declared to be int, another two bytes are added to the stack, but no value is placed in these bytes.

137

3. The address of the called function, which is kept in a special area of memory set aside for that purpose, is loaded into the instruction pointer, so the next instruction executed will be in the called function.

4. The current top of the stack is now noted and is held in a special pointer called the *stack frame*. Everything added to the stack from now until the function returns will be considered "local" to the function.

5. All the arguments to the function are placed on the stack.

6. The instruction now in the instruction pointer is executed, thus executing the first instruction in the function.

7. Local variables are pushed onto the stack as they are defined.

When the function is ready to return, the return value is placed in the area of the stack reserved at step 2. The stack is then popped all the way up to the stack frame pointer, which effectively throws away all the local variables and the arguments to the function.

The return value is popped off the stack and assigned as the value of the function call itself, and the address stashed away in step 1 is retrieved and put into the instruction pointer. The program therefore resumes immediately after the function call, with the value of the function retrieved.

Some of the details of this process change from compiler to compiler, or between computers, but the essential ideas are consistent across environments. In general, when you call a function, the return address and the parameters are put on the stack. During the life of the function, local variables are added to the stack. When the function returns, these are all removed by popping the stack.

Having looked at this process, you should now understand why recursive functions that don't end produce errors. Because data is never removed from the stack, the stack will eventually exceed its size limit.

The following chapters examine other places in memory that are used to hold data that must persist beyond the life of the function.

The Least You Need to Know

➤ A function is a subprogram that can return data to the main program.

➤ Functions can be called repeatedly, even from within the same function.

➤ Programs interact with the stack, a specific group of memory locations.

Chapter 9

Classes and Objects

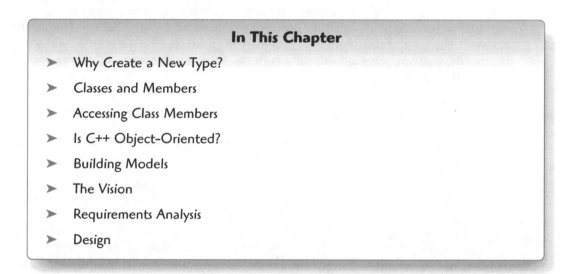

In This Chapter

➤ Why Create a New Type?

➤ Classes and Members

➤ Accessing Class Members

➤ Is C++ Object-Oriented?

➤ Building Models

➤ The Vision

➤ Requirements Analysis

➤ Design

The past several chapters discussed numbers as viewed by computer programs. The variables described so far have been from a limited number of "types," including characters and integers. The type of the variable tells you quite a bit about it. For example, if you declare Height and Width to be unsigned short integers, you know that each one can hold a number between 0 and 65,535, assuming an unsigned short integer is two bytes. That is the meaning of saying they are unsigned integers; trying to hold anything else in these variables causes an error. You can't store your name in an unsigned short integer, and you shouldn't try.

Just by declaring these variables to be unsigned short integers, you know that it's possible to add Height to Width and to assign that number to another number.

The type of these variables tells you

➤ Their size in memory.

➤ What information they can hold.

➤ What actions can be performed on them.

More generally, a type is a category. Familiar types include car, house, person, fruit, and shape. In object-oriented languages, the programmer can create any type needed, and each of these new types can have all the functionality and power of the built-in types.

Why Create a New Type?

Programs are usually written to solve real-world problems, such as keeping track of employee records or simulating the workings of a heating system. Although it is possible to solve complex problems by using programs written with only integers and characters, it is far easier to grapple with large, complex problems if you can create representations of the objects that you are talking about. In other words, simulating the workings of a heating system is easier if you can create variables that represent rooms, heat sensors, thermostats, and boilers. The closer these variables correspond to reality, the easier it is to write the program.

Classes and Members

In C++ and Java, you make a new type by declaring a *class*. A class is just a collection of variables—often of different types—combined with a set of related functions.

Steep Grade Ahead

This chapter covers advanced concepts in object-oriented analysis and design. If you find this heavy going, you may want to check the bibliography for a book offering more complete coverage of the subject. In any case, feel free to skim, and don't panic if you don't understand all of it. Actually, that goes for everything in life.

One way to think about a car is as a collection of wheels, doors, seats, windows, and so forth. Another way is to think about what a car can do: It can move, speed up, slow down, stop, park, and so on. A class enables you to encapsulate, or *bundle*, these various parts and various functions into one collection, which is called an *object*.

Encapsulating everything you know about a car into one class has a number of advantages for a programmer. Everything is in one place, which makes it easy to refer to, copy, and manipulate the data. Likewise, clients of your class—that is, the parts of the program that use your class—can use your object without worrying about what is in it or how it works.

A class can consist of any combination of the variable types and also other class types. The variables in the class are referred to as the member variables or data members. A Car class might have member variables representing the seats, radio type, tires, and so forth.

Member variables, also known as data members, are the variables in your class. Member variables are part of your class, just like the wheels and engine are part of your car.

The functions in the class typically manipulate the member variables. They are referred to as member functions or methods of the class. Methods of the Car class might include Start() and Brake(). A Cat class might have data members that represent age and weight; its methods might include Sleep(), Meow(), and ChaseMice().

Member functions, also known as methods, are the functions in your class. Member functions are as much a part of your class as the member variables. They determine what your class can do.

Geek Speak

The Head of the Class

A class defines a new type. An object is an instance of that type. Therefore: Dog is a type, Milo is the object sitting at my feet shedding on my carpet. Dogs have the attribute weight. The weight value for Milo is five pounds more than is any good for his health, but I've cut back on his food and I'm giving him lots of exercise, so stop nagging me, will ya?

Declaring a Class

In C++, you declare a class by writing the keyword **class** followed by an opening brace, and then listing the data members and methods of that class. End the declaration with a closing brace and a semicolon. Here's the declaration of a class called Cat:

```
class Cat
{
    unsigned int   itsAge;
    unsigned int   itsWeight;
    void Meow();
};
```

Declaring this class doesn't allocate memory for a Cat. It just tells the compiler what a Cat is, what data it contains (itsAge and itsWeight), and what it can do (Meow()). It also tells the compiler how big a Cat is—that is, how much room the compiler must set aside for each Cat that you create. In this example, if an integer is four bytes, a Cat is eight bytes big: itsAge is four bytes, and itsWeight is another four bytes. Meow() takes up no room, because no storage space is set aside for member functions (methods).

A Word on Naming Conventions

As a programmer, you must name all your member variables, member functions, and classes. As you learned in Chapter 6, "Parts of a Language," in the section "Variables and Constants," these should be easily understood and meaningful names. Cat, Rectangle, and Employee are good class names. Meow(), ChaseMice(), and StopEngine() are good function names, because they tell you what the functions do. Many programmers name the member variables with the prefix its, as in itsAge, itsWeight, and itsSpeed. This helps to distinguish member variables from nonmember variables.

House of Style

It's common for development companies to have house standards for many style issues. This ensures that all developers can easily read one another's code.

You should treat your programming language as if it were case sensitive, whether or not it is. All class names should follow the same pattern. That way, you never have to check how to spell your class name; was it Rectangle, rectangle, or RECTANGLE? Some programmers like to prefix every class name with a particular letter—for example, cCat or cPerson—whereas others put the name in all UPPERCASE or all lowercase. The convention that I use is to name all classes with initial capitalization, as in Cat and Person.

Similarly, many programmers begin all functions with capital letters and all variables with lowercase. Words are usually separated with an underscore—as in Chase_Mice—or by capitalizing each word—for example, ChaseMice or DrawCircle.

The important idea is that you should pick one style and stay with it through each program. Over time, your style will evolve to include not only naming conventions, but also indentation, alignment of braces, and commenting style. Remember that consistency is the key.

Defining an Object

You define an object of your new type just as you define an integer variable:

```
unsigned int GrossWeight;      // define an unsigned integer
Cat Frisky;                    // define a Cat
```

This code defines a variable called GrossWeight, whose type is an unsigned integer. It also defines Frisky, which is an object whose class (or type) is Cat.

Classes Versus Objects

You never pet the definition of a cat; you pet individual cats. You draw a distinction between the idea of a cat, and the particular cat that right now is ripping up your curtains. In the same way, C++ differentiates between the class Cat, which is the idea of a cat, and each individual Cat object. Thus, Frisky is an object of type Cat in the same way in which GrossWeight is a variable of type unsigned int.

An object is an individual instance of a class.

Accessing Class Members

After you define an actual Cat object—for example, Frisky—you use the dot operator (.) to access the members of that object. Therefore, to assign 50 to Frisky's Weight member variable, you would write

```
Frisky.itsWeight = 50;
```

In the same way, to call the Meow() function, you would write

```
Frisky.Meow();
```

When you use a class method, you call the method. In this example, you are calling Meow() on Frisky.

Assign to Objects, Not to Classes

You don't assign values to types; you assign values to variables. For example, you would never write

```
int = 5;                  // wrong
```

The compiler would flag this code fragment as an error, because you can't assign 5 to an integer. Rather, you must define an integer variable and assign 5 to that variable. For example,

```
int  x;                   // define x to be an int
x = 5;                    // set x's value to 5
```

This code is a shorthand way of saying, "Assign 5 to the variable x, which is of type int." In the same way, you wouldn't write

```
Cat.itsAge=5;             // wrong
```

The compiler would flag this statement as an error, because you can't assign 5 to the age part of a Cat. Rather, you must define a Cat object and assign 5 to that object. For example,

```
Cat Frisky;               // just like  int x;
Frisky.itsAge = 5;        // just like  x = 5;
```

If You Don't Declare It, Your Class Won't Have It

Try this experiment: Walk up to a three-year-old and show her a cat. Then say, "This is Frisky. Frisky knows a trick. Frisky, bark." The child will giggle and say, "No, silly, cats can't bark."

If you wrote

```
Cat  Frisky;           // make a Cat named Frisky
Frisky.Bark()          // tell Frisky to bark
```

the compiler would say, "No, silly, cats can't bark." (Your compiler's actual wording will vary.) The compiler knows that Frisky can't bark because the Cat class doesn't have a Bark() function. The compiler wouldn't even let Frisky meow if you didn't define a Meow() function.

Is C++ Object-Oriented?

C++ was created as a bridge between object-oriented programming and C, the world's most popular programming language for commercial software development. The goal was to provide object-oriented design to a fast, commercial software development platform.

C was developed as a middle ground between high-level business applications languages such as COBOL and the pedal-to-the-metal, high-performance but difficult-to-use Assembler language. C was to enforce "structured" programming, in which problems were "decomposed" into smaller units of repeatable activities called *procedures*.

The programs being written at the end of the 1990s are far more complex than those written at the beginning of the decade. Programs created in procedural languages tend to be difficult to manage, hard to maintain, and impossible to extend. Graphical user interfaces, the Internet, digital telephony, and a host of new technologies have dramatically increased the complexity of our projects at the very same time that consumer expectations for the quality of the user interface are rising.

In the face of this increasing complexity, developers took a long, hard look at the state of the industry. What they found was disheartening, at best. Software was late, broken, defective, bugridden, unreliable, and expensive. Projects routinely ran over budget and were delivered late to market. The cost of maintaining and building on these projects was prohibitive, and a tremendous amount of money was being wasted.

Object-oriented software development offers a path out of the abyss. Object-oriented programming languages build a strong link between the data structures and the methods that manipulate that data. More important, in object-oriented programming, you no longer think about data structures and manipulating functions; you think instead about objects. Things.

144

The world is populated by things: cars, dogs, trees, clouds, flowers. Things. Each thing has characteristics (fast, friendly, brown, puffy, pretty). Most things have behavior (move, bark, grow, rain, wilt). We don't think about a dog's data and how we might manipulate it—we think about a dog as a thing in the world, what it is like and what it does.

Building Models

If we are to manage complexity, we must create a model of the universe. The goal of the model is to create a meaningful abstraction of the real world. Such an abstraction should be simpler than the real world but should also accurately reflect the real world so that we can use the model to predict the behavior of things in the real world.

A child's globe is a classic model. The model isn't the thing itself; we would never confuse a child's globe with the Earth, but one maps the other well enough that we can learn about the Earth by studying the globe.

There are, of course, significant simplifications. My daughter's globe never has rain, floods, globe-quakes, and so forth. But I can use her globe to predict how long it will take me to fly from my home to Indianapolis should I ever need to come in and explain to my editors why my manuscript was late ("you see, I was doing great, but then I got lost in a metaphor and it took me hours to get out").

A model that is not simpler than the thing being modeled is not much use. There is a Steven Wright joke about just such a thing: "I have a map on which one inch equals one inch. I live at E5."

Object-oriented software design is about building good models. It consists of two significant pieces: a modeling language and a process.

Software Design: The Process

A *methodologist* is someone who develops or studies one or more methods. Typically, methodologists develop and publish their own methods. A *method* is a modeling language and a process. Three of the leading methodologists and their methods are Grady Booch, who developed the Booch method, Ivar Jacobson, who developed object-oriented software engineering, and James Rumbaugh, who developed Object Modeling Technology (OMT). These three men have joined together to create *Objectory*, a method and a commercial product from Rational Software, Inc. All three men are employed at Rational Software, where they are affectionately known as the *Three Amigos*.

In Objectory, the process of software design is *iterative*. That means that as we develop software, we go through the entire process repeatedly as we strive for enhanced understanding of the requirements. The design directs the implementation, but the details uncovered during implementation feed back into the design. Most important, we do not try to develop any sizable project in a single, orderly, straight line; rather, we iterate over pieces of the project, constantly improving our design and refining our implementation.

Iterative development can be distinguished from waterfall development. In waterfall development, the output from one stage becomes the input to the next, and there is no going back. In a waterfall development process, the requirements are detailed, and the clients sign off ("Yes, this is what I want"); the requirements are then passed on to the designer, set in stone. The designer creates the design (and a wonder to behold it is) and passes it off to the programmer, who implements the design. The programmer in turn hands the code to a QA person who tests the code and then releases it to the customer. Great in theory, disaster in practice.

In iterative design, the visionary comes up with a concept and then we begin to work on fleshing out the requirements. As we examine the details, the vision may grow and evolve. When we have a good start on the requirements, we begin the design, knowing full well that the questions that arise during design may cause modifications back in the requirements. As we work on design, we begin prototyping and then implementing the product. The issues that arise in development feed back into design, and may even influence our understanding of the requirements. Most important, object-oriented programmers design and implement only pieces of the full product, iterating over the design and implementation phases repeatedly.

All of this must be leavened with a strong commitment to shipping the product and getting it into the hands of the end-user. Analysis paralysis, over-design, and perfectionist coding can be risks as great as haphazard analysis, quickie design, and all-night coding sessions.

Although the steps of the process are repeated iteratively, it is nearly impossible to describe them in such a cyclical manner. Therefore, I will describe them in sequence: vision, analysis, design, implementation, testing, rollout. Don't misunderstand me—in reality, we run through each of these steps many times during the course of the development of a single product. The iterative design process is just hard to present and understand if we cycle through each step; so I'll describe them one after the other.

Here are the steps of the iterative design process:

1. Conceptualization
2. Analysis
3. Design
4. Implementation
5. Testing
6. Rollout

Conceptualization is the "vision thing." It is the single sentence that describes the great idea. Analysis is the process of understanding the requirements. Design is the process of creating the model of your classes, from which you will generate your code. Implementation is writing it in code (for example in C++); testing is making sure that you did it right, and rollout is getting it to your customers. Piece of cake. All the rest is details.

The Vision

All great software starts with a vision. One individual has an insight into a product he or she thinks would be good to build. Rarely do committees create compelling visions. The very first phase of object-oriented analysis and design is to capture this vision in a single sentence (or at most, a short paragraph). The vision becomes the guiding principle of development, and the team that comes together to implement the vision ought to refer back to it—and update it if necessary—as it goes forward.

Requirements Analysis

The conceptualization phase, in which the vision is articulated, is very brief. It may be no longer than a flash of insight followed by the time it takes to write down what the visionary has in mind. Often, as the object-oriented expert, you join the project after the vision is already articulated.

Some companies confuse the vision statement with the requirements. A strong vision is necessary, but it is not sufficient. To move on to analysis, you must understand how the product will be used, and how it must perform. The goal of the analysis phase is to articulate and capture these requirements. The outcome of the Analysis phase is the production of a requirements document. The first section in the requirements document is the use-case analysis.

Use Cases

The driving force in analysis, design, and implementation is the use case. A *use case* is nothing more than a high-level description of how the product will be used. Use cases drive not only the analysis, but also the design. They help you find the classes, and they are especially important in testing the product.

Creating a robust and comprehensive set of use cases may be the single most important task in analysis. Here you depend most heavily on your domain experts; the domain experts have the most information about the business requirements you are trying to capture.

Use cases pay little attention to user interface, and they pay no attention to the internals of the system you are building. Any system or person who interacts with the system is called an *actor*.

147

Geek Speak

In the Black

A black box is something you can't look inside of. You give it data and it spits out an answer, but you have no idea what is going on inside. For all you know, Albert Einstein is inside, scribbling down answers.

A use case is a description of the interaction between an actor and the system itself. For purposes of use-case analysis, the system is treated as a "black box."

A use case for an automatic teller machine might look like this: Get Cash. The user approaches the machine, puts in his card, enters his password by pressing buttons, chooses Get Cash, and enters the amount wanted, and money comes out with a receipt and the user's card is returned.

The system itself is a black box; we have no idea what the computer does. For all we know, there is a teller inside, reading the request and stuffing money into the slot.

Create the Domain Model

After you have a first cut at your use cases, you can begin to flesh out your requirements document with a detailed domain model. The *domain model* is a document that captures all you know about the domain (the field of business you are working in). As part of your domain model, you create domain objects that describe all the objects mentioned in your use cases. For example, suppose you were designing a new automatic teller machine. It could include these objects: customer, bank personnel, back office systems, checking account, savings account, and so forth.

Application Analysis

In addition to creating use cases, the requirements document will capture your customer's assumptions, constraints, and requirements about hardware and operating systems. Application requirements are your *particular* customer's prerequisites—those things that you would normally determine during design but that your client has decided for you. For example, I normally choose which operating system my software will run on after I know what it is I'm trying to build and I've designed much of the solution. If my client tells me that I *must* run on Windows 98, that requirement goes into Application Analysis.

The application requirements are often driven by the need to interface with existing (legacy) systems. In this case, understanding what the existing systems do and how they work is an essential component of your analysis.

Ideally, you'll analyze the problem, design the solution, and then decide which platform and operating system best fits your design. That scenario is as ideal as it is rare. More often, the client has a standing investment in a particular operating system or hardware platform. The client's business plan depends on your software running on the existing system, and you must capture these requirements early and design accordingly.

Systems Analysis

Some software is written to stand alone, interacting only with the end user. Often, however, you will be called on to interface to an existing system. *Systems analysis* is the process of collecting all the details of the systems with which you will interact. Will your new system be a server, providing services to the existing system, or will it be a client? Will you be able to negotiate an interface between the systems, or must you adapt to an existing standard? Will the other system be stable, or must you continually hit a moving target?

These and related questions must be answered in the analysis phase, before you begin to design your new system. In addition, you will want to try to capture the constraints and limitations implicit in interacting with the other systems. Will they slow down the responsiveness of your system? Will they put high demands on your new system, consuming resources and computing time?

Planning Documents

After you understand what your system must do and how it must behave, it is time to take a first stab at creating a time and budget document. Often, the timeline is dictated, top-down, by the client: "You have 18 months to get this done." Ideally, you'll examine the requirements and estimate the time it will take to design and implement the solution. That is the ideal; the practical reality is that most systems come with an imposed time limit and cost limit, and the real trick is to figure out how much of the required functionality you can build in the allotted time—and at the allotted cost.

Here are a couple guidelines to keep in mind when you are creating a project budget and timeline:

➤ If you are given a range, the outer number is probably optimistic.

➤ Liberty's Law states that everything takes longer than you expect—even if you take into account Liberty's Law.

Given these realities, it is imperative that you prioritize your work. *You will not finish*—it is that simple. It is important that, when you run out of time, what you have works and is adequate for a first release. If you are building a bridge and run out of time, if you didn't get a chance to put in the bicycle path, that is too bad; but you can still open the bridge and start collecting tolls. If you run out of time and you're only halfway across the river, that is not as good.

An essential thing to know about planning documents is that they are wrong. This early in the process, it is virtually impossible to offer a reliable estimate of the duration of the project. After you have the requirements, you can get a good handle on how long the design will take, a fair estimate of how long the implementation will take, and a reasonable "guesstimate" of the testing time. Then you must allow yourself at least 20 to 25 percent "wiggle room," which you can tighten as you move forward and learn more.

Don't Abuse Wiggle Room

The inclusion of "wiggle room" in your planning document is not an excuse to avoid planning documents. It is merely a warning not to rely on them too much early on. As the project goes forward, you'll strengthen your understanding of how the system works, and your estimates will become increasingly precise.

Beta Release

A prototype of a software product designed to be tested and have errors reported and suggestions made by its users.

Visualizations

The final piece of the requirements document is the visualization. The visualization is just a fancy name for the diagrams, pictures, screen shots, prototypes, and any other visual representations created to help you think through and design the graphical user interface of your product.

For many large projects, you may develop a full prototype to help you (and your customers) understand how the system will behave. On some teams, the prototype becomes the living requirements document; the "real" system is designed to implement the functionality demonstrated in the prototype.

Design

Analysis focuses on understanding the problem domain, whereas design focuses on creating the solution. *Design* is the process of transforming our understanding of the requirements into a model that can be implemented in software. The result of this process is the production of a design document.

The design document is divided into two sections: Class Design and Architectural Mechanisms. The Class Design section, in turn, is divided into static design (which details the various classes and their relationships and characteristics) and dynamic design (which details how the classes interact).

The Architectural Mechanisms section of the design document provides details about how you will implement object persistence, concurrency, a distributed object system, and so forth. The rest of this chapter focuses on the class design aspect of the design document; other chapters in the rest of this book explain how to implement various architecture mechanisms.

What Are the Classes?

Formal design methodology requires you to separate the class you create in a programming language from the design class, although they will be intimately related. The class you write in code is the implementation of the class you designed. These are isomorphic: Each class in your design will correspond to a class in your code, but don't confuse one for the other. It is certainly possible to implement your design classes in another language, and the *syntax* of the class definitions might be changed.

That said, most of the time we talk about these classes without distinguishing them, because the differences are highly abstract. When you say that in your model your Cat class will have a Meow() method, understand that this means that you will put a Meow() method into your C++ or Java class as well.

The biggest stumbling block for many novices is finding the initial set of classes and understanding what makes a well-designed class. One simplistic technique suggests writing out the use-case scenarios and then creating a class for every noun. Consider the following use-case scenario:

> **Customer** chooses to withdraw **cash** from **checking**. There is sufficient cash in the **account**, sufficient cash and **receipts** in the **ATM**, and the **network** is up and running. The ATM asks the customer to indicate an **amount** for the **withdrawal**, and the customer asks for $300, a legal amount to withdraw at this time. The **machine** dispenses $300 and prints a receipt, and the customer takes the **money** and the receipt.

You might pull out of this scenario the following classes:

➤ Customer
➤ Cash
➤ Checking
➤ Account
➤ Receipts
➤ ATM
➤ Network
➤ Amount
➤ Withdrawal
➤ Machine
➤ Money

You might then aggregate the synonyms to create this list, and then create classes for each of these nouns:

➤ Customer
➤ Cash (money, amount, withdrawal)
➤ Checking
➤ Account
➤ Receipts
➤ ATM (machine)
➤ Network

Transformations

What you began to do in the preceding section was not so much extract the nouns from the scenario as to begin transforming objects from the domain analysis into objects in the design. That is a fine first step. Often, many of the objects in the domain will have *surrogates* in the design. An object is called a surrogate to distinguish between the actual physical receipt dispensed by an ATM and the object in your design that is merely an intellectual abstraction implemented in code.

You will likely find that most of the domain objects have an isomorphic representation in the design—that is, there is a one-to-one correspondence between the domain object and the design object. Other times, however, a single domain object is represented in the design by an entire series of design objects. And at times, a series of domain objects may be represented by a single design object.

Other Transformations

After you have transformed the domain objects, you can begin to look for other useful design-time objects. A good starting place is with interfaces. Each interface between your new system and any existing (legacy) systems should be encapsulated in an interface class. If you interact with a database of any type, this is also a good candidate for an interface class.

These interface classes offer encapsulation of the interface protocol and thus shield your code from changes in the other system. Interface classes enable you to change your own design, or to accommodate changes in the design of other systems, without breaking the rest of the code. As long as the two systems continue to support the agreed-upon interface, they can move independently of each other.

Data Manipulation

Similarly, you will create classes for data manipulation. If you have to transform data from one format into another format (for example, from Fahrenheit to Celsius, or from English to Metric), you may want to encapsulate these manipulations behind a data manipulation class. You can use this technique when messaging data into required formats for other systems or for transmission over the Internet—in short, any time you must manipulate data into a specified format, you will encapsulate the protocol behind a data manipulation class.

Devices

If your system interacts with or manipulates devices (such as printers, modems, scanners, and so forth), the specifics of the device protocol ought to be encapsulated in a class. Again, by creating classes for the interface to the device, you can plug in new devices with new protocols and not break any of the rest of your code; just create a new interface class that supports the same interface (or a derived interface), and off you go.

Models

Once you have established your preliminary set of classes, it is time to begin modeling their relationships and interactions.

The specifics of these techniques are well beyond the scope of this book but the essential lesson is that the more you model in your design, the more easily you can implement it all in code.

The Least You Need to Know

➤ Variables come in several types; the variable's type determines what information it can hold.

➤ Object-oriented programming uses classes and objects, which are categories and examples of the category.

➤ You can define classes and objects to describe and manipulate the data for your specific purpose.

➤ The software design process defines a need and creates programs to meet the need.

Quality Assurance Testing and Debugging

Quality Assurance is to programmers what lower taxes is to politicians: a touchstone truth, a shibboleth, and a promise, observed more in the breach than in fidelity.

True quality is achieved by the programmer testing and debugging his code, and by the application of professional Quality Assurance expertise. This chapter will consider code quality from inception through delivery.

Quality Assurance Testing

Quality Assurance (QA) is used in two ways: as a noun and as a verb.

As a noun ("Did you perform QA on that?"), QA refers to the art of testing software to make sure that it performs as expected, and meets the requirements established during Analysis. Programmers turn this phrase into a verb and ask, "Did you QA that code?" By this they mean, "Did you perform QA on this code?"

Many programmers think they can QA their own code, but they are almost certainly wrong. First, QA is an expertise in its own right, and second, no one can fully test his own code, as the programmer is too close to the design to anticipate all the ways a user will interact with the system. Or in other words, nothing can be made foolproof, because fools are so ingenious.

Some years ago, I was working on software for an online service when the director of QA called me and told me that a module I'd submitted for review was crashing. "Impossible," I said with great confidence, "I tested it fully." She walked to my desk and said, "Fire it up." I did. "Click here." I did that, too. "Now enter 5 here." Before I could stop myself, I blurted out, "No one would do that!" She just walked away chuckling.

It is the job of QA to test all the ways someone might use your product despite the fact that "no one would do that." Of course, the minute you give your software to real users, they will, in fact, do all those things you never though they might, and your code had better be able to handle their actions gracefully. Mine didn't, but thankfully the QA department found the problem before 10,000 angry users did.

Catching Bugs Early

Professional Quality Assurance Engineers ought to be involved in the development process from the very beginning. Gone are the days when programmers analyzed the requirements, designed a solution, implemented the solution, and then handed their completed but untested code off to QA for final testing just before shipment. This process had a dismal track record; QA was handed large, complex products to test, and had little opportunity to identify bugs until they were so embedded in the system that it was difficult, if not impossible to extract them.

Experience and research shows that the earlier you catch a bug in the development process, the less expensive it is to fix. A professional Quality Assurance team will put procedures in place to ensure that bugs are caught as early in the process as possible. I'll discuss how they do so in a moment.

Quality Assurance in Analysis

The role of Quality Assurance begins in the Analysis phase in which the use cases are created, as described in Chapter 9. These use cases drive not only the design of the product, but the testing requirements as well. The use-case analysis predicts how the product will be used, and serves as the perfect foundation for test plans to ensure that the final product can in fact be used as expected.

Such a plan might include a set of tests designed to ensure that each scenario plays out as expected in the final product. Use cases typically describe preconditions (conditions which must be true in order to begin the use case) and post-conditions

156

(conditions which must be true after the use case completes for it to be a success). A test plan might establish the following steps:

1. Test that the preconditions have been fulfilled.
2. Run a specific scenario (variation) of the use case.
3. Test the post-conditions to ensure they've been met.

This would be repeated for every possible scenario within the use case, and a complete set of scenarios would constitute one test of a use case. Each use case would have a similar suite of tests.

In addition to describing use cases, a good requirements document will detail performance, reliability, and robustness criteria, all of which should be validated during Quality Assurance. A full requirements analysis will also include visualizations—that is, descriptions of the User Interface which can be tested by QA. Every element in the UI must be tested to ensure it is represented in the final product.

More important, the QA engineer will ensure that the requirements document captures what behavior is expected for every possible user interaction. Specifically, the document will detail what is expected to happen if the user chooses any menu choice, pushes any key combination, clicks on any button, and so forth. A complete user-specification document will be a necessary starting point for a comprehensive test plan.

Final acceptance testing, necessary before product release, will depend on the work done during analysis. Throughout the product cycle, as the project enters design and implementation, the requirements will evolve as the customer better understands his specific needs and as information is fed back from design and implementation. It is imperative that the analysis documents and the test plan be kept up to date with these changes, so that QA can ensure that what is tested is what is really required. Alan Cooper has an excellent analysis of this process in *The Inmates Are Running the Asylum* (Sams 1999, ISBN: 0-672-31649-8).

Quality Assurance in Design

During the design phase, the developers are focused on designing the classes they will need during implementation. It is at this phase that the more advanced QA test designers will discuss test planning with the developer. In an ideal development environment, every class will be created with testing in mind.

The entire class interface—that is the contract the class makes with its clients—will provide a specification of what information must be provided to each method of the class, and what the impact or outcome is expected as a result. Every class, perhaps every method, ought to include a set of tests that can be run against an instance of the class to ensure that it is fulfilling its contract. Every instance of the class—that is, every object—can be tested using the tests associated with that class.

After objects are shown to work, the developer goes on to test the interactions among objects; and so these interactions must be documented in the requirements. After these interactions are tested, we test the entire component to ensure that it works as a whole. When the components are working, we move up the hierarchy of complexity until we are testing the entire application.

Testing and Debugging During Implementation

While testing during implementation is the responsibility of the developer, today's sophisticated development environments go a long way toward simplifying the problem of finding and fixing bugs.

Integrated Development Environments (IDEs) provide powerful tools for finding and detecting errors in the program. One of the most powerful of these tools is the compiler itself (for compiled languages such as C++).

Well-written code invites the debugger to help you find bugs. This is a smart approach, as compile-time bugs will fail reliably. Runtime bugs often hide and lurk in your code long after you're released your program to the public, only to be found by tens of thousands of frustrated users.

When you do suspect a runtime bug, the most powerful tool for tracking it down is the debugger. To get a sense of how this works, let's examine a simple C++ program with a subtle but common bug in it. You don't need to know C++ to follow this example; I'll talk you through it. Listing 10.1 shows debugDemo.cpp.

Listing 10.1 Debugging a Simple C++ Program

```
0:   #include <iostream>
1:   using namespace std;
2:
3:   void Swap(int x, int y);
4:
5:   int main()
6:   {
7:    int firstValue = 5;
8:    int secondValue = 7;
9:
10:         cout << "firstValue: ";
11:         cout << firstValue;
12:         cout << ". second value: ";
13:         cout << secondValue;
14:         cout << "Calling swap…" << endl;
15:
16:         Swap(firstValue,secondValue);
17:
```

```
18:            cout << "Back in main. firstValue: ";
19:            cout << firstValue;
20:            cout << ". second value: ";
21:            cout << secondValue;
22:            cout << endl;
23:            return 0;
24:
25:    }
26:
27:    void Swap(int x, int y)
28:    {
29:            int temp = x;
30:            x = y;
31:            y = temp;
32:    }
```

Output

```
firstValue: 5. second value: 7. Calling swap...
Back in main. firstValue: 5. second value: 7
```

Analysis

The intent of this program is to demonstrate a tiny function that swaps two integer values. Let's start by looking at the code.

Lines 0 and 1 set up some housekeeping for C++ that we won't bother with here. Line 3 declares that we will use a function named Swap(), which will take two integers (int x and int y).

Line 5 begins the main() function, the first function to run in any C++ program. On lines 7 and 8, we declare a couple variables, and initialize their values to 5 and 7. On lines 10-14, we print these values to the screen (cout handles the printing for us).

The first line of printout shows that firstValue is 5 and secondValue is 7, as we expected.

On line 16, we call the Swap function, which, you will remember, means that we jump to line 27 where the Swap() function is implemented. Note that on line 16 we pass in the values firstValue (5) and secondValue (7) but on line 27 they are called x and y. That's fine; x will be assigned the value of firstValue and y will be assigned the value of secondValue.

On line 29, we create a temporary integer named temp and initialize it with the value now in x. Therefore, at this very moment, temp = 5, x = 5, and y = 7.

On line 30, we assign to x the value in y, so temp = 5, x =7 and y = 7. Finally, on line 31, we assign to y the value held in temp (5), and so after line 31 runs, we have swapped the values: x is now 7 and y is now 5.

159

We exit Swap() and resume processing on line 18, where we print the values of firstValue and secondValue, with the hope that these also have been swapped. Checking the printout, however, shows that we failed. The second line of the print-out shows that firstValue is still 5 and secondValue is still 7. What went wrong?

To find out, we'll set a breakpoint on line 16 in main(). A breakpoint is an instruction to the debugger that when we run the program we want to stop *here*. This illustration illustrates the breakpoint—the dot in the margin next to the line on which we want to stop.

The breakpoint is where the debugger will cease executing code.

You can now tell the debugger to run, and it will process our code right up to the breakpoint, and then it will stop. This figure shows what the IDE looks like when the debugger stops on line 16.

Take a look at this window in some detail. The topmost window contains the source code, and in the left margin you can see the dot indicating a breakpoint and an arrow within the dot indicating that this is the current line of execution. In the lower-left corner, we see a window with the variables, and we can see that firstValue is 5 and secondValue is 7. In the middle, we see the call stack. The call stack window shows which function has called the current function, but this has no information of interest yet. In the far-right corner is a window in which we can place variables we want to keep an eye on.

Our next task is to step *in* to the Swap() function. The next illustration shows what things look like after executing the three lines in Swap(). As you can see, the arrow now points to the closing brace. I've added the three values of interest to the watch window on the far right. As we expect, temp now has the value 5, x has the value 7, and y has the value 5. Clearly the swap works here in the Swap() function.

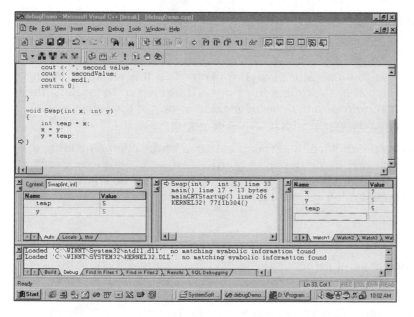

When the debugger stops on line 16, you'll see something like this.

After you execute the Swap() *function, you'll see this.*

You might also want to note that the middle window on the bottom, which shows the call stack, indicates that Swap() was called by main(), passing in the values 7 and 5, just as we would expect.

We now know the right values are passed in, and that they are swapped in the Swap function. We continue stepping through the code and find ourselves back in main(), but firstValue and secondValue are not changed, as illustrated here.

When the program returns to the main() *functions, the numerical values are unchanged.*

Having used the debugger to look inside Swap(), we know that it is working, but the values are not being swapped in the calling functions. This causes us to examine the parameters to Swap(), and to realize that we are making a copy of the values passed in, rather than passing in references, which can be changed.

With that insight, fixing the problem is trivial. If you aren't fully comprehending the details of the C++, don't worry at all; the point of this discussion is not to understand the details of this program, but rather to see that the debugger can be an invaluable aid in revealing what would otherwise be hidden and obscure.

Quality Assurance Testing

Sooner or later, the helpless and pathetic programmer must hand over code that he thinks is fully tested, to the satanically twisted souls in Quality Assurance. These demented denizens of denigration work late into the night in their dark and foreboding bastions of torture, where they apply a variety of sadistic techniques to torment our helpless code. They toil relentlessly, lightning flashing outside their window, never resting until they can prove that every last lurking bug, aphid, insect, or arachnid of computer ineptitude has been found, and its life squished out between their virtual tweezers.

Manual Black-Box Testing

The simplest form of Quality Assurance is to test a product by using it. A smart, well-organized person can test a product quite thoroughly by working with the product extensively, and perhaps exhaustively.

Although this was the preferred method for software testing in the past, the greater complexity of modern software makes this approach increasingly inefficient and unrealistic. Event-driven programs, in which the user can choose any number of menu items, and move freely and in no particular order through the program, make for software that is tremendously difficult to test exhaustively.

Nonetheless, there are still many QA engineers doing nothing but manual black box testing, and at times it is these very people who surface not only simple misbehaviors in the system, but logical inconsistencies that might otherwise confuse end users.

Employers looking for manual black box testers are looking for the ability to follow a test plan, to report problems accurately, and to write coherent bug reports. It helps if the tester has experience working with GUI applications and a strong sense of what makes software usable for the target audience.

Using Software-Testing Tools

The next rung up the skills ladder for QA professionals is the ability to develop test scripts in a fourth-generation language or a test-application program, such as Rational Test Suite.

While developing these scripts does not require advanced technical or programming skills, it does require that you be able to think logically about programming tasks.

Employers hiring test writers are looking for the same skills as for black-box testing, with the addition of scripting language skills.

This skill can be expanded upon to create test scripts in other, more advanced scripting languages such as SQL, Perl, Python, and so forth.

Using these scripts, testers can create *capture and playback* scripts which mimic the behavior of a potential user, but which can exhaustively test every combination of keystrokes and record the results.

API Testing

Finally, skilled C++ and Java programmers may work with QA to develop tests that interact with specific modules of the code in order to test their performance. Such testing may include building a "test harness"—that is a suite of tests to which new code will be subjected each time a module is added.

API test developers need all the skills of the other testers, augmented by an ability to program in the language in which the application being tested is developed. API testers typically work closely with the programming team; often under a matrix management by the development team leader and the director of Quality Assurance.

The Least You Need to Know

➤ Quality Assurance is a critical task in the production of software.

➤ QA has a role to play in every phase of development.

➤ The earlier you catch bugs, the less expensive it is to fix them.

Chapter 11

What Are Frameworks?

In This Chapter

➤ The Microsoft Foundation Classes

➤ Issues in Preemptive Multithreading

➤ String Manipulation Classes

➤ Time Classes

➤ Documents and Views

The great, unrealized promise of object-oriented programming is code reuse. The idea of OOP was to create classes that could serve as the foundation on which new programs could be built. Components could be plugged into a new architecture just as electronics are plugged into a circuit board. By and large, however, things haven't worked out that way, with one significant exception—application framework libraries.

An application framework is a set of classes and associated methods that provide a starting point for building your application. These classes encapsulate the common foundation on which all applications are built, and they provide low-level services that you would otherwise have to build yourself.

The vast majority of successful application framework libraries are those that facilitate the creation of applications in a windowing environment such as Windows NT or X Window. By far the most successful such library is the Microsoft Foundation Classes (MFC), Microsoft's application framework for writing Windows applications. This chapter focuses on the MFC as an example of what such an Application Frameworks library can provide.

Monstrous Proportions

The MFC is large and powerful and necessarily complex. No single chapter can fully introduce all its functionality—let alone provide a comprehensive tutorial. The intent of this chapter is not to teach you how to use the MFC but rather to dip into the MFC here and there to examine some of the universal issues common to all such application frameworks.

The Microsoft Foundation Classes

The Microsoft Foundation Class library (called *the MFC*) is an application framework that provides a structure and a set of classes with which you can build an application for Windows. The MFC provides standard user-interface implementations of windowing classes as well as a set of utility classes to assist you in the manipulation of certain kinds of objects, such as String and Time.

The Casserole Approach

The material in this chapter is adapted from my book *C++ Unleashed.*

Getting Started

The MFC goes beyond providing a set of application-level classes and actually provides a framework within which you can use these classes. You can see the power of this approach when you use the wizards that facilitate the creation of Windows applications. For example, you can see here how a new project can be created using the Application Wizard.

The Application Wizard creating a new project.

After you start the Application Wizard, it asks a series of questions to help you design your application within the Document/View architecture. The next figure shows the first question: Are you building a Single Document interface or Multi-Document Interface (MDI) application, or do you just need a simple dialog-box interface?

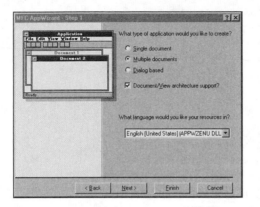

The Application Wizard asks what type of application to create.

Subsequent pages of the wizard ask you to choose among various options: database support, COM support, support for Internet access, and so forth. After the Application Wizard has run, a number of classes are created that constitute the initial framework for your application.

Note that each class contains a number of standard methods. Often, these methods provide simple boilerplate code and then indicate where your customizing code should be added, as shown in this sample output from the Application Wizard:

```
BOOL CCareerDoc::OnNewDocument()
{
    if (!CDocument::OnNewDocument())
        return FALSE;

    // TODO: add reinitialization code here
    // (SDI documents will reuse this document)

    return TRUE;
}
```

The details of the code don't matter; what is important here is the comment beginning with "TODO: add reinitialization..." The wizard spits out useful starter code, and identifies where you, the programmer, must fill in the details.

At times, the code provided by the wizard is extensive; it can save you significant development time and simplify your interaction with the more complex aspects of Windows programming.

The initial framework contains the number of classes created after the Application Wizard has run.

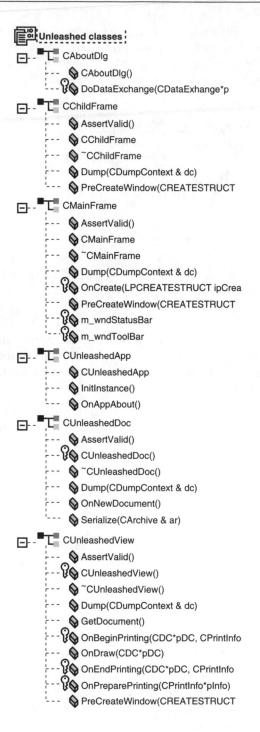

Other Wizards

In addition to the Application Wizard, the MFC provides wizards that create and manipulate classes and the methods and members of those classes as well as wizards that hook up methods for responding to user actions such as button clicks. The MFC also provides wizards that interact with databases and that use COM.

Multithreading

The MFC provides a set of classes for managing multithreading. Although the specifics of how the MFC implements these classes may differ from how, for example, the XOpen libraries for windowing on UNIX handle multithreading, the essential tasks and objectives are universal in all application frameworks.

The term *thread* is shorthand for *thread of execution*. The Windows operating system (and most modern operating systems) allows your application to have more than one thread of execution in a single program. It *appears* as though your program were running two or more tasks at one time, although most often what is really happening is that the computer is switching among the threads, offering the illusion of simultaneity. As a matter of fact, this is exactly how the illusion of multiprocessing is accomplished on your computer. When you run your word processing program, your Internet browser, and your spreadsheet program, the processor just switches among them.

A program represents a process, and each process may have more than one thread. The principal difference between a process and a thread is the "overhead" of each—it takes more time to switch among processes than it does to switch among threads. This is why threads are sometimes referred to as *lightweight processes*.

The thread *context* is the information the computer needs to make the switch among threads. The thread context consists of a stack (for temporary variables and the return addresses of subroutines), a kernel stack (to hold addresses for interrupt service returns), and a set of registers. In the registers, there are, among other things, the instruction pointer and the stack pointer. The instruction pointer tells the CPU where to find its next instruction (as it works its way through your source code), and the stack pointer tells the CPU where it can store or retrieve the next local variable.

The CPU is rather dumb; it just works its way through the code. The operating system (in this case, Windows) tells the CPU when to effect a thread or process switch. The operating system is said to manage *time slicing*—affording each thread its own little "slice of time" in which to execute.

Cooperative Versus Preemptive Multithreading

Earlier operating systems, such as Windows 3.x or the earlier versions of the Macintosh, used a form of multithreading called *cooperative multithreading*. This primitive form of multithreading allowed for more than one thread, but each thread was required voluntarily to release control of the processor periodically to allow other threads to run.

The problem with cooperative multithreading is that a single thread can "hog" the processor, causing all other threads to run very slowly. Worse, the thread can "hang," causing the entire application—or even the computer—to grind to a halt.

Preemptive multithreading takes advantage of the CPU's ability to signal when it is time to switch among threads. This more sophisticated mechanism involves cooperation between the operating system (for example, Windows NT) and the CPU chip (for example, the Pentium) to ensure that each thread is allocated a preset amount of processor time (typically measured in milliseconds). The operating system rapidly switches among threads, allocating a "slice" of time based on the thread's priority.

The advantage of preemptive multithreading is that no thread can consume a dispro-portionate share of the system processing time—and if a thread hangs, the remaining threads can continue working.

Issues in Preemptive Multithreading

Creating programs that run in a multi*processing* environment such as Windows is fairly straightforward: You write your program as if you had uncontested access to the CPU, the disk, the database, and so forth. You leave it to the operating system to keep everything straight—you just plow ahead as though yours were the only program running.

Writing a multi*threaded* application is somewhat more complicated. Actually, it is a *lot* more complicated, because suddenly your code can be interrupted at any time (which is always true). More important, more than one thread can *reenter* your code so that the same code can be running in two different threads. This can happen if functions in two different threads each call into your code.

The MFC provides a set of classes to help manage these issues and to ensure the integrity of your data. I'll consider these classes in a moment, but the short advice on multithreading is this: If you can avoid writing multithreaded code, do so. Don't use multithreading unless and until you have no choice. It makes your code more com-plex and far harder to maintain. It dramatically increases the likelihood of bugs—and most of the time, it decreases performance. After all, it takes time to stash away the thread context and to switch threads. Add enough threads, and the CPU spends a sig-nificant portion of its time just switching among them—and proportionally less time getting any useful work done!

Suppose that you have a program that takes a lot of data in, calculates the sum of the data, and then uses that sum in a second equation. "Aha!" you say, "Two tasks! I'll create two threads." The problem is that the second thread can't begin until the first thread is done working. Even if you could calculate them "at the same time," if you can't use the data until both are done, why not let them run in series rather than in parallel? Running the tasks together buys you nothing, and the cost of switching between the tasks may be high.

So when *do* you use multithreading? The classic scenario is one in which one task will take a long time and the second task does *not* depend on the first. Suppose that you must save data to disk and also display it on-screen. You'd hate to wait for the data to be saved before you can put it on the screen—after all, writing to disk can take a while. Why not put the "write it to disk" task into a separate thread and get on with the more important job of interacting with the user? Why not, indeed.

Synchronization

If you do decide to use multithreading, the principal obstacle will be making sure that your data integrity is protected. The MFC provides a number of objects to help with this task, including critical sections, mutexes, and events. (What's a *mutex*? Don't worry; I'm coming to that.)

Each of these objects is designed to ensure that only one thread is talking to your critical data at a time. Your thread can check the status of each of these objects (other than critical sections) to see whether the object is signaled or unsignaled (often called *cleared*). When a synchronization object is signaled, it indicates that your thread may have access. Until the object is signaled, your thread "waits." When a thread is waiting, it is doing nothing and is blocked.

Critical Sections

Critical sections are the simplest, easiest to use, and most limited of the synchronization objects. Your thread obeys a simple rule: When it wants to touch an area of code to be synchronized, it first asks for a lock on its `CriticalSection` object. It then blocks execution of its thread until the `CriticalSection` object can be locked. If another thread has already locked the object, your thread waits until the other thread unlocks the `CriticalSection`. The `CriticalSection` thus synchronizes access to the specified area of code.

Mutexes

Critical sections are great. For many purposes, they are all you need. They are fast, lightweight, and easy to use. They are, unfortunately, also limited. Their biggest limitations are that they are visible only in one process, and that you cannot wait a specified amount of time for them to unlock.

A more sophisticated synchronization device is the mutex. The word *mutex* is derived from the words *mutually exclusive*, with the implication that if two (or more) objects share a mutex, they have mutually exclusive access to whatever that mutex controls.

A mutex is very similar to a critical section: Either you own it (and can access the area of code it protects) or you do not (and you must wait). Unlike a critical section, however, a mutex can be shared across processes; your code can also specify how long to wait for the mutex to become available before you "time out."

Events

Event objects are useful for waiting for an event to occur. Event objects are unsignaled until some other object sets them to signaled. Threads can wait for an event to become signaled, allowing you to say to a thread "start running when this event occurs."

Typically, you create an event in the unsignaled state and then tell one or more threads to wait for that event to become signaled. You might set such an event to notify threads when printing is complete, when a file has been downloaded, when there is a message in the queue, and so forth.

String Manipulation Classes

Another application framework, the Standard Template Library, provides a string class that is now part of the C++ language. Java has its own string class, as does Visual Basic. The point of all of these classes is to allow you to manipulate strings of characters.

Typically, an application framework allows you to copy strings, find out how long they are, and search for letters or substrings. It is not uncommon also to want to be able to concatenate strings, so that you can write

```
string newString = helloString + worldString;
```

so that if `helloString` has "hello" and `worldString` has "world," then `newString` will have "hello world."

Time Classes

Another popular set of utility classes provided by the MFC and many other application frameworks assist with manipulating time. The ANSI standard provides for a `time_t` data type. This class represents an absolute time and date within the range January 1, 1970 to January 18, 2038, inclusive. Time classes typically include utility functions to convert to and from Gregorian dates and between 12-hour and 24-hour clocks. Additional methods assist you in extracting the year, month, day, hours, minutes, and so forth from a given time value.

Many libraries provide a timespan class that provides relative time values—that is, time spans. When one time object is subtracted from another, the result is a timeSpan object.

Documents and Views

Of course, dialog boxes and threads are not the heart and soul of any application framework. The real reason for the existence of an application framework such as the MFC is to help you manage the creation and manipulation of windows—onscreen views of your data. To do this, many application frameworks use *documents* (to manage data) and *views* (to manage windows and controls).

The MFC's *document/view* design pattern is a simplification of the Model/View/Controller (MVC) design pattern originally used to build user interfaces in Smalltalk-80. In MVC, you create an object that represents your data; this object is called the *model*. You then assign responsibility for viewing that data to various *views*, and decouple viewing from the responsibility for controlling or manipulating the data, which is assigned to the *controllers*.

Microsoft's variant on the MVC design pattern is the somewhat simpler Document/View pattern. In Microsoft's approach, the data (document) is still separated from the view, but the view and the controller are merged. Document/View is so intrinsic to the Microsoft Foundation Classes that it is sometimes a challenge to write programs that ignore this pattern.

It is important to note that in both the MVC and the Document/View patterns, the *model*, or *document*, is any data your program uses. Documents need not be word processing documents—they can be collections of records, tables, or amorphous data structures.

Views

The views in the MFC are represented as windows and *widgets*, or *controls*. The class CWnd is the base class for all the views, including dialog boxes, CFrameWnd (which manages the frame of a window), and CMDIChildWnd (which manages multidocument-interface windows—that is, multiple subwindows within a single frame as you might see by opening more than one document in Microsoft Word). CWnd is also the base class to CView as well as the base to all the controls such as CButton, CListbox, and so on.

The CDocument and CView classes encapsulate the Document/View design pattern and work with the CWnd-derived classes to display the contents of the CDocument. The CView class can be extended in many powerful ways, and the MFC provides you with a family of derived classes. These classes include CScrollView (for scrolling through large documents), CEditView (for building text documents), CRichEditView (for creating documents with rich text such as FORMATTING, **bold**, *italic*, and so on), CFormView (for creating onscreen forms), CRecordView (for working with databases), and CTreeView (for creating structured views of hierarchical data).

173

CView is the parent class of all these derived views, and it provides a number of virtual functions for your derived class to override. The most important CView functions are probably OnInitialUpdate(), OnUpdate(), and OnDraw().

OnInitialUpdate() is called the first time the view updates itself. Every time a document changes, it notifies all the views currently attached to it. MFC calls OnInitialUpdate() the first time and calls OnUpdate() on all subsequent calls.

The default behavior for the update methods is to invalidate the window and then to invoke OnDraw(). This approach gives you tremendous flexibility in how you render your view, but also provides boilerplate code that can be used to implement default drawing functionality.

The Least You Need to Know

➤ Each vendor may supply its own frameworks.

➤ The MFC provides a powerful set of utilities.

➤ Good frameworks are highly encapsulated and robust.

Databases

When you strip away the flashy user interface, the overwhelming majority of computer programs exist for just one reason—to present, manipulate, edit, add to, or remove data. Data—information—is the driving force behind most programs, and the heart of any such program is the database.

We have become used to building databases to house everything from our collection of recipes to the list of books in the National Archives. Commercial databases may represent a business's most precious resource, and for many businesses, the database *is* their business.

A sales organization may keep records on all of its contacts; a warehouse may keep all of its inventory. Writing solid, reliable, fast, and efficient databases is a well-developed science; and the role of the database designer and database administrator is a critical role in any large organization.

What Is a Database?

A database is nothing more (and nothing less!) than an organized collection of information. There are many ways to organize large amounts of data, and database theory has evolved to find the most efficient approach to this problem. Efficiency is defined along two axes: speed and size. Speed refers to how quickly you can add, retrieve, edit, and delete data, and size refers to how much disk space and memory the database consumes.

In general, speed is more important, but when you are talking about hundreds of thousands or even millions of records, size is also important, both for its own sake and because it affects speed!

Another often-overlooked but highly critical criterion of a successful database is data integrity. What can you do to ensure that when you retrieve the data, what you get back is an accurate and reliable reflection of what you've stored away? The loss of critical data can be financially ruinous. Imagine if a credit card company were to lose the record of even a part of one day's transactions!

Types of Databases

Although databases can be organized in many ways, the three principal forms of databases in use today are

Flat databases

Relational databases

Object databases

Flat databases are used for storing relatively small amounts of data, such as the membership list for a club, or your CD collection. The advantage of flat database programs is that they are simple to use and to understand. Although they fill an important niche, they are not of concern to the commercial database programmer and won't be considered further.

Object databases are designed to work with object-oriented languages, and they will become increasingly important over time. Object-database technology is still in the early days of development, however, and the tools and technology are still primitive. Few database professionals are proficient in object-database technology, and it will be a few years before we see many large-scale projects using an object database. Again, from the view of learning to be a professional programmer, this technology is beyond the scope of this book and of only marginal interest.

The heart of database programming is and remains relational database programming. A **R**elational **D**atabase (RDB) is one in which the data is stored in tables, and the relationship among the data in various tables is made explicit.

Relational databases are capable of representing large and complex relationships among your data. I'll examine this concept in detail, but to get started, I need some data to work with.

By modeling these relationships, you can extract meaningful reports out of your data. For example, you might ask for a report on which products are most popular, or what the purchasing trends have been recently. Proper database design is critical to managing your data effectively.

Starting with Access, Moving Up from There

There are any number of programs to manage databases, depending on what you want to accomplish and how much data you need to manage. From the perspective of learning about database technology, the best place to start is with Microsoft Access.

Access has the advantage that it is part of the Microsoft Office package, so if you already know Word or Excel, you're halfway home. More important, just about all the work you do in Access will apply to learning about SQL Server. Make no mistake, however, if you are serious about a career in database development, Access is too limited, and you need to learn about SQL Server or one of the programs with which it competes, such as Oracle. However, as a learning tool, it is second to none.

Tables, Rows, and Columns

It all begins with tables. A table represents a cohesive set of data. Each column represents one attribute of information, called a *field*. Each row represents one *record* in the database. Here's an example to make this arrangement understandable. Access and SQL Server both come with the same sample database: NorthWind. The Northwind database contains data for a mythical Northwind Traders company, which imports and exports gourmet foods from around the world.

Let's take a look at the customer table. The columns in this table represent fields or attributes of each customer's record, including such data as their name, address, phone number, and so forth. Each row represents a different customer.

In a relational database, each column represents a field, or type of data, and each row represents one record.

Customer ID	Company Name	Contact Name	Contact Title	Address	City	Region	Postal Code	
ALFKI	Alfreds Futterkiste	Maria Anders	Sales Represent	Obere Str. 57	Berlin		12209	G
ANATR	Ana Trujillo Emparedac	Ana Trujillo	Owner	Avda. de la Con	México D.		05021	M
ANTON	Antonio Moreno Taquei	Antonio Moreno	Owner	Mataderos 231	México D.		05023	M
AROUT	Around the Horn	Thomas Hardy	Sales Represent	120 Hanover Sq	London		WA1 1DP	UI
BERGS	Berglunds snabbköp	Christina Berglund	Order Administra	Berguvsvägen 8	Luleå		S-958 22	S\
BLAUS	Blauer See Delikatess	Hanna Moos	Sales Represent	Forsterstr. 57	Mannheim		68306	G
BLONP	Blondel père et fils	Frédérique Citeaux	Marketing Mana	24, place Klébe	Strasbour		67000	Fr
BOLID	Bólido Comidas prepar	Martín Sommer	Owner	C/ Araquil, 67	Madrid		28023	S|
BONAP	Bon app'	Laurence Lebihan	Owner	12, rue des Bou	Marseille		13008	Fr
BOTTM	Bottom-Dollar Markets	Elizabeth Lincoln	Accounting Man	23 Tsawassen E	Tsawasse	BC	T2F 8M4	C:
BSBEV	B's Beverages	Victoria Ashworth	Sales Represent	Fauntleroy Circi	London		EC2 5NT	UI
CACTU	Cactus Comidas para l	Patricio Simpson	Sales Agent	Cerrito 333	Buenos A		1010	A
CENTC	Centro comercial Moct	Francisco Chang	Marketing Mana	Sierras de Gran	México D.		05022	M
CHOPS	Chop-suey Chinese	Yang Wang	Owner	Hauptstr. 29	Bern		3012	S\
COMMI	Comércio Mineiro	Pedro Afonso	Sales Associate	Av. dos Lusíads	São Paulc	SP	05432-043	Br
CONSH	Consolidated Holdings	Elizabeth Brown	Sales Represent	Berkeley Garde	London		WX1 6LT	UI
DRACD	Drachenblut Delikatess	Sven Ottlieb	Order Administra	Walserweg 21	Aachen		52066	G
DUMON	Du monde entier	Janine Labrune	Owner	67, rue des Cin	Nantes		44000	Fr
EASTC	Eastern Connection	Ann Devon	Sales Agent	35 King George	London		WX3 6FW	UI
ERNSH	Ernst Handel	Roland Mendel	Sales Manager	Kirchgasse 6	Graz		8010	A
FAMIA	Familia Arquibaldo	Aria Cruz	Marketing Assis	Rua Orós, 92	São Paulc	SP	05442-030	Br
FISSA	FISSA Fabrica Inter. S	Diego Roel	Accounting Man	C/ Moralzarzal,	Madrid		28034	S|
FOLIG	Folies gourmandes	Martine Rancé	Assistant Sales	184, chaussée	Lille		59000	Fr
FOLKO	Folk och fä HB	Maria Larsson	Owner	Åkergatan 24	Bräcke		S-844 67	S\
FRANK	Frankenversand	Peter Franken	Marketing Mana	Berliner Platz 4	München		80805	G

Record: 1 ▶ ▶| ▶* of 91

Unique five-character code based on customer name.

This rows-and-columns arrangement of data is a very powerful way to manipulate a large amount of information at once. A single table, however, does not make a relational database. The true power in relational database management is in tying together related tables of information.

Records and Fields

Record—a row in the table representing one complete entry in the database.

Field—a column in the table, representing a single category of data, such as last name or order date.

Datatypes

Every column or field is made up of data. Databases typically support a number of different datatypes. For example, Access supports numeric data, and strings of written data. Written data is divided into text, used for addresses, Social Security numbers, phone numbers, and so forth, and memos, which are large blocks of text.

Like many databases, Access also supports special advanced data types such as dates, currency, yes/no fields, and so forth. These advanced types make storing your data simpler, as you don't have to do the work of converting text or numbers into these more abstract interpretations.

Relations and Joins

The true power in a relational database comes from creating relationships between data in various tables. For example, in the NorthWind database, there is a second table called Employee in which all the employees are listed, and a third table named Orders, in which every order is listed.

Because Access is a relational database, you can create a listing of your employees and associate that information to your other records.

You can create as many tables as you have types of data to categorize.

179

Let's examine the relationship among these three tables in some detail. We note that the customer table tells us all about the customer, and the employee table tells us about the employee. No surprises there. The Orders table tells us about orders (what else?) with each row representing a different order. The details of what are in the order are in a different table. Here we learn only about the order date, who ordered the product, when they need it, where to ship it to, and so forth.

Notice that the second column here is the customer name, and the third column is the employee name. These entries tie each order to a specific customer and a specific employee. There is no need, here in the order, to make columns for the employee's phone numbers; if we need that information, we can use the employee name to look up the employee record in the employee table, and get the information we need. This linkage is the essence of a relational database. Here's the key concept: Each table represents a set of data, and there is no need to duplicate that data anywhere else in the database. We'll cover this in detail in a moment, when we talk about normalization.

Efficient Data Storage

The Access version of NorthWind keeps this data in a very inefficient way. There really is no need to keep the employee's name. A name is a lot of text, and more important, names can be duplicated. In a large company, such as AT&T or Citibank, there may be hundreds of people named John Smith. Each employee, however, does have a unique employee ID that is guaranteed to be unique. It is more efficient and more reliable to store this data rather than the employee name.

Similarly, it is more efficient and more reliable to store the customer's unique customer ID than to store the customer's name in each order. This, in fact, is how SQL Server manages the same table.

Records in a relational database each have a unique ID that can distinguish them from similar entries.

Here we see that only the customerID is stored, not the customer name. We can get the name by looking it up in the customer table. Similarly, we keep only the EmployeeID—if we need the name, it is easy to get from the employee table. This is what database programmers expect to see in a database table.

Elimination of duplicate information and efficient storage of information are two hallmarks of a good database. The third is data integrity.

Diagramming the Relationships

Advanced database tools, such as those provided with SQL Server, Oracle, and other powerful databases, can help you visualize these relationships.

Keep Information Consistent

Data integrity—All the data in the database is consistent among all the tables. For example, the information about an employee identified in one table is consistent with the information about that same employee when it appears in any other table.

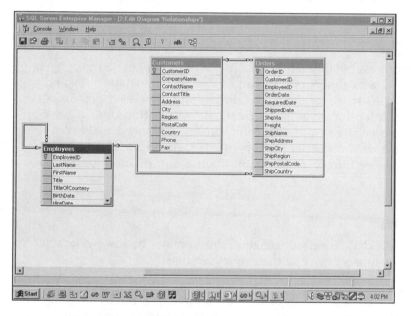

Advanced database tools illustrate the links between tables in your database.

Although this simple diagram may not provide much help, after your database grows in complexity, a diagram can provide great insight into the relationship among the tables. For example, the diagram of the complete NorthWind database does show a bit more information than could be relayed in just a few sentences.

This diagram shows the relationship of the records in the NorthWind database.

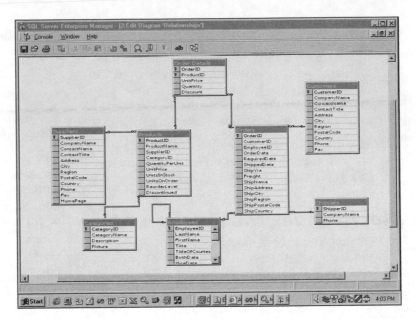

Normalization

Normalization is the process of eliminating various forms of duplication from your database. This process creates a more efficient and more reliable database. Typically, serious database developers strive for the third normal form (described as follows), although at times we'll intentionally *denormalize* the database—that is, drop back down to the second or even the first normal form, because advanced analysis of the database may prove that we'll get better performance. Programming is always an art of tradeoffs, and at times we'll trade greater duplication of information for better overall performance.

First Normal Form

In the first normal form (1NF), we eliminate all multiple values in any given table. Therefore, no employee appears twice in the employee table.

Although eliminating duplicates of employees is fairly straightforward, it's easy to find that you have duplicate lines for an order. For example, you might have an order that includes two items purchased, and to move your table into the first normal form, you'd have to ensure that the order appears only once in the table. The way to do that is to create a row for the order, and then to create a second table that holds the details. In that second table, you'd have two entries, one for each item purchased in the single order.

Second Normal Form

In the second normal form (2NF), we must fulfill all the requirements of the first normal form, and then we add the requirement that each row in a table must be uniquely identifiable.

This requirement is typically accomplished by assigning each record a unique identifier. Thus, every employee has a unique employee ID, and every order has a unique order ID.

Third Normal Form

Tables in the third normal form (3NF) must, of course, meet all the criteria for the first normal form and the second normal form. In addition, in tables in 3NF you eliminate redundancy among the tables. Specifically (get ready—this is tricky the first time you read it): You eliminate all redundant nonkey information in your table that relies on nonkey information in another table! In plain English, you want to eliminate duplication of information. For example, suppose you have an employee table that includes some insurance information:

Table 12.1 Employee Insurance Table

Employee ID	Insurance Company	Deductible
00011	Acme Insurance	$500
00012	Beta Insurance	$750

This data is not in 3NF because the name of the insurance company and the amount for the deductible depends on information in the insurance company table. If we change the deductible in the insurance company table, the data in the employee table might get out of sync. We fix this by normalizing the tables to 3NF:

Table 12.2 Normalizing the Tables to 3NF

Employee ID	Insurance Company ID	
00011	027	
00012	035	

Insurance Co ID	Insurance Co Name	Deductible
027	Acme Insurance	$500
035	Beta Insurance	$750

Now there is no duplication. If we need to know the deductible for the insurance for employee 11, we look up his Insurance Co ID and then use that to find the deductible.

Keys

A key is a unique identifier. The key to the employee table is the Employee ID. It is called a key because it opens up the information. By using the Employee ID, you can find the employee record.

The Power of 3NF

The third normal form eliminates duplication by using keys to refer to information stored in other tables. Therefore, the order table does not need to store any information about the employee who recorded the order except the *key*—the Employee ID.

This elimination of duplicate information results in far more reliable databases. It's impossible for information about an employee in the order table to get out of sync with that same information in the employee table, because we've eliminated all employee information in the order table!

Let's say the employee changes his phone number. If he had recorded his phone number in the order table (so that we could call if there is a problem with the order), we'd have to update both the order table and the employee table with the new phone number. If we forget to update the order table, then we have corrupted data: The phone number in one table, the employee table, is out of sync with the same information in another table, the order. By removing this information from the order table, it is not possible for the data to get out of sync. If we need to call the employee, we look up his ID in the order and use that as a key into the employee table, where we find the phone number.

The Great Space Waster

To get an idea of how much space you'd waste by keeping several copies of a table, imagine a phone book containing listings by first name, address, and phone number in addition to last name. It would be the size of a phone booth!

Indexing Information

Typically, you'd like to be able to get to your information quickly. You may want to look up an order by the order number, by the employee who took the order, by the customer who placed the order, or by date.

If the table is not in order, and you have tens of thousands of orders to search through, it can take a long time to find this information. One way to accomplish easy data location is to keep multiple copies of the table, each ordered in the way you might want to get at it. Therefore, you can keep a copy ordered by customer name, another copy ordered by employee, another by date, and so forth.

This is insanely expensive in terms of disk space, and it raises the question of data integrity. How do we keep all these tables in agreement with one another? The answer is, we don't do it this way.

We keep the table ordered by the most common way of searching, and then we build indexes that solve our quick searching. For example, we might order the table by order ID, and then build another table, an index table, ordered by customer ID. Such an index might look like this:

CustomerID	OrderID
CHOPS	10254
HANAR	10250
HANAR	10253
RICSU	10255
SUPRD	10252
TOMSP	10249
VICTE	10251
VNET	10248
WELLI	10256

As you can see, this table is arranged by Customer ID. Associated with each CustomerID is an OrderID. To find a customer's order, you search this table (which is very quick), find the CustomerID, look up the OrderID, and use that to search the Order table. Because the index is *ordered* (in this case, alphabetical), it is a very fast process, far faster than a brute-force search of the Order table for every instance of a given CustomerID.

Note that the index table will be built and maintained by the database itself; this is not something you must do by hand. You simply indicate to the database program which tables and fields you want indexed; the database does the rest.

Database Integrity

There is much more to say about database integrity, and entire books have been written on the art of designing efficient and reliable databases.

There are two ways to work with databases as a programmer. You can learn the fundamentals of database design and programming, or you can decide to develop your expertise in this specialized area. If that is your interest, you'll want to learn about transaction processing and database theory. The glossary lists a few books to get you started.

The details of database integrity are beyond the scope of this book, except to note that database design and programming remains an important and lucrative field for software engineers.

Queries

After you've designed your database, how do you get information in and out of it? The first and most fundamental task is to search for data.

Each database has its own language, its own syntax to master. This "tower of babble" has presented a serious challenge to the industry, and in recent years a standard has emerged that virtually every major database vendor supports: Structured Query Language (SQL).

SQL provides full access to all the functionality of your database, in a common language supported across platforms. SQL has transformed the industry, and a great deal of technology has been built on top of SQL to make SQL available in increasingly powerful environments.

Using SQL

SQL is a large, complex language with a great deal of power. I'll be able to skim only the most superficial surface of SQL here, but I do want to give you a flavor of what it is like.

The essence of SQL is to create, manipulate, and define databases. I'll focus on the most common use of SQL—to extract information from a database. Specifically, SQL is most often used to select information from one or more tables, and to create a table of results. Not surprisingly, the keyword for this task is SELECT.

For example, you can use SELECT to pull out a subset of information from the Orders Table. Here's the result of entering

```
select OrderID, CustomerID, EmployeeID, ShipName from orders
```

The purpose of this SELECT statement is to extract all the records from orders, but only the columns listed. While this is convenient, the real power is in the where clause:

```
select OrderID, CustomerID, EmployeeID, ShipName from orders
where customerID = "VINET" or customerID = "ROMEY"
```

This time I've used the where clause to narrow our results, answering the question "What is the orderID, customerID, employeeID, and shipName for every order in which the customerID is ROMEY or VINET?"

SQL lets you extract records from a database using a sentence-like syntax.

The SELECT statement lets you narrow your results based on criteria you specify with a where *clause.*

Careful use of the SQL Select statement and its clauses such as where and order-by can allow you to create powerful reports. The syntax of SQL is quite demanding, however, and many developers use tools which make accessing this data far easier.

Accessing DBs from Programs

All the work we've done to date has been in accessing this data through the SQL or Access tools themselves. It is possible, however, to work with data directly from within programs. Here is an example of a quick project in Visual Basic that opens the NorthWind database and iterates through its records, printing to the debug window:

```
 0:   Sub Main()
 1:   Dim oCompany As NorthWind.Companies
 2:   Set oCompany = New NorthWind.Companies
 3:      Dim rs As ADODB.Recordset
 4:      Set rs = oCompany.doLoad
 5:
 6:      Dim Company As String
 7:
 8:      While Not rs.EOF
 9:          Company = rs("CompanyName")
10:           Debug.Print Company
11:            rs.MoveNext
12:        Wend
13:   End Sub
14:
15:   Public Function doLoad() As Recordset
16:      Dim rs As ADODB.Recordset
17:      Set rs = New ADODB.Recordset
18:      Call rs.Open("select * from customers", "North Wind")
19:      Set doLoad = rs
20:   End Function
```

Let's analyze this code. I don't expect you to follow the syntax—this is fairly advanced Visual Basic—but I suspect you will find the ideas fairly comfortable.

On line 2, I create a variable called oCompany, which is of type NorthWind.Companies. This is a type I created, a little object which knows how to interact with the companies table in the NorthWind database. On line 3, I create an ADODB.RecordSet object. This is an object provided by Microsoft for iterating through the results of a select statement, and on line 4 I set that object to point to the result of calling doLoad on my NorthWind.Companies object.

This pointer jumps to line 16 where I create another record set object to point to the results of calling

```
select * from customers
```

on the NorthWind database, and pass that result back to the calling function on line 4. In short, I've opened a SQL statement and received back results, which are now stored in the result set I declared on line 3. On line 8, I begin a while loop that will display these results, line by line, until I've shown them all.

Again, don't worry about the Visual Basic; there is lots of confusing syntax here. The point of this exercise is to show that it can be done, quite easily in fact, from within VB.

Interestingly, it isn't hard to do the same thing from within ASP, which we covered in Chapter 5, "Internet Programming."

```
0:   <TR>
1:           <TD>#</TD>
2:           <TD>CustomerID</TD>
3:           <TD>CompanyName</TD>
4:       </TR>
5:   <%
6:       Dim rs
7:       Set rs = Server.CreateObject("adodb.recordset")
8:       call rs.Open("select * from customers", "North Wind")
9:       Dim i
10:       i = 1
11:       while not rs.EOF
12:
13:       %>
14:
15:
16:       <TR>
17:           <TD><%=i%></TD>
18:           <TD><%=rs("CustomerID")%></TD>
19:           <TD><%=rs("CompanyName")%></TD>
20:       </TR>
21:   <%rs.MoveNext
22:   i=i+1
23:       wend %>
```

Once again, don't worry very much about the syntax, just the general idea. On line 0, I create a row in a table, and on lines 1-3, I put in some column headings: #, CustomerID and CompanyName. On line 6, I create a recordset which we populate on line 8, using the same select statement I called from VB. This time, I call it directly from the ASP page.

On lines 11-23, I iterate over the results, printing them into a table that I can view in a browser.

Web browsers can display the results of an ASP database query.

#	CustomerID	CompanyName
1	ALFKI	Alfreds Futterkiste
2	ANATR	Ana Trujillo Emparedados y helados
3	ANTON	Antonio Moreno Taquería
4	AROUT	Around the Horn
5	BERGS	Berglunds snabbköp
6	BLAUS	Blauer See Delikatessen
7	BLONP	Blondesddsl père et fils
8	BOLID	Bólido Comidas preparadas
9	BONAP	Bon app'
10	BOTTM	Bottom-Dollar Markets
11	BSBEV	B's Beverages
12	CACTU	Cactus Comidas para llevar
13	CENTC	Centro comercial Moctezuma
14	CHOPS	Chop-suey Chinese
15	COMMI	Comércio Mineiro
16	CONSH	Consolidated Holdings
17	DRACD	Drachenblut Delikatessen

More to Study

There are many other aspects to writing an efficient database program, and, of course, there is a great deal to know about setting up and optimizing the database itself. Until recently, database programming has been a somewhat obscure specialty. Database programmers and applications programmers were distinct, with somewhat disparate skill sets. This is changing as more and more people are challenged with making large databases available on the Web and building interactive database intranet and Internet applications.

The Least You Need to Know

➤ A database is an efficient way to store your information.

➤ Relational databases consist of rows (records) and columns (fields).

➤ Databases can be normalized to eliminate duplication of information and make them more reliable.

➤ Databases can be indexed to make retrieval of information fast.

Part 3

Getting a Job

If you've come this far, you know there are good jobs waiting and you have an idea of what you must learn. How do you find the right job? In this section, I'll explore looking for work by networking, using newspapers and the Internet, and employment agencies. I'll give you tips on preparing your résumé and on interviewing well.

Chapter 13

Looking for Work

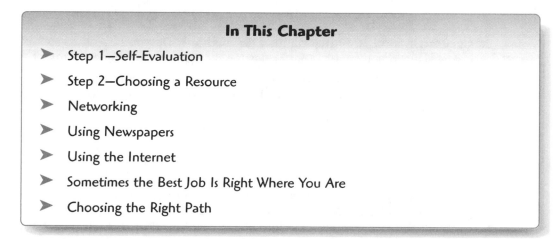

In This Chapter

➤ Step 1—Self-Evaluation

➤ Step 2—Choosing a Resource

➤ Networking

➤ Using Newspapers

➤ Using the Internet

➤ Sometimes the Best Job Is Right Where You Are

➤ Choosing the Right Path

Now that you are convinced there are market opportunities, and you've acquired the necessary skills, where do you find work? Getting that first job is, of course, always the hardest task; although finding a career path is a challenge at every stage.

There are a number of resources we'll consider in this chapter, including friends and family, agencies, the Internet, and other media. Which you choose depends in large measure on where you are in your career, and what you value most in a job.

Step 1—Self-Evaluation

The very first step in finding work is to engage in a ruthless self-evaluation. What are your strengths and weaknesses? In this evaluation, consider not only your technical skills, but also your interpersonal skills, business acumen, experience, and other emotional and intellectual resources. Table 13.1 includes a self-evaluation checklist to use as a starting point.

Table 13.1   Self-Evaluation Checklist

1. **Skill check.** What are your programming skills? Include programming languages you know and level of expertise: novice, solid programmer, advanced skills, guru. What projects have you built with each language? How long have you been programming in this language? What role have you played on development teams? If this is your first job, consider internships or large projects you've built in school.

   Also include experience with software packages, hardware skills, networking, knowledge of the Internet, protocols, drivers, and so forth.

   _____
   _____
   _____
   _____

2. **Credentials.** What formal training do you have? Do you have a degree? What credentials do you have? What professional organizations do you belong to?

   Also include achievements in other fields. Many of the best programmers are well-rounded people with advanced expertise in music, psychology, medicine, and other unrelated fields.

   _____
   _____
   _____
   _____

3. **Learning style.** Do you need formal training, or do you teach yourself? How do you like to learn? Do you enjoy college classes, professional classes, or reading the book? Do you learn by doing or by reading theory? What skills have you acquired in the past year? Five years? Ten?

   Consider your learning style. Do you like to acquire a solid expertise before undertaking a project, or do you prefer to learn as you go? Are you good at finding your own way, or do you prefer to work with a guide? Do you learn well in large classes, or do you prefer individual mentors?

   _____
   _____
   _____
   _____

4. **Technical experience.** What is your technical experience? What projects have you worked on and what was the result? Consider both paid and unpaid work, internships, and other projects.

Here we're not looking for specific technical expertise as much as *experience*. What have you actually done; what projects have you worked on? Did you build something? If so, how did it work out? What problems have you solved with technology and what was your approach?

_____

_____

_____

_____

5. **Business experience.** What are your business skills and experience. Consider work experience, management, and leadership positions. Don't ignore marketing and business development experience.

    A limiting factor in the careers of many technical people is that they can't see past the technology to the underlying business concerns. Are you able to understand budgets, profit and loss, and business priorities? Do you understand marketing and sales? Can you interact with end users and customers to ascertain their driving concerns?

_____

_____

_____

_____

6. **Interpersonal skills.** What are your interpersonal skills? Are you good with people? Are you a leader? Are you someone who helps bring a team together or generates new ideas?

    Most commercial programming is done in teams. While some highly qualified programmers can get away with being a prima donna for a while, the simple reality is that interpersonal relationships among the members of the team cannot be ignored, nor should they. In the end, these teams are not only building software, they are building teams and relationships.

_____

_____

_____

_____

7. **Creativity.** Are you creative? Do you work well from a blank sheet of paper, creating solutions from scratch? Are you thorough and detailed? Do you carry through to the final delivery? Are you better at innovation and development, or production and follow-through?

    There is no best answer here, but an honest self-assessment is critical. Some folks enjoy working on a new, undefined project; they see it as a limitless opportunity for creativity. Others panic; they thrive given enough direction, but flounder when the task is open-ended and unbounded. Both types of people can succeed in software, but knowing which you are helps avoid setting yourself up for frustration and failure.

_____

_____

_____

8. **Self-promotion.** How are you at selling yourself? Can you talk your way into any job even if you aren't qualified? Are you someone who doesn't interview well but is great in the job when given a chance? Are you better at writing or speaking?

   Some people can walk into an interview and sell themselves so well that their specific qualifications and skills really are secondary. They "click" with the person making the hiring decision, and it is obvious they can acquire whatever skills they need. Others are highly qualified and would do well in the job, but they are so uncomfortable in an interview that they never get the opportunity. Knowing which of these better describes you will help you decide how much you need to rely on the help of others, and how you will approach selling yourself to prospective employers.

   _____

   _____

   _____

   _____

9. **Financial Needs.** What do you need financially? What is your minimum salary? Are you looking for a high-risk, high-potential gain with stock options, or a lower-risk, lower-reward salaried position? Do you prefer salary, commissions, or consulting fees? How long can you go with no salary at all?

   Some people are simply willing to tolerate more risk than others. This may be a function of personality, or specific life conditions. A father who is the sole supporter of a young family may need a steady income from a large company where he can feel a high level of job security. A young college graduate with no other responsibilities may be able to tolerate a job with little or no salary in exchange for stock options in a high-risk but potentially very lucrative startup.

   _____

   _____

   _____

   _____

10. **Working Conditions.** Now consider what working conditions you need and what you're willing to put up with. Do you mind working 60-hour weeks, or do you want to work 35? Do you need your own office, or can you survive in a cube?

    This subject is an often-overlooked area of concern, but ignoring these considerations can be fatal to your happiness in the job you take. If you have a young family and being home a lot is important to you, a job that requires long nights and weekends with lots of travel may not be the right position no matter how appealing it is otherwise.

    _____

    _____

    _____

    _____

11. **Perfection.** Before you go further, describe the perfect job. Is it pitching for the Red Sox? President of the United States? Chairman of Microsoft? Now what is the ideal job in programming? President of a small startup? Salaried programmer? Team lead on an Internet Commerce project?

_____

_____

_____

_____

You can't evaluate the steps along the way if you don't know where you want to end up. Don't be constrained by reality; engage in a flight of fantasy: What would be the absolute dream job? After you know this, you can think about which jobs will help you move toward your goal.

Step 2—Choosing a Resource

There are a number of ways to look for work, and which you choose will depend on your work experience, your goals, and the quality of the resources available to you. These include

➤ Family and friends

➤ People with whom you've worked in the past

➤ Newspaper classifieds

➤ The Internet and World Wide Web

➤ Your current employer or school

➤ Full-time employment agencies

➤ Contract and temporary agencies

Let's consider each of these in turn. If you are looking for your first job, you will almost certainly have to rely on family and friends to a very large degree. There is an old saying, often said disparagingly: "It's not what you know, it's whom you know." I would turn this around and say: "It's not only what you know, it is what folks think about you." Said that way, it isn't an insult; it is a recognition that your reputation is critically important.

Your friends and family may not know anything about your technical skills, but they know you, and, you may hope, they know you to be a responsible, hardworking, eager, energetic, and motivated person. You can capitalize on their good feelings by asking them to help you find an opportunity to put these skills to work.

Networking

Networking with former associates, friends, and family is not a passive activity of "asking around" to see whether anyone knows about a job. That approach rarely gets you a job in any reasonable amount of time, and leads to frustration and despair.

If you are looking for work, you must go about it aggressively and actively. You must make your first job, getting a job, and you must work at it as hard and for the same long hours you expect to work on the actual job itself.

You start by making a list of everyone you know. This task is not as easy as it sounds. We're not only talking here about the people you see every day, but everyone you've met, everyone you talk with, every acquaintance. We're talking about all your aunts and uncles and cousins, your friends from school, others you've ever talked with, local merchants, the person whose dog you once walked, that nice old woman whom you went shopping for back in the Scouts. Everyone.

Create a database. Using something such as Access or FoxPro is ideal, but paper and pencil can work fine. (Of course, any opportunity to practice a valuable computer skill is good!) I used the Access Database Wizard to create a contact database, and it was nearly perfect for this. Here you can see the entry form I use to keep track of each contact.

Create a database of potential work contacts.

Be sure to fill in all the phone numbers you can find. Clicking the Page 2 button at the bottom brings up the supplemental form, as shown here.

Create a form enabling you to enter miscellaneous information about your contact, including the vital Contact Type field.

Note the Contact Type entry. You can edit this field by double-clicking on it. This field enables you to differentiate among family, friends, former associates, referrals from family, and so forth. Be sure to fill in the supplemental personal information, such as Spouse Name and children's names. It is always impressive when you can "remember" these names in subsequent conversations. Nothing is worse than forgetting Uncle Harry's younger son's name. Take extensive notes. If you are comfortable with Access, consider expanding this field, and adding new fields to track relevant information. As you use the database, you'll discover information that you want to keep for each contact.

This database also tracks every call, noting the time and date and subject as well as the outcome. This information is critical; you will be talking to a lot of folks and you want to keep straight who said what, and when.

While you're at it, add all of these people to your phone list, and make the following resolution: The phone list is written in permanent, indelible ink. No one is ever erased. Ever. You can't predict when you'll want that number again. I've been doing this for 10 years; no one is ever erased. My current phone book has over 2,000 names in it. I'm constantly amazed at how often I need to call someone with whom I've not talked in five or even 10 years. Even if their number has changed, I at least have a starting point in tracking them down.

This Is Work

First, set a schedule for yourself. This is your job—finding a job. You must start work early in the day and plan to work late into the evening. This work is the hardest you will ever do, and you will succeed only by sheer determination.

When you get to work in the morning, review your notes from the day before. With whom did you talk? Did they give you a lead? Did you write up your notes, or do you need to edit them? Make a plan for the day. Construction people have a slogan that you should adopt immediately for this work and for your job after you get it: "Plan your work, and work your plan." Be sure you have a detailed plan of what you are going to do, and then let that guide your work, adjusting and fixing the plan as you go.

People have different tolerances for when you can call them. Some folks are up early and prefer you to call before they set out for their workday. Others sleep in, or are busy in the morning getting kids ready for school. Be very sensitive to these needs. If you are unsure, don't call before 10 a.m. or after 8 p.m. If you are calling them at work, consider calling mid-afternoon, as that affords the person you're calling an opportunity to get things under control in the morning.

Plan to make a specific number of calls every day. What is realistic? You can certainly call 10 people a day. Can you call 20? 40? Push yourself; how many people can you talk with and not sound exhausted? The simple reality is that the more folks you speak with each day, the more quickly you'll find work.

Making the Calls

Before you pick up the phone, know what you want to say. Is this someone you know or is this a referral? If the person might not know who you are, think through how you'll identify yourself, and what you want to say. Get to the point. "Hello, this is Jesse Liberty. You may not remember me but we met at a party last December and you said I should give you a call when I graduate...My uncle, Moe Brown, suggested I give you a call...

"I'm calling because I'm eager to find a job as a C++ programmer...I'm calling because I'm looking for work in software and I thought you might be able to point me in the right direction...I'm calling because I thought you might be able to give me advice about finding work as a programmer..."

Here's the rule: Either they bring you in for an interview, or they refer you to at least two other people who might be of help. "You're not hiring now? Would it be okay if I send you my résumé anyway, to keep on file? Great, I wonder whether you know of one or two people whom I might call to ask about work?" "You don't make the hiring decisions? Can you refer me to the right person in your company who might be able to help me?" "I know you're not in the field, but I wondered whether you knew anyone who is whom I might call?"

If they do give you a name, try to get as much information as you can. What is their phone number? Address? Title? Job responsibility? Best time to call them? What else should you know about them? Log all this information and be sure to track who referred you. "I'm calling at the recommendation of Moe Brown..."

Keep extensive notes on every call. Even dead-ends contain valuable information. "Didn't someone tell me yesterday that there is a new company opening in Riverdale? I didn't care about it when he said it, but now that I know Joe is moving to Riverdale, maybe I should look into it. Where is my note on that?"

You Never Know Where You'll Find Work

It never fails. You set out to find work in a systematic way, and you end up getting a job because you happened to mention your job search to someone in the laundromat and you were overheard by Bill Gates who was just dropping off his shirts. Talk to everyone; rule no one out. The guy who sells you chopped liver in the deli might very well have a brother who owns an Internet services company.

Here's an important fact: Many jobs never get to an agency and never appear in the newspaper. Perhaps the company is too small or too financially constrained to afford an agency. Perhaps the company doesn't want to read through 500 résumés; they want to find someone by word-of-mouth. Or perhaps the job hasn't officially opened yet, but if you happen along at the right moment, they might make you an offer.

The Advantages of Networking

The single greatest advantage of networking with friends, family, and acquaintances is that they can "speak for you." They can make the recommendation that means so much more than your specific skills. They can make the phone calls that open doors otherwise closed to you.

When a prospective employer has an opportunity to hire someone on a recommendation, that carries a great deal of weight. It reassures the employer that you are a known quantity, and helps him manage the risk that you are misrepresenting yourself or that he might misjudge you in what is, after all, a relatively brief encounter of an interview or two.

The Disadvantages of Networking

Here's the problem: After your friend or your uncle recommends a job to you, you may feel obliged to take the job if it is offered. Don't do it! If the job is not right for you, you are not doing your friend a favor if you say yes.

If a friend or a former co-worker referred you, they might stand to get a referral bonus if you take the job. Do not let this influence your decision. The $500 they receive cannot make up for your making the wrong job decision. Put yourself in their shoes; you might want someone to take the job if you'll gain from the referral, but you don't want it to the point that you'd encourage them to make a poor career decision.

There is one other disadvantage to this kind of networking. Not every job works out. There may turn out to be a bad "fit" between you and your boss. In the long run, the job may end with some acrimony or disappointment, and you want to ensure that the person who recommended you does not feel the brunt of that frustration and anger.

I knew someone who recommended a former co-worker to his boss. The interview went well and the boss offered the job. The applicant accepted the job, and then, the day the job was supposed to start, a family emergency cropped up that prevented the applicant from taking the job after all. Now the company was stuck; they were on deadline and they had to start the hiring all over again, costing them time and money. The fellow making the recommendation couldn't help feeling responsible and it hurt his relationship with both his boss and the former co-worker.

Be careful; there is a lot riding on your friend's recommendation. Although you don't want to take a job out of a sense of obligation, you do need to be sensitive to the potential fallout from your actions.

Using Newspapers

Some years back, the buses and trains of New York City were plastered with ads showing people at work with the tagline, "I got my job through the *New York Times*." This trend was lampooned by a cartoon showing Richard Nixon saying, "I lost my job through the *Washington Post*," but that is another story altogether.

Newspaper job ads are a time-tested resource, but they have distinct disadvantages that you must consider. Companies typically advertise in the paper because they want to reach a very wide audience. They will receive, if they are successful, hundreds, sometimes thousands of résumés in response to one large ad in the paper.

The company will sift through this deluge of résumés, and only the truly extraordinary ones will surface to the top and be contacted. Chasing jobs offered in newspaper ads can be a frustrating experience, as you'll need to respond to many ads before you'll get a single response. Writing a world-class résumé and accompanying cover letter is a skill considered in a later chapter, but writing a résumé that stands out from the crowd will be essential if this is the path you follow.

I've Ad It!

I'll talk more about answering newspaper ads with a killer résumé later on, but there's one tip I wanted to present right here. Don't be content with simply mailing a résumé. Call to confirm that the proper person received it, speaking directly with him or her if possible. This extra effort alone can bring you to a hiring manager's attention.

You also have a tough job of sifting through the ads and separating out those with promising jobs from those for which you are unqualified, or about which you are uninterested. Be on the lookout for agencies masquerading as employers. Often you send in your résumé for what sounds like a great job only to find that you've actually sent it to an agency that doesn't actually have that job available but that is eager to "help you find something else." This kind of bait-and-switch ought to be a sharp warning about the integrity of the agency. Of course, by the time you call, a given job may be filled, but watch out for ads that are nothing more than unrealistic come-ons designed to bring you in as a candidate.

Using the Internet

Ten years ago, if you wanted to find a job without an agency or referral, the newspaper was your only choice. Today, you can find literally thousands of jobs on the Internet.

First, you can go to any of the national newspapers, such as the *New York Times* or the *San Jose Mercury News*, and review their classified ads. Many of the display ads can be viewed through your Internet browser, as you can see in these two examples.

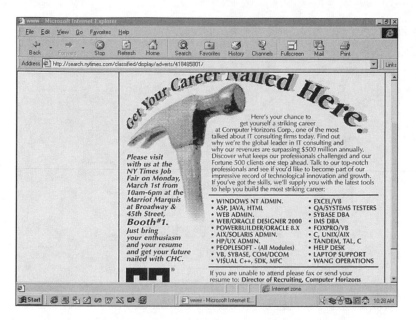

You can often browse classified ads in online versions of newspapers such as The New York Times...

...and the San Jose Mercury News.

In addition, there are now nationally recognized sites on the World Wide Web, dedicated to serving as intelligent classified advertising centers. One of the more famous is monster.com, whose home page is shown here.

The home page for
`monster.com`.

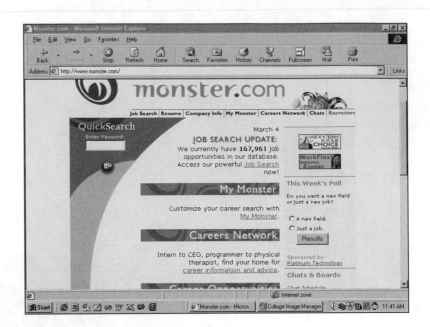

`monster.com` claims to list more than 170,000 jobs with 30,000 employers. They offer extensive job-searching capabilities. Let's pursue a job as a C++ programmer in Boston. Clicking on job search bring us to the screen shown here.

You can search
`monster.com` *for jobs in a specific location.*

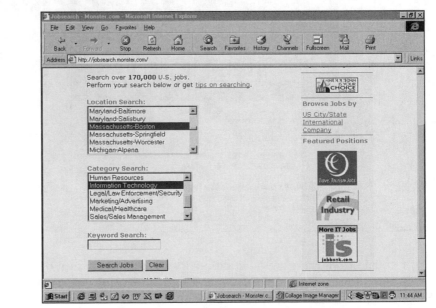

We'll choose Boston and Information Technology, and on the day I tried this, `monster.com` came back with more than 2,000 jobs, as you can see here.

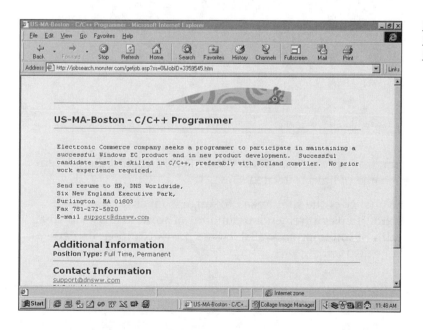

The hard part is not so much finding a job as sorting through the multiple possibilities.

I clicked through a few ads and quickly found this listing.

Here's one of more than 2,000 IT jobs in the Boston area.

With five minutes' work, I had a first lead on a job as a C++ programmer in the Boston area. Note that the ad specifically says, "No prior work experience required." Great stuff!

205

Through monster.com and many other online job sites, you can file cover letters, résumés, and related personal information and then use these to apply for jobs listed on the board. In addition, they offer advice columns, Q&A, chat rooms, and other services relating to looking for and getting a great job. monster.com is a great example of the kind of incredible services available free on the Web, and it is certainly not the only one offering these services.

The Web is awash in information about employment. I went to www.yahoo.com and clicked on Business and Economy, and then on Employment. There were more than 1,800 listings, as shown here.

You can find still more job prospects by searching a different site, such as Yahoo!

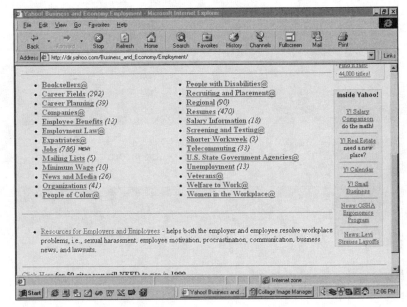

Clicking on Employment, Careers and Vocations, Career Planning, and then Recent Grads led me to a cornucopia of links to related sites.

As you might guess, the quality of the sites linked to range from abysmally useless through incredibly helpful. It takes a tremendous amount of work to chase down all these leads, but the wealth of information available does provide unprecedented opportunities to find your next job.

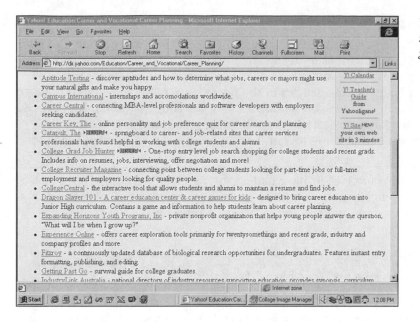

Yahoo! offers a set of job sites tailored for recent graduates.

The Disadvantages of the Internet

The very thing that makes the Web so powerful—its incredible profusion of information—also makes it difficult to deal with. Sifting through the information, separating the kernels of useful information from the overwhelming chaff of irrelevant and unhelpful detail can be a daunting task.

Sometimes the Best Job Is Right Where You Are

If you are looking to break into software, but all your work experience is in another field, how do you get started? Before you start reading ads, and networking with friends, consider staying right where you are.

If your company is happy with your work, why not ask them to help you in the transition. They may very well be willing to guide you through a process of changing jobs within your company. This tactic has the advantage of reducing the stress you'll experience as you take on new work, and providing you with an ideal first experience for your résumé.

If you choose to look elsewhere, you must be prepared to answer the legitimate question, "Why couldn't you find this work from within your existing company?" A prospective employer must be concerned; if your work wasn't good enough for your current company to want to keep you, why should the new employer want to take the risk?

Choosing the Right Path

Many people find that an employment agency is their best alternative when looking for work. The significant advantage of using an employment agency is that you will be able to draw on the expertise and advocacy of a professional. I'll consider the advantages and disadvantages of agencies in the next chapter, but they may not be an option for you. If you are currently in school, looking for your first job, most agencies won't be able to expend a great deal of energy helping you find work, because their customers, the companies that hire programmers, typically don't list entry-level jobs with agencies.

If you are at the top of your class, or have had an internship which has given you a lot of real world experience, you may want to try an agency, but in all likelihood you'll be best off with friends and families, ads, or the Internet.

The Least You Need to Know

➤ Depending on where you are in your career and what you value most in a job, there are a number of resources available to help you find satisfying work.

➤ A thorough self-evaluation is critical in assisting you with identifying your ideal job that matches your particular attributes.

➤ Make getting a job your first job—you must actively and aggressively go about it as hard as you expect to work on the actual job itself.

Chapter 14

Working with Agencies

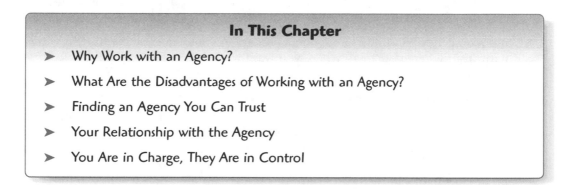

In This Chapter

➤ Why Work with an Agency?

➤ What Are the Disadvantages of Working with an Agency?

➤ Finding an Agency You Can Trust

➤ Your Relationship with the Agency

➤ You Are in Charge, They Are in Control

Employment agencies offer a tremendous opportunity for you to receive professional assistance in your job quest, but finding the right agency is critical. A good agency acts in your best interest, and is dedicated to building a lasting and profitable relationship with you and with the companies they represent. This chapter will focus on how you can find a great agency, and use it effectively.

Why Work with an Agency?

The single most compelling reason to work with an employment agency is this: Your area of expertise is software, theirs is employment. The goal is to leverage their expertise, experience, and advice. In the best of all possible worlds, your relationship with an agency results in a win/win/win situation: You get a great job, the company gets a great employee, and the agency gets a fee.

How an Agency Helps

If you are working with a *good* agency, their help should go way beyond simply finding a good group of companies that might be interested in interviewing you. They should be able to help you prepare for the interview and tweak your résumé. They should be your advocate and they ought to be a conduit back to you for honest and helpful feedback. A good agency should be able to negotiate for you and should keep your best interests at the forefront.

Articulating Your Goals

Long before the agency sends you on your first interview, they should be working actively to help you articulate your goals and requirements. A good agency will work with you to set your priorities; and to determine the kinds of jobs you want to find and the kinds you want to avoid.

Some of what they will discuss with you is the material you already considered in the last chapter: What is your dream job, what salary do you need, and how much risk can you handle?

A good agency will understand where you are in your career, and will help you plot a path from where you are to where you want to be.

Tweaking Your Résumé

Your agency ought to help you prepare your résumé, making sure it is professional and well-written, but they should not write it for you. An agency can give you a great deal of advice about targeting your résumé to a particular industry or company. In the next chapter, I'll get you started with tips on writing a great résumé, but your placement counselor can help you hone your résumé for a particular job.

The agency can also help ensure that your résumé highlights the most important and relevant facts. It is not their job, however, to distort your experience or expertise. Nor should you make it *your* job to do so. You want to be honest, but focused.

There's a subtle but important distinction here: What you want is to ensure that the employer learns the most favorable and relevant facts about you. You are not trying to present yourself as someone you are not, but rather as the person you *really* are.

Because we are all complex, multifaceted people, and because the potential employer has very specific needs, it is the agency's job to help highlight those facets of your experience and skills that most closely match the needs of the prospective employer.

Preparing for the Interview

The agency ought to prepare you for each company, reviewing what you might expect in the interview and briefing you on the details of the company so that you are fully prepared for the questions you might need to answer. For the agency to be able to do this job well, they must know a great deal about the company to which they are referring you.

Ideally, your placement counselor can tell you about what the company is looking for in a candidate, and what business problem they are trying to solve. He can tell you a great deal about the overall business goals of the company and about the corporate culture. All of this information helps you prepare for the interview so that you can present yourself at your very best. In the next chapter, I'll discuss how you want to prepare yourself for an interview, how to dress, and how to interact with your prospective employer.

Your Advocate

The agency is also your advocate. Before your interview, they should clear the ground ahead of you, preparing the company for your arrival and giving them advanced notice of why you will be a strong candidate. They should be on the phone, pitching you to the employer, explaining your advantages, and overcoming any objections to an interview.

Receiving Honest Feedback

After your interview, they should be back on the phone, obtaining feedback from the company about your interview, and surfacing any possible obstacles to a second interview or an offer. The agency acts as a facilitator between you and the company; a third party with whom the company can be brutally honest.

It is *imperative* that you find out if you are not interviewing well, but many companies will be very reluctant to say that to you directly. "I'm sorry, we'd like to hire you, but your pathetic attempts at humor came across as juvenile and obnoxious." Difficult to say to the candidate directly, but perhaps something they might share with your placement counselor. You need to hear it, however, even if it is painful. You want to be sure you incorporate this feedback into your next interview.

"You were much better this time," your agent might say after a subsequent interview with a new company, "only this time you were so sober they thought you were a bit stiff. Lighten up; don't make jokes but try to be personable. Oh, and next time leave the teddy bear at home, okay?"

Negotiating for You

Toward the end of the process, the agency can be helpful in providing advice when you're negotiating your salary and other benefits. They have experience across the industry, and can leverage that experience to help you realize that a company is not offering quite enough to attract someone with your qualifications. Frankly, they can also help *you* to get a good sense of whether your expectations are realistic. A good agency will *never* pressure you into taking a job, or accepting a particular salary, but they can help you evaluate your options and understand what the market is like across different companies.

211

What Are the Disadvantages of Working with an Agency?

Many people are reluctant to work with agencies. They see placement agents as middlemen; brokers who add nothing to the transaction between an employee and an employer, but who extract a fee, hurting both sides of the equation.

Others are concerned that employment agencies are agents of the employer. After all, it is the employer who pays the fees, so ultimately the agency must be responsive to the needs of the employer, not unlike a real estate agent who ultimately works for the seller, not the buyer.

In this section, I'll discuss some of the potential problems in working with an agency, and how you might overcome these concerns and problems.

A Lower Salary?

Some applicants worry that if they take a job through an agency, they will get a lower salary, because the company will want to recover their agency fees.

Fortunately, this scenario is unlikely. Even if a company were inclined to do so, they would be hard-pressed to get away with it, because they must complete in the same environment as everyone else, hoping to attract the same candidates as companies not making that decision. The salary they must pay is not dictated by their fees: Instead, it's driven by market imperatives: competition, and supply and demand.

You can protect yourself from this problem in two ways: First, do your own market survey of what similar jobs pay. Use the Internet, talk with your friends, and study ads in the newspaper. As you interview, and especially after you have a few offers, you'll get a firmer sense of the going rate.

More important, if you are working with an agency you trust, ask *them* what the going rate is, and what you can realistically expect. And if you are not working with an agency you can trust, find a new agency!

If the rate you are offered is lower than you expected, talk with the agency about what might be driving the difference. Ask them whether *they* think the company might be trying to cover the fees. Again, if you trust your agency, then surface these concerns openly.

Shotgun Approach

Some applicants are concerned that an agency will fire out their résumés to dozens of companies indiscriminately. An agency that works this way adds little value to what you can do yourself with a Web browser and the Sunday *Times*.

212

If you feel your agency is not targeting your job search adequately, you must work closely with them to narrow their search, or find a new agency that'll be more responsive to your needs. Later in this chapter, I'll cover how to find an agency that you can trust and that will send your résumé only to companies that are highly likely to meet your needs.

Use You As a Lead Generator

Unprofessional agencies have been known to use some applicants as a tool for finding new companies they can solicit. Here's how it works: At your interview with the agency, they say to you, "So, where else have you looked already?" They say they need to know this to ensure that they don't send your résumé to a company that has already seen you. That question can be entirely legitimate, but in this scenario, their hidden agenda is that they will contact these companies to see whether the company wants to list their jobs with the agency. They have, in effect, used you to find companies that are hiring in your field.

A good firm, on the other hand, will review what other companies you've interviewed with to provide information helpful to your process. This information can also help provide a baseline for what jobs interested you and which did not. The essential difference is that a good firm has only one goal: to help you find a job, not to make a placement.

Once again, this comes down to finding a good professional agency you can trust. Before we cover how this is done, let's look at one other significant area of concern: the conflict of interest.

Potential Conflicts of Interest

A company typically hires an agency to help them find an employee. The agency is paid a percentage of the employee's starting salary, if and only if they fill the job. This arrangement has the potential to set up a conflict of interest.

Imagine this scenario: Acme Software hires your agency, Personnel Inc., to help them hire a new software engineer. Personnel Inc. is paid only if Acme hires one of their applicants; if Acme hires an applicant from a competing agency, Personnel Inc. gets nothing.

You go for an interview and you are interested in working for Acme, but the job isn't quite what you were looking for. You like the project, but you won't have a chance to learn anything new, and the salary is 10% below your target. Your agent from Personnel Inc. tells you that the interview went well and a solid offer is on the table.

You agonize about the decision—should you take it or keep looking for something better? You very much want to ask your agent for advice, but now the conflict of interest rears its ugly head.

Your placement counselor gets a commission only if you take the job. Acme has been interviewing other candidates from other agencies. Your counselor has been working on the Acme job for three months, and hasn't been meeting her own sales goals for a while. Two other promising candidates for this job have already turned it down after weeks of careful hand-holding, you are the third, and perhaps last, chance of her getting a commission

Is it possible that her desire to close the deal will cause her to begin to "sell" the job to you? Might she see opportunities for you in this job that exist more in her wishful thinking than in the reality? Might she inadvertently underestimate your ability to get a better job if you just wait a while longer?

The agent doesn't have to be evil or duplicitous for this inherent conflict of interest to become a problem. It is built into the payment structure of the system itself, but there is a solution, which I've alluded to already and will cover in the next section.

Trust

You must decide, long before you are on the phone agonizing over a job offer, whether or not you really can trust your agency. If you believe they are profoundly committed to developing long-term relationships both with their corporate clients as well as with you, then you can trust that they will have your best interests at heart. A good, professional agency will see that it would be short-sighted for them to encourage you into the wrong job; they'd receive their fee, but at the cost of damaging their relationship with you and with the company.

If they want a long-term relationship with both the company and with you, then the conflict of interest is greatly diminished. Of course, you must always look out for your own interests, but if your agency is honestly dedicated to their long-term relationships, then their interests will be closely aligned with your own.

Such an agency is not interested in the quick-sale, get-in-get-out, take-the-commission approach to placement. They are more interested in the "put them in a great job and they'll be a client for life" approach to their job. That is the kind of agency you are looking for.

Finding an Agency You Can Trust

There is great potential for an agency to abuse their relationship with you and to mishandle a very critical step in your career. Finding the right agent is obviously critically important. So, how is it done?

Reputation and Word of Mouth

It starts, as so many things do, with reputation. Begin by asking for recommendations. Ask your friends and colleagues whether they use an agency, and whether they are happy with the agent. If they are, ask more questions. Do they trust their agent, and if so why? How long have they dealt with the agency? How has the agency handled their interactions? How much does their agent know about *them:* their career history, their goals, limitations, skills, and requirements? Of course, you may need to be careful not to signal the people with whom you work that you are about to change jobs. You might want to talk with friends in other companies first.

Ask Potential Employers

Don't stop there—begin a process of active exploration. Call companies in your field and talk to the personnel office. Say something to the effect of, "I'm not looking for work right now, but I am looking to establish a relationship with the best agency. Which agencies do you like to work with and why?" You'll be surprised how responsive many companies will be to this question. (Who knows, you might impress them so much they'll bring you in for an interview!)

Interview Agencies

After you have a few leads, call the agencies *before* you are looking for work. Tell them that you are not actively looking for a job yet, but want to find an agency for a long-term relationship. See what they say.

Here's the wrong answer: "Okay, well, call us when you're ready." Not much better is, "Why don't you send us a résumé, and we'll keep it on file until you're ready to start looking." Pass these agencies by.

The better answer is "Great, let's schedule an interview and we'll get to know each other."

Actually, the very best answer is "Okay, tell me a bit about yourself so that I can figure out if I'm the right person to help you. If so, I'll ask you to come in and meet me and discuss your goals; if not, I can refer you to someone else."

Now *that* is an agency I want to deal with.

What to Ask an Agency

When you do go in to meet with the placement counselor, arrive prepared with a list of questions. Ask about how big the agency is and how many people are employed. Find out whether you'll always work with the same person, or whether you will be shunted among a number of different counselors.

Ask about how long their placement counselors have been in the field, and how long they've been at this agency. Quick turnover should be a red flag. If they have low turnover, ask whether there are clients with whom you might speak, to get references about their agency.

Ideally, you'd like to talk with one or two people they've placed, and one or two companies they've worked with.

Perhaps they can refer you to people who've been dealing with their agency for a long while and who can speak to their professionalism, stability, and longevity.

Ask them about their overall approach to placement. You want to hear a strong dedication to long-term relationships, and you want them to make you believe it.

Do You Get Out Much?

After you are convinced that this agency has the right attitude about their relationship with *you*, it is time to find out about how they relate to their companies. Do they visit the firms they work with? How can they tell you about what it would be like to work in that company if they've never walked around in the office?

Do they know what the firm does, what it produces, and how it relates to the rest of the industry? Are they interested in software development? Do they know much about it?

You are looking for work in a highly technical and esoteric field. If your agency is clueless about software, how can they possibly help you find an appropriate job that will further your career and build on your skills?

What professional seminars have they attended? How much do they know about the field? Are they out there talking with personnel directors to find out what is in demand? Are they following up with the people they place to find out how things are going?

You Are Hiring a Consultant

The placement agent is applying for a job *with you*. She wants you to hire her to represent you, and if you're going to use her services, you had better interview her and be convinced that she is the very best person for this very important job.

Is She a Professional?

Does she see herself as a professional? Do you sense a commitment to her work and to the integrity of her relationship with her client?

Talk with your potential employment consultant about her peripheral vision. Is she looking around, keeping current and keeping an eye out for changes and new developments? What does she do to improve her skills?

Does the Consultant Know the Field?

How much does your consultant know about the Information Technology industry? What does he know about software development?

You need for your consultant to know a great deal. He must know a lot about sales, and selling and employment, so that he can market you effectively.

He should know about résumés and interviews and helping you target your job search, find the right position, and get it with the terms and conditions you need.

Your consultant must also know a great deal about technology. He represents programmers; he had better know about the new trends. If your consultant knows nothing about object-oriented programming and you are a C++ programmer, he may not be able to help you find the right job. Does he know about the Internet? Client/server applications? N-tier components? Is he working to keep current?

You want your consultant connected and wired in to the industry as a whole. What organizations does he belong to? Is he a member of the local software professional organization? Here's a partial list of the kinds of organizations you're hoping he belongs to:

➤ Arizona Software Association

➤ Chicago Software Association

➤ Colorado Software Association

➤ Indiana Software Association

➤ Maine Software Developers Association

➤ Massachusetts Software Council

➤ Minnesota Software Association

➤ NC Electronics & Information Technology Assn.

➤ New Hampshire High Technology Council

➤ New York Software Industry Association

➤ North Bay Software and Info. Tech. Assn.

➤ Northern Virginia Technology Council

➤ Pittsburgh High Technology Council

➤ San Diego Software Industry Council

➤ Software Association of Oregon

➤ Software Council of Southern California

➤ Software Entrepreneurs Forum

➤ Software Valley Corporation

➤ Southeastern Software Association

➤ Suburban Maryland High Tech. Council

➤ Technology Council of Central PA

➤ Technology Council of Greater Philadelphia

➤ Utah Information Technologies Association

➤ Washington Software Association

What about professional organizations for placement agencies? Does your agency belong to the local Association of Personnel Services or the local Professional Placement Consultants organization? Look for this kind of membership as an indication of the agency's commitment to a professional approach.

If your consultant is a true professional, he is also paying a lot of attention to employment practices in general and in the industries and companies he represents.

If you have a world-class consultant, he's interested in management theory and he can talk intelligently about the impact of organizational structure on product development. He is tuned in to the entire *process* of creating software, and understands how your particular skills might fit in with various organizations he represents.

There aren't many consultants who live up to this idealized vision of the perfect employment consultant, but you do want to probe to find the strengths and weaknesses of the person in whose trust you will place your career.

What Services Do They Offer?

Before you sign up with an agency, find out what services they offer. Are they restricted just to finding a job, or can they help you understand the market as well?

Ask the agency how they can help you become more marketable. Are they interested in guiding your career development and course of study? Can they make recommendations on what skills you ought to acquire?

How sensitive are they to issues of corporate culture and finding the right fit for you? Are you a button-down, pressed-suit, big-ticket Wall Street financials kind of person, or a baggy jeans, dirty sneakers, futon-on-the-floor type? Are they interested in these issues and can they help you find a good fit?

What Are They Promising the Company?

Here's a great final check: See whether you can get a handle on how they sell themselves to companies. Are they selling their professionalism? How much do they help the company assess their specific needs?

A truly world-class agency is involved with their companies, helping them plan for their needs and helping them assess the shifts and currents within their industry. Does your agency help their companies identify technological changes and plan for them?

In short, does your agency act as a consultant to these companies, or does it simply act as a body shop?

Take a Look at Their Web Site

Even before your first interview with the agency, you may be able to answer many of these questions by reading through their Web site carefully. Take a look at the sections targeted at others, either companies or people in fields other than your own. The objectivity you bring to this review may be greater than when the marketing material is targeted right between your eyes.

If they are going to help you find a great job, they need to know a lot about technology. Does their Web site look like it? Is this an agency filled with people who get a charge out of technology, or would they be just as happy representing lawyers?

Your Relationship with the Agency

After you find an agency you like, tell them everything they need to know about you. Think long and hard about the perfect job, and then describe it to them so that they can know where you want to end up.

Talk with your agency about the path you envision and solicit feedback and suggestions. They can give you good advice on what is possible, and they may help you think through which options you'd like to pursue in your career.

If you've established a relationship of trust with your agency, then let them know your concerns as they arise. You may find that your needs change suddenly in the face of a job offer. You wouldn't be the first person to suddenly discover you need a higher salary after a more modest salary offer is on the table.

You Are in Charge, They Are in Control

Many people are reluctant to work with agencies because they don't want to give up control. But being in control is not the same as being in charge. You are the final decision maker; and neither you nor the agency ought ever to forget that. After all, it is *you* who must live with the consequences of any employment decision.

Being in charge doesn't mean that you can't yield control of the process to the experts you've hired. It is *their* job to pace the presentations, to schedule the interviews, and to manage the process toward the desired outcome. What's important is that the process leaves you in a satisfying job that meets your current needs.

The Least You Need to Know

➤ Agencies can offer their expertise in finding work.

➤ Agencies can help you hone your presentation and can offer honest feedback.

➤ It is imperative that you find an agency you can trust.

➤ A good agent is eager to establish a long-term relationship with you, not just make a placement.

Chapter 15

Getting the Interview

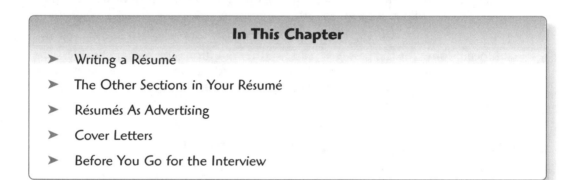

In This Chapter

➤ Writing a Résumé

➤ The Other Sections in Your Résumé

➤ Résumés As Advertising

➤ Cover Letters

➤ Before You Go for the Interview

In Chapter 13, I talked about using newspapers, the Internet, and friends and family to find work. In Chapter 14, I talked about working with agencies. However you conduct your search, sooner or later you'll find a company with a job you're interested in.

How do you write the cover letter? What should your résumé have and what should you leave out? How do you prepare for that first interview? What can you expect them to ask you, and more important, what should you ask them?

This chapter covers the entire process of getting a job from sending in your first résumé through the final handshake.

Writing a Résumé

Writing a résumé is such a difficult skill that there is a whole industry dedicated to helping you get it right. A quick search of Amazon.com returned nearly 300 books on the subject, including such titles as *101 Tips for a Dynamite Résumé*, *The Complete Idiot's Guide to the Perfect Résumé*, and *The Damn Good Résumé Guide*.

You wouldn't think it would be that hard: Just write down your work and educational experience and explain your skills. Yet, writing a good résumé turns out to be frightfully difficult, and more disturbing, writing a terrible résumé is surprisingly easy.

I'll try to review a few of the most important points about writing a good résumé, and I'll supply a couple of examples to get you started.

Chronological, Not Functional

The cardinal rule in résumés is that you list your experiences in chronological order, not by functional groupings. That is, list each job you've had, starting with the most recent, and working your way backward in time.

It is tempting to aggregate your programming jobs in one section and your support or marketing jobs in another section, but this is very disconcerting to your prospective employer and makes for a very confusing résumé.

The person reading your résumé is trying to answer the question, "What has this person been doing for the past few years?" Other questions the reader considers are "How long does he stay at a job? " and "What did she accomplish at each job?" The reader may also want to know whether you've worked on the kind of project (or used the kind of technology) that you'll be working on in the new job.

Responsibilities and Accomplishments

For each job you place on your résumé, tell the reader both what your responsibilities were, and also what you accomplished in the job. It is best if you can express the accomplishments in terms of the benefit received by your employer.

Thus, rather than writing, "simplified user interface," consider writing something such as "simplified the user interface, which cut the number of customer support inquiries about this part of the program by 80%." That is an accomplishment a manager can understand, and can translate into dollars and cents.

What to Write About Each Job

For every job you list in the résumé, be sure to indicate your position, your responsibilities, what work you actually did, what technology you used, what problem you solved, exactly what you delivered, and what benefit the company received.

This example of an entry from a résumé provides each of these details.

9/96 - 12/98   Acme Software Incorporated **Software Engineer**

Acted as a member of the software team in the deployment of new imaging applications and assisted with the implementation of new product features. Developed a new Windows NT software module written in C++ to provide workflow processing between an Intelligent Character Recognition system and a data entry system, and a COM module to provide an interface between the Visual Basic front end and the SQL Server database. Developed a file-staging feature for the imaging system which provided a significant performance advantage over the competition and which was cited by many customers as a significant reason for their purchase of the product.

Responsibilities included object-oriented analysis and design and independent software development.

The **position** of this job is Software Engineer.

The **responsibilities** are detailed in the final paragraph.

The **work actually done** is described in the first sentence: "Acted as a member of the software team in the deployment of new imaging applications and assisted with the implementation of new product features."

The **technology used** is spread throughout the first paragraph, including Windows NT, COM, C++, VB, SQL.

The **problem solved** is explained in the first sentence: deployment of new imaging applications, and the design and implementation of new product features.

What was delivered is described throughout the first paragraph, including "a data entry system" and "a COM module to provide an interface between the Visual Basic front end and the SQL Server database" and "a file-staging feature."

The **benefit the company received** is carefully detailed: "a significant performance advantage over the competition."

Ideally, each entry in your résumé should include all of these points.

The Other Sections in Your Résumé

Of course, your résumé is not simply a list of your jobs and accomplishments. You'll want sections that detail your skills and your education, and you might want a section with your career objectives. This example illustrates a typical résumé for someone with a good bit of technical experience.

223

STEPHEN M. PRESCOTT

1234 Main St.
Mytown, IN 43210
317-555-0111
prescott@isp.net

➤ **Objective:** A challenging position on the cutting edge of object-oriented Internet development, leveraging my expertise in Java, C++, and multithreaded distributed application development and with an opportunity to learn new skills.

➤ **Technical Skills:** Technical team leading, object-oriented design and programming, threaded design and programming, database design, Web programming, client/server software architecture design and implementation, UNIX, Windows NT, C++, Java.

➤ **Additional Skills:** Comfortable in both leadership and team roles, and possess strong writing, presentation, and negotiation skills.

EXPERIENCE

Liberty Associates, Inc.   October 1997 - present

Principal Software Engineer   www.libertyassociates.com

System Architect and Technical Team Leader, Outage Reporting System, Electric Utility

➤ Responsible for design, development, and rollout of browser-based three-tier intranet application using Java 1.1 applets, custom application server, Oracle 7.3, JDBC, Windows NT, Microsoft ASP, and JClass GUI components.

➤ Led team of four consultants and mentored developers in object-oriented design and multithreaded Java programming. Performed design and code reviews.

➤ Designed and built multithreaded, networked database application server in Java, including remote administration tools and scheduled database loaders.

➤ Managed deliverables schedule and project plan. Reported to client's project manager and group manager on team's progress and technical issues, with recommendations for functionality and scope management.

Acme Technology Partners, Inc.   April 1996 - September 1997

Senior Developer   www.acme.com

Senior Developer, Custom Fault-Tolerant CTI Call Center, Emergency Response Industry

STEPHEN M. PRESCOTT
Page Two

➤ Built custom object-oriented, multithreaded CTI application for a fault-tolerant call center with Java and Genesys Labs' telephony software. System involved unique, proprietary hardware elements, HP UNIX, Java, JDBC, and stored procedures in an Oracle database. Emergency response nature of the application required 100% fault-tolerant design.

➤ Development Phase: Custom CTI Server Team Lead, responsible for correct implementation of system design and mentoring less senior developers in the system's architecture, Java programming, and general object-oriented design and software engineering. Report to project manager on team's progress, difficulties, and development needs. Review code for efficiency, thread safety.

➤ Design Phase: Primary system designer for entire custom CTI server application. Used Singleton, Producer-Consumer, and State Machine design patterns extensively. Thoroughly researched threading issues in Java, including attendance at COOTS '97 conference, Portland, Oregon.

➤ Proof-of-Concept Phase: Integrated proprietary hardware, custom code, and Genesys telephony software. Investigated, evaluated, and recommended use of Java as the language of implementation.

Senior Developer   Marketing/Customer Service Web site,
                                          Telecommunications Industry

➤ Designed and built object-oriented middle tier server to handle requests for information and orders from the user interface to the back-end database server. UNIX, C++, extensive error checking and handling for fault-tolerant behavior, logging, data dictionary use, creation and use of a textual markup language for client/server communication.

➤ Played significant role in prototype development.

➤ Participated in client-requirements discussions and creation of scope document.

Senior Developer   Internet Software Distribution System,
                                          Marketing Industry

➤ Designed and documented pieces of an object-oriented online order system.

➤ Responsible for developing and organizing the design presentation.

➤ Facilitated client requirements discussions in the scoping phase.

Online University, Cambridge, MA   March - May 1997
C++ Instructor   www.online.com

➤ Answer questions and provide examples for two eight-week Internet-based C++ programming classes with 500 students each. *(Part-time work)*

STEPHEN M. PRESCOTT
Page Three

| **BigTelCo, Cambridge, MA** | October 1994 - April 1996 |
| Software Engineer | www.BigTelCo.com |

➤ Maintained and improved relational database loading system for a client/server online service.

➤ Managed and maintained production and QA release process and large software source code control system for a team of 15 software engineers.

MiniComputer Corporation, Maynard, MA	June 1993 - October 1994
Development Program Participant	www.MiniComputer.com
Systems Analyst	

➤ Engaged in 18 months of significant professional training for leadership, team-building, facilitation, communication, and presentation skills as a member of a team-oriented development program for future IT managers. Job rotations provided technical experience and exposure to technical management issues.

➤ Designed, built, and maintained network system management tools for use by Digital's support groups. Tools facilitated system performance reporting.

EDUCATION

MS, Computer Science, Boston University, Boston, Massachusetts

December 1997, GPA: 3.8

Coursework: Object-Oriented Analysis and Design, Object-Oriented Programming, Advanced UNIX Programming, Client/Server Systems, Database Systems, Expert Systems, Software Engineering, Computer Organization, Data Communication

BA, Computer Science, Middlebury College, Middlebury, Vermont

June 1993, *cum laude* honors

Résumés As Advertising

Your résumé is your marketing material; its job is to intrigue the reader and cause him or her to want to take a closer look. You don't accomplish this with "cutesy" gimmicks; you accomplish it by targeting your material at the employer's needs.

If the person you will be applying to needs someone to work as a team leader, then accent your leadership abilities. If they need someone who understands distributed computing, or multithreaded environments, then target these aspects of your experience. If you are a beginner, then put the accent on your internship or projects you've completed. Don't oversell yourself (be honest!) but give the employer a reason to want you rather than the next person.

> **Color by Numbers**
>
> You want your résumé to stand out by its content. Don't resort to gimmicks such as printing your résumé on Day-Glo paper. They're hard to read and are often not favored by hirers.
>
> However, you might consider choosing paper that's either a little heavier than normal or a shade off white. These small factors can subtly distinguish your résumé from the others in a pile.

Know the Employer

You can't focus your résumé appropriately if you don't know anything about the person you are sending it to. If you are using an agency, they can help you understand the company and their needs.

If you are chasing ads in newspapers or on the Internet, then be prepared to do some research before you send in your résumé. They'll get only one first impression of you; it is up to you to knock their socks off.

Tactical Planning

When a law firm has a lot riding on a multimillion-dollar lawsuit, they don't come into the courtroom unprepared, figuring they'll try to understand the plaintiff during initial testimony. They do months of research in advance of the trial, learning all they can about their adversary.

Finding the right job is the single most important career step you'll take, and it demands a bit of work up front. Find out everything you can about the company you're interested in. Check their Web site, do some research into the kinds of products they develop, and speculate on where they might be headed. If you can, try to find out more about the job they're advertising—see how the generic ad fits in with their other ads. The more you know about what they want, the more likely it is you can focus your résumé and cover letter to stand out as a powerful candidate.

You want only one thing from your résumé; you want it to generate a face-to-face interview. After you have your foot in the door, it is up to you to make the sale.

Cover Letters

The first question is how you are going to deliver your résumé. Are you going to send it in the mail, or will you deliver it by email, the Internet, or in person?

The second question is: What do you say in your cover letter?

The cover letter has only one purpose—to get the employer to look at your résumé for long enough to decide to bring you in for an interview. Cover letters can't help you much, but they can do a lot of harm. Poor cover letters with misspellings and grammatical errors are the kiss of death. Have someone else proofread your cover letter twice; make sure you get it right.

After you have it right, save it on your computer and generate all subsequent cover letters as a rewrite of your perfected original. Do the same for your résumé. Your process will be to open each prototype, edit it for the particular job you are interested in, save the new copies under new names, and print them.

Getting the Cover Letter Right

The most important thing to check on your cover letter is whether you spelled the person's name right. When I get mail to Jessie Liberty (note the *i* in the first name, which does not belong there, and which so many people put there), it subconsciously annoys me and makes me ill-disposed toward the person who sent it. You do not want your prospective employer to dislike you before he or she ever meets you.

If you are sending hard copy, have it printed on a very high-quality printer, using high-quality and expensive paper. The feel of good paper in your hands makes you think of high-quality people; the feel of cheap copier paper makes you think of something to throw away. (You might consider taking your résumé to a copy shop to have several duplicates made on good paper.)

Your cover letter should be crisp, professional and—most important—brief. Not just brief, it should be little, tiny, diminutive, dwarfish, minute, microscopic, Lilliputian, wee. Did I mention that it should be brief? The following short example illustrates a good cover letter:

Mr. John Caffrey
Director of Personnel
Acme Software Development
100 Park Avenue
Boston, MA 01234

March 1, 2004

Mr. Caffrey,

I am writing to apply for the position of Software Engineer, advertised in this morning's Sunday *New York Times* (ad reference number 17325).

Enclosed please find my résumé. I look forward to talking with you at your earliest convenience about this opportunity.

Thank you,

Jesse Liberty
Liberty Associates, Inc.
One Till Drive
Acton, MA 01720
617-747-7301
Fax: 978-635-9599
Email: jliberty@libertyassociates.com

The letter is addressed to the right person, his name is spelled correctly, and it is dated, as all letters ought to be. The date is important—it indicates that I wrote the letter the day the ad appeared, showing the right level of enthusiasm and interest.

A Word About Appellation

First, never, ever succumb to the temptation to use the prospective employer's first name. "Dear Jack," you might write, in the false hope of establishing a rapport. What comes across is sham-friendliness; the smarmy sensibilities of a used-car salesman. Use the last name (did I mention that you ought to be sure to spell it right?).

Second, get the title right. If the person has a doctorate, it is Dr. Smith; if not, Mr., Mrs., Miss, or Ms. For women, if you absolutely can't find out which is preferred, go with "Ms." On the other hand, it is much better to make a call to the company and find out which title she prefers. Some folks don't like Ms. at all; they prefer Mrs. Others hate Mrs. (and especially Miss) and use Ms. Find out which, and then use it consistently.

What the Cover Letter Says

The job of the body of the letter is to identify which job you're interested in (Software Engineer), where you saw the job advertised (this morning's Sunday *New York Times*), and which ad you're referring to (ad reference number 17325).

The second paragraph is your one opportunity to tell him that the ball is now in his court ("at your earliest convenience") and that you're politely eager to talk with him.

The signature is critical—people think they learn a lot about you from your signature; be sure it is at least slightly readable. Below the signature is your contact information; make it easy for them to find you!

Think about the phone number you provide on your résumé and cover letter. Does it have a cutesy answering machine that plays a funny message? Get rid of it and replace it with a businesslike brief recording: "Hello. You've reached Jesse Liberty. I'm unable to take your call at the moment, but please leave your phone number and a brief message and I will return your call as quickly as possible. Thank you."

(You probably want to substitute your own name, rather than Jesse Liberty, to reduce confusion.)

Sending Your Résumé by Email

If you are sending your résumé by email, you face a number of difficulties. You can't predict what kind of email software will be in use on the other end of the wire, and your carefully laid-out letter and résumé may be garbled in translation. Therefore, use belt-and-suspenders redundancy (which should also help prepare you for a career in computer programming).

Send the cover note in plain text, and attach a nicely formatted copy as a file. You may want also to refer the reader to a copy you've posted on the Internet. This gives them three chances to see your résumé, and at least one of the copies will look very sharp.

You may want to consider sending a copy of your résumé in the U.S. mail in addition to sending an email copy. This action provides you the fast access of email coupled with the security that they'll have a hard copy in hand a few days later. Be sure to mention that you've sent the hard copy in your email message. The arrival of the hard copy may constitute a second chance for them to see your résumé, but make sure your cover letter indicates that this is the hard copy of the letter already received in email.

Before You Go for the Interview

Like a pilot running through his preflight checklist, you want to anticipate an interview by making sure you are ready to take full advantage of this opportunity. Before you go, you will ensure you know as much as possible about the company, that you are ready to answer their questions, and that you know what you want to ask them.

Doing the Research

Now is the time to do some serious preparation in advance of the Interview. Does the company have a Web site? Read through it thoroughly, and take notes for yourself. Are you applying to a publicly traded company? Find out all you can from Dun and Bradstreet (`http://www.dbisna.com/`) or other corporate information services.

A D&B report can tell you the corporate headquarters, its number of employees at a given location and worldwide, as well as their net sales and net worth figures. The report will tell you what businesses they are in and will familiarize you with the principals (officers and founders) of the company. In addition, the report will tell you the significant milestones in the company's history (founding date, when it went public, and so forth).

Far more extensive corporate profiles are on file with the Federal Trade Commission for publicly traded companies, and if you are applying to a large company, you can call their corporate headquarters and ask for their annual report.

Check Your References

The interview goes well, they're ready to make you an offer, and just before you leave they say "Oh, we need three references." You rattle off a few names, but they want people you've worked for, or they want people who've worked for you. You scramble to come up with the names they need, certain that your former co-workers won't let you down.

Unfortunately, when they call, your co-worker isn't quite as enthusiastic as you might have hoped. Perhaps he has been harboring a grudge against you and sees this as an opportunity to get even. More likely, he isn't out to sink you at all, but in a fit of brutal honesty he provides a lukewarm endorsement of your ability to lead a team.

Before you give anyone's name as a reference, you must ask that person if he or she is comfortable providing a reference, and then you must find out what your prospective reference is going to say. One way to do this is by having your agency check your references. They'll call and interview the reference, and if the person isn't sufficiently enthusiastic, they'll let you know.

Actually, they won't let you know because that would compromise their responsibility to the person giving the reference. Instead, what they'll say is, "Joe was great, but I think you need someone with a different perspective to round out your references; someone who knew you longer or had a different relationship." It is possible they are saying exactly what they think; it is also possible that what they are really saying is, "This guy would sink you like a toy ship. Let's find someone else."

If you are not using an agency, you have a more difficult task: You must get someone else to check your references. Find a friend with a business and ask him to make a background check for you. However you do it, make sure you know what your references are going to say before they call.

Review Your Résumé

The morning of your interview, reread and study your résumé. Be sure you can talk intelligently about every job you've had. When they ask you about a project you worked on, you don't want to stare back at them in bewilderment, struggling to remember what exactly you did on that project. You want to rattle off an impressive summary of the problem you were trying to solve and the incredibly creative and innovative solution you implemented.

If you need to, review the design or even the code of your past projects. Do whatever it takes to reacquaint yourself with the details of each of your projects so that you can talk about them. It may be that something you worked on five years ago is very similar to a project your prospective employer has in mind; if you can explain what you did, he may let you do it again!

Make Yourself Ready

On the day of the interview, get up early, shower, eat a full breakfast. Comb your hair, use deodorant, brush your teeth, polish your shoes. Do not apply perfume, aftershave, or other scents—you never know when your employer will be allergic.

Ideally, you'll have cut your hair one week before the interview. The day before is fine; the day after is (surprise!) too late.

Wear a dark, professional suit. Here's the rule; you can only underdress; you can never overdress. If they tell you business casual, go up one notch. Let them know you are eager.

Everything you wear should be crisp; nothing wrinkled. Look in the mirror; pretend you are back in second grade and your mother is checking you over before sending you in to take class pictures. Are your nails clean? Are your hands washed?

If you must eat immediately before the interview, eat lightly and don't eat onions or anything else your interviewer will hate. You know the drill; you don't want to send subtle signals saying "unpleasant to be near."

Arrive early. Earlier than that. There are no excuses at an interview. If you are late, they won't care whether you were stuck in traffic because a volcano spontaneously erupted on the way in to the city. If you can't get to the interview on time, how can they possibly believe you'll deliver software on time?

Bring a book or magazine. Think carefully about what you're reading. When they come out to get you, will you be reading a racy novel or will you be reading a technical book or industry journal? Worse, if they're hiring you as a C++ guru, you had better not be reading a primer unless you wrote it!

If someone offers you a cup of coffee, decline. You don't want to juggle the cup when your interviewer arrives, you don't want it on your breath, and you don't want to have to get rid of it before the interview is over.

Oh, by the way, relax. You'll be fine. Now get in there—they're waiting.

The Least You Need to Know

➤ Your résumé is your marketing material—you want it to generate a face-to-face interview.

➤ For every job you list, express your accomplishments in terms of the benefit received by your employer.

➤ The cover letter provides an introduction to your prospective employer—its only purpose is to get the employer to look at your résumé.

WELCOME
ABOARD!!

Chapter 16

Getting the Job at the Interview

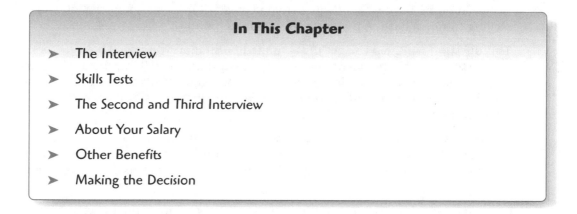

In This Chapter

➤ The Interview

➤ Skills Tests

➤ The Second and Third Interview

➤ About Your Salary

➤ Other Benefits

➤ Making the Decision

The Interview

The key pop-psychology fact to know about an interview is that for many people a favorable or unfavorable impression is made very quickly; usually within the first 10 minutes of the interview. This means you want to connect with the interviewer quickly, but you need to realize that the person conducting the interview may not be terribly well prepared, and may be more nervous than you are.

They are making a big investment, but taking the time to read the résumé and think clearly about what they need to know may not be possible in the middle of their busy day. More often than not, you'll be talking to a harried middle-manager. Your job is to help him or her settle into the interview so that you have a chance to tell him or her what you can do.

Here's a second pop-psychology fact: When two people meet for the first time, the talker usually has a favorable impression of the listener. In an interview, you are supposed to be the talker, but you can even things out by asking a few well-targeted questions such as, "How long have you been with the company?"

Getting Started

Typically, you'll be met in a waiting area, and the walk to the office is a good time for light chitchat. "How was the traffic; did you find everything okay?" Whatever the reality, your answer is, "no problem getting here; oh yes, quite easy, your directions were perfect," and so forth. Now is not the time to discuss the annoying habits of drivers on the interstate, or to whine about the flat tire you got in their parking lot. The atmosphere you want to establish right away is "no problem."

After you are seated, resist the temptation to launch into a monologue. Sit quietly a few minutes, lean slightly forward, and listen. If the interviewer needs to rustle some papers or read your résumé, let him. Relax. But don't start looking around; watch the interviewer, but don't stare. The overall goal is to help the interviewer know you are ready, but not pressing.

When asked the first question, remember that chemistry is everything. A typical opening question might be, "So tell me about yourself." If asked a vague general question such as this say, "Yes, I'd be happy to; I'm quite excited about some of the work I've been doing but I wonder whether you could tell me a bit about the job you are seeking to fill. What was it you saw in my background that interested you?"

This question will help you get the accurate information you need about the position, and it will help the interviewer become more comfortable, talking about what he is comfortable with and knowledgeable about—the job he wants to fill. This also gets the interviewer talking and answering and lets you listen; a valuable technique in establishing rapport.

The trick is, however, that you must really listen. It isn't your job to parrot back what you've heard, but you want to be sure that you don't say things that suggest either you didn't listen to what you were told or that you don't care about what you were told.

It is important that you find an opportunity to answer the original question, however. You might consider following the interviewer's statement with, "Great, let me tell you a bit about my background and how it might fit in with what you are looking for." This makes it clear that you will focus your rendition in terms of the issues the interviewer has raised.

About Your Strengths

At some point in the interview, you will be asked about your strengths. Now is not the time for false humility, but you must find the delicate balance between confidence and arrogance.

Begin with something like, "I may be proudest of the work my team did solving the sign-on problem for... Management was faced with unacceptable costs because... We put together a team to... We decided to approach this by... As a result we were able to bring down customer service inquiries about sign-on from 60% of the customer inquiries to less than 5%, with an estimated annual savings of..." and so forth.

Note the persistent use of the plural ("we did"). You can mitigate any suspicion of arrogance by attributing the accomplishment to the group you were a part of. This shows you are a team player and allows the listener to assume you did the bulk of the thinking and hard work without your tooting your own horn too loudly.

Be sure you can talk about specific strengths such as leadership or design ability, rather than skills such as mastery of a particular technology. You may want to soften this with phrases such as "I think I'm good at..." or "I've been told I'm effective at..." The latter is particularly useful as it implies this is feedback you've received during management evaluations.

Never, Ever Complain About People You've Worked With

There is an old story about a traveler approaching the gates of a city. He walks up to the guard at the gate and says, "What kind of people live in this city?" The guard asks, "What kinds were there in the city you came from?"

The man scowls and says, "That's why I'm here. In that city were nothing but scoundrels and cheats. People there were quick to condemn you and slow to embrace you or to help. They were a mean and narrow-minded people and that is why I left."

The guard shakes his head in sympathy and says, "I advise you to keep going, then, my friend, as the people here are no better; they are much the same." The man walks on dejectedly.

An hour later a second man approaches the guard and also asks about what kinds of people are in this town. In answer to the guard's query about the town from which he comes, the man answers, "Oh, I hated to leave that city; the people there were the salt of the earth. Always quick to lend a hand, never a sharp word, they were my neighbors and friends and I shall miss them dearly."

The guard smiles and says, "Fear not, stranger, here you will find people of much the same character. Enter our city and be welcome."

Your prospective employer must judge your ability to work with others on her team during a very short interview. She would be foolhardy to think that if you hated the people at your last job, you'll get along any better here. Never complain, and especially never complain about your boss.

You would be amazed how many people answer the question, "Why did you leave your last job?" by moaning about what an idiot they worked for. That is certainly not the way to convince your prospective new boss that you'll be a great addition to his team. No one wants to be your next idiot.

About Your Weaknesses

Nearly every interviewer in America will ask the inevitable interview question: "What is your greatest weakness?"

Take a moment before your first interview to think this through. Find a real weakness, but one with a compensating strength. In fact, you can often express your weakness as the flip side of the strengths you cited earlier.

Don't focus on a lack of knowledge or skill. The fact that you don't know Assembler is not a weakness.

Do yourself a favor; don't answer, "I work too hard," or "I'm too responsible." They've all heard it and it rings false. You might say something more realistic such as, "Sometimes I get so focused on the technology that I lose focus on the user's requirements. I'm working on that by spending a bit more time reading through the early specifications, and when possible talking directly with the customer or users."

This weakness reveals a major compensating strength: a sensitivity to an issue to which many developers are oblivious. It also segues the conversation into issues about user requirements and the proper role of the developer.

Overcoming Objections

We are not all perfect for every job. What do you do if there is something in your background that the prospective employer is likely to object to?

Of course, it depends on the problem. If you have a felony arrest for murdering your previous employer, that is more difficult to overcome than if the problem is that you don't have the skill he's looking for (well, it depends; in some startups, the murder might be less of a problem!).

The first rule is never to deny their concerns; but rather to acknowledge the legitimacy of their concerns and then work to overcome them. For example, rather than saying, "It isn't a problem that I don't know Windows programming because I know the Mac," you might say, "I know you need a Windows programmer and I don't have that skill, but I do know the Mac and I'm sure I can make the transition." It is a subtle difference, but in the latter statement you are acknowledging their legitimate concern.

Handling Serious Problems in Your Background

What do you do if there are very serious problems in your background, such as being fired or even having been convicted of a crime? The short answer is not to hide it and not to deny that the employer might see this as a very serious problem. You might approach an answer along the lines of, "If I were in your place I'd have the same concern, if I hadn't learned anything from it, that concern would be justified, but let me tell you what I learned from that experience."

Many things that look to you like a fatal flaw are just a warning flag to your potential employer. If you can manage that flag, confront it, and overcome the concern, then it need not stop you cold. One manager told me, "Why not hire a person who learned on the other manager's nickel? This way, I get an experienced, wiser person and I didn't pay for the lesson."

What If They Need a Skill You Don't Have?

Resist the temptation to fake it, and doubly resist the temptation to say, "I don't know that, but I can learn it." There is no reason for your prospective employer to want to pay you while you learn.

Before you deny knowing the skill in question, clarify what they mean. Frequently the employer will ask, "Do you know SQL?" and you'll think they're asking whether you are a guru, and what they really want to know is, "Have you heard of SQL; do you know what it is for?" If you are going to say you don't know it, be clear what you mean. "I know what SQL is for, and I've worked with it just a little, but I'm not yet an expert with it by any means" is a lot better than "no."

If you have related expertise, make that clear as well. If asked about Oracle which you don't know, you might say, "I haven't worked with Oracle, but I have experience with SQL-Server, and I'd guess that many of the issues are the same."

Body Language

Don't discount body language; we're all trained to take it seriously and so we do. Remember what you mother used to say: Don't slouch and sit up tall in your seat. Many studies have shown that people trust tall, thin people. You can't make yourself taller or leaner, but you can sit and stand straight and give yourself every advantage.

Keep an eye on the interviewer. Most people give away their discomfort when they hear something they don't like. Don't immediately veer off into what you think is a safer answer; but stay attuned to their concerns—perhaps they've misunderstood you or you can clarify. In any case, don't be too eager to please; it is fine if they disagree with you about a few things as long as you appear to have thought things through.

If you see them shaking their head or otherwise sending a signal that you've blown it; remain calm and ask. "I sense you think that isn't right; which aspect of my answer concerns you?" Why not be direct? It gives them a chance to express their concerns and it gives you a chance to clarify and reduce misunderstanding.

Interview Questions

Interview questions come in a few different categories. There are the get-acquainted questions:

➤ So, tell me about yourself.

➤ What have you been working on recently?

➤ What kind of job are you looking for?

Expect to be asked about your work history in some detail: What were you working on at this job? Why did you leave this job? What were your responsibilities? These are questions you should be able to answer quickly, easily, and with confidence.

Asking about your goals helps the interviewer understand your values and direction:

➤ What kind of work would you like to be doing in a few years?

➤ Do you like to work in C++ or do you prefer Java?

➤ What are your long-term goals?

You face an interesting dilemma here. You want to be honest, but if your answer reveals goals wholly impossible for this company, you send a difficult message in your first interview. Try to be responsive but be sure you are open to many possibilities. If you are fairly early in your career, make it clear that you know you have much to learn; perhaps even a bit more to learn before you settle on a particular direction.

Many interviewers like to get a sense of how your mind works. There are a number of standard questions to get you thinking aloud so that the interviewer can do a quick, intuitive IQ test:

Why are manhole covers round? I suspect this question is asked to throw you for a loop and see what creative answers you can generate. The real answer, by the way, is that they are easy to roll, they won't fall down into the hole, and they can be laid on top of the hole from any angle.

How many gas stations do you think there are in America? This question gets at your ability to estimate and perhaps to grapple with large numbers. One way to go at it is to suggest that if there are 250 million Americans, and each gas station has about 250 customers, there are about a million gas stations. Now, does that even make sense? Let's see, the average person drives about 12,000 miles per year, and gets about 20 miles per gallon; therefore, the average driver buys about 600 gallons of gas. If the station make 10 cents a gallon profit, that's $60 per year per driver. 250 drivers at $60 profit would be $15,000 profit, from which they must pay for their rent and they must pay the attendant who pumps the gas. I'm guessing a gas station owner wants to make about five times that, so I'll reduce my estimate by dividing by five, and guess 200,000 gas stations. A quick call to my library reveals there were about 141,000 gas stations in the United States in 1992. Not bad.

The important thing in this exercise is not to get the right answer, but to show a reasonable line of thinking.

Skills Tests

Some employers will ask you to demonstrate your skills. They may do this with a formal test, or through an informal set of questions. When I interview programmers, I often probe for the outside of the envelope of their expertise. I was looking for four things:

1. How much does this person know?
2. Does that match what he says he knows?
3. Is he going to try to fake it?
4. How does he reason through the areas he is uncertain about?

If I asked about pointer-to-member functions (an advanced concept in C++) and the person didn't know what they were, I was hoping for an honest but creative answer. I'd like to hear something along the lines of, "I am not familiar with them, but based on the name, I can guess that they are a way of calling member functions indirectly. I'm not quite sure I see when you might use them, however." That's a great answer; if he's lucky, I'll become engaged showing him how they're used, and if he becomes enthusiastic about them, then we've hit a rapport, which is worth far more than his already having the knowledge.

As soon as you get back from the interview, sit down and write your interview a thank-you note. Do it now. And don't forget to mail it!

The Second and Third Interview

The first interview is your chance to sell yourself to the employer. It is important to realize that in this interview you are selling and they are buying. Now is not the time to ask about salary, incentives, benefits, and vacation; now is the time to talk about what you bring to the table and how you can help them meet their goals. Simply put, you can't sell and buy at the same time. Concentrate on selling; assume you'll love the job—there's plenty of time to find out otherwise after they start selling and you start buying.

A second interview may be required so that senior management can meet you and be made to feel sufficiently comfortable that an offer will be forthcoming. You are still selling, they are still buying, but you're getting closer to closure.

If the process is going well, and if the employers know how to do their business, they won't make an offer unless they're pretty certain you will accept. At some point, probably during the second interview, or at the latest, during the third, the balance will begin to shift; you will now become the buyer and they will start selling you on why this is a great company to work for.

It still isn't time to think about compensation and benefits, but it is time to start focusing on what your job will be and what career growth opportunities exist.

About Your Salary

If you are asked about your salary expectations, you need to have an answer ready. It can be helpful to put the answer into a larger perspective. Point out that you know that salary is only one aspect of compensation, which also includes growth opportunity and the chance to learn new skills, work on interesting topics, and eventually to have leadership opportunities.

That said, you do have to have a salary in mind. To do that, you need a good sense of what the market really is. If you're not working with an agency, then you must study a lot of ads, and talk with a lot of people. After you have a number, be sure you are comfortable with it. The worst thing that can happen is to ask for $50,000, have the employer say fine, and then kick yourself and be miserable.

If $50,000 is your number, then say you were looking for something in the $50s. Don't say something in the range of 50,000 because that includes 45,000 and if you can't live with that number, don't get that offer.

When thinking about salary, many people get caught between what they want, and not wanting to be seen as a fool. It's a terrible thing when you go home proud of your new job and your best buddy says, "Well, they saw you coming; my neighbor has the same job and he makes $15,000 more than you."

Don't worry about being made a fool; companies generally pay what the market will bear, and you may well decide to take a somewhat lower salary than you might get elsewhere if the opportunity has compensating factors. If you can learn a lot, have an opportunity to take on greater responsibilities sooner, and generally thrive in a job you'll love, it may well be worth settling for a slightly lower salary than you might get elsewhere.

And remember, people lie about what they're earning.

Stock Options

When computing your salary, be sure to take into account every aspect of your compensation. For example, many jobs in the industry today offer stock options, often in lieu of greater salary.

Here, in brief is how it works. A stock option is a guarantee that you may buy the stock at a particular price. If the company is a startup and therefore not currently traded, this option has zero value until and unless the company is either bought or "goes public" at some time in the future.

If the company is already publicly traded (for example, on the New York Stock Exchange), the option will probably be for a value greater than its current trading value.

Let's take an example. Suppose you work for Acme Software (stock symbol ACMEX) and it is currently trading for $120 a share. Your options may be to buy 1,000 shares at 150. It would be silly to exercise these options today (even if you were allowed to) because they would cost you $150 per share and you'd be able to sell them only for $120 per share.

If you hold on to the options for a few years, the stock may rise to 170. You'd be betting that your participation in this great company would drive the value up. When the stock is at 170, you might choose to "exercise" your options. This would allow you to buy 1,000 shares at 150, and sell them immediately at 170, or make $20,000 profit.

Typically you are not "vested" in your shares when you first get them. That means they are set aside for you, but you don't own them yet. A typical vesting scheme works so that you gain ownership at 20% per year, so that after five years you are "fully vested"—that is, you really own the options and can exercise them when you want.

For many startups, you will receive a tiny fraction of the company; say 1/4 of 1%. If the company goes public one day and is valued at $100 million, your 1/4 of 1% will be worth $250,000. If the company goes bankrupt, your options will make a very nice cage lining for that parrot you've always wanted.

Microsoft has probably made millionaires of more people through the allocation of options than any company in history, and while the industry is thrilled by these get-rich stories, the reality is that most programmers never make very much money on their options.

That said, options are a great way to increase an employee's investment in the company and they balance the incentives to scurry from one job to the next in times of high demand for programmers.

Incentives and Bonuses

In addition to salaries and stock options, many companies offer bonuses. There are many ways to structure a bonus program, but there are four common bonuses that constitute the overwhelming majority of plans.

Sign-On Bonus

Companies often offer sign-on bonuses to meet a specific goal: hiring a particular developer who is otherwise hard to attract without raising the base salary.

If the company's compensation program allows them to offer a senior developer only $70,000 per year, but that is insufficient to attract a star candidate, they may find it useful to offer a $10,000 sign-on bonus. This is highly attractive to the candidate, but keeps the base salary manageable for the company.

Performance Bonus

This is typically an annual bonus tied to an individual's performance in the job. With salespeople, this is easy to measure; with a developer, it may be somewhat more arbitrary. Individual performance bonuses are not common for software developers.

Team Bonus

Far more common is a bonus tied to the company's overall performance. This amounts to a form of profit-sharing; as the company does well in the market, all the players participate in that success through a bonus plan.

Golden Handcuffs

Software is an industry in which the company's most precious and valuable resources are people, not equipment. If the company is interested in being sold, it faces an interesting dilemma. How does the buyer know that the key players won't quit one week after the sale? After all, it hardly makes sense to spend $100 million to buy the best talent in the industry if they'll all leave and what you have left is code no one can properly support.

Because the Supreme Court has taken a rather obstinate view regarding indentured servitude, it is difficult to prevent an exodus through threats or punishment, but it is not impossible to accomplish this goal using incentives.

Golden Handcuffs is a term for an incentive program structured to encourage employees to stay through the transfer period. For example, the bonus program might be written so that if the employee is still employed on the second anniversary of the sale, she will be awarded 1% of the sale price. Typically, golden handcuff arrangements include a bonus should the venture fail and the employee is laid off.

Together, the possibility of a big payout sometime down the road and protection against failure make a powerful incentive to the key employees to stay with the company through the transition. Clever bonus schemes don't fall off a cliff at the end of two years, but rather have cascading benefits for staying longer, so that there is no sudden exodus at payout.

Other Benefits

In addition to salary and bonuses, there are many other forms of benefits, which together may represent a significant fraction of your total compensation. These include the various forms of insurance commonly offered by employers, including health, dental, life, and disability.

Each of these benefits can be better or significantly worse than those offered by the competition, and they may be more or less important to you depending on your life circumstances. For example, if you are single and healthy, life insurance may not be a

244

major concern, but if you are middle-aged, with three kids and a mortgage, then a solid life insurance package is something you'd otherwise have to pay for and amounts to money in your pocket.

Time off is important to everyone, and some companies offer only one week of vacation whereas others offer four. In addition to the stated amount of vacation, you'll want to get a sense of the culture: Do people actually take their vacation, or is vacation better in theory than in reality? If vacations are missed, can they be cashed out? This is tricky, however: Often it is better to get the time off than to get the extra money; be careful that they aren't using this as a way to get 52 sixty-hour weeks a year out of their development staff.

What is their policy on holidays, sick days, and personal days? How do they support family leave, and do they offer child-care arrangements? What are their travel policies? While you're at it, will you be expected to travel much?

In a larger company, they will be able to provide you a complete benefits package; in a small startup, these offerings may be rather Spartan.

While you are considering your working conditions, find out whether you'll be in a cube or an office, and how easily you can work from home. Does the company have a policy about telecommuting?

There are other benefits often overlooked, such as tuition reimbursement, parental leave, child care, job-sharing, a book allowance, opportunities for training and professional development, and so forth. Finally, don't forget to consider the corporate culture and dress code: Can you wear your comfortable clothes to work, or will you have to spend a hunk of your salary on new suits?

Making the Decision

Okay, the offer is on the table, and now it is time for you to accept or turn it down. If you've done your homework, you know a lot about the company, and you've had every possible question answered.

If you feel you still have questions, don't call and ask them; you'll just think of more. Spend 24 hours writing down everything you need to know and then call and say, "I'm very close to a decision, but there are a few things I'd like to know."

Ideally at the end of that conversation, you'll be ready to give your answer, but if not, at least let them know when you will have the answer: "Thanks for clarifying these points. May I call you by 4:00 with my answer?" If you set a deadline, be sure to be early. If the deadline is 4, be sure you call by 3; if they're out of the office, you want time to reach them before they call someone else.

Don't be pressured into taking a job, but understand that they will need your answer in a timely manner. If you are undecided, try the Ben Franklin approach: Draw a line down the middle of a blank sheet of paper and put all the things you like about the job on one side, and all your concerns and objections on the other.

Don't count which side has more, but use the paper to help you think through the problems. Can the objections be overcome? Perhaps your single biggest objection is that you won't have an office. If that is really the stumbling block, then you have to decide how important it is to you.

If it is a critical, show-stopping, drop-dead requirement that you have an office—if you're ready to turn the job down because you can't have one—then call them back and tell them that you're ready to accept but you can't quite bring yourself to take a job sitting in a cube. It can't hurt to try; you've already decided to give up the job. But don't do this as a ploy; if they won't give you the office, it may be hard for you to take the job after saying that. And don't say it unless you are certain you do want the job if they meet your terms; you'll make them crazy if they give in on the office and you then say, "Great, and I also need one more thing…"

If you decide you will take the job, and you are not working with an agency, then be sure to call them and tell them in person. They should send you a formal offer in the mail; ask when you might expect it. If they don't do this, send them a quick note thanking them for the job offer and expressing your enthusiasm.

Congratulations; and remember to be early your first day of work!

The Least You Need to Know

➤ A favorable or unfavorable impression is made very quickly in an interview—come prepared, arrive on time, and realize that the interviewer may be more nervous than you.

➤ Establish rapport by asking questions and listening to the response.

➤ Emphasize specific strengths rather than skills; phrase your response as if it were feedback you had received during management evaluations.

Extended
Glossary

BASIC   Beginner's All-Purpose Symbolic Instruction Set. A programming language.

Binary   A system with only two choices. Binary math consists of only 1s and 0s.

Bit   Binary Digit (1 or 0).

Bug   An error in a computer program.

Byte   8 bits.

Case Sensitive   If a language is case sensitive, then words are differentiated by the case of the letters.

Class   A user-defined type.

Clear   A bit is clear when its value is false or 0.

Code   The instructions that make up a computer program.

Compiler   A program that takes human-readable and turns it into machine-readable code.

Constant   A data storage location with an unchanging value.

Cookie   In Web programming, a small file created by a server and stored on the client machine.

Data   Information and values stored in your program.

Data Integrity   All the data in a database is consistent among all the tables.

Debugger   Software that helps a programmer find bugs in a program.

Easy to maintain   This phrase suggests that as business requirements change, the program can be extended and enhanced without great expense.

Editor   A program for editing programming code.

Event driven   Programs that respond to events such as the user clicking on a button, choosing from a menu or otherwise spontaneously interacting with the program.

Expression   Anything that evaluates to a value.

Field   In a database, a column representing a single attribute.

HTTP   HyperText Transport Protocol.

Iteration   Doing the same thing repeatedly.

Linker   A program that links together multiple parts of a single program.

Literal   A numeric value used as a constant.

Nybble   4 bits.

Object   An object is a thing to a programmer; an object is an instance of a type the programmer has created. Objects have characteristics and behavior.

Polymorphism   The ability for many related objects each to respond to the same message differently yet appropriately.

Procedure or function   An identified block of instructions, executed one after another.

Programming   Writing a program in a programming language.

Protocol   An agreed-upon convention; in this case, a protocol describes the order in which information is sent, the parts of the header, and so forth.

Prototype   In C++, a prototype defines a function and tells the compiler its return type, name, and parameter list.

Record   In a database, a single entry in a table (a row).

Semantics   The meaning of the program and its purpose.

Server   A computer whose job is to provide information to client machines. In this case, a Web server's job is to "serve" pages to client machines.

Set   A bit is set when its value is 1 or true.

Structured programming   A technique of dividing a program into short procedures and controlling the flow of the program among these procedures.

Syntax   The precise rules for how programs are written.

Tag   In HTML, a special word or symbol set in text indicating how the text that follows should be displayed.

Type of a variable   Tells the compiler how much room to set aside in memory to hold the variable's value.

URL   Uniform Resource Locator—the address of an item on the World Wide Web.

Variable   A named location in memory in which you can store a value.

White space   Blank areas of program code created by spaces, tabs, and new lines.

Wintel   An acronym for Windows and Intel—refers to the kind of machine that has an Intel processor (or work-alike) and Microsoft Windows.

WYSIWYG   What You See Is What You Get—an environment in which you see the text as it will be displayed, rather than working with tags directly.

Reading List

If you have decided you are serious about a career in programming, this is not the last book you'll read on the subject, but rather the first. The following reading list is far from comprehensive; it can cover only the books with which I'm personally familiar.

To find more books that will be of use, talk with friends and colleagues and keep your eyes open for reviews in professional magazines. Many Internet bookstores offer reviews both by professional reviewers and by readers of the book—although any one review can be misleading, when you see a book where the overwhelming majority of readers feel one way or another, that can be a good indicator of the quality of the book.

Which Language?

The first decision you must make is on which language to focus. The next few sections recommend books for each of the various languages considered in Part 2. It is difficult enough to learn a programming language; trying to learn more than one at a time is not realistic. Focus on your first language to the exclusion of all others; you can always pick up a second language when you have a year or two's worth of experience in the first.

General Style

Whichever language you choose, you'll want to find at least one and perhaps two good primers. Before you buy, visit your local bookstore and examine the choices carefully. Pick up each book and thumb through it, reading at least a few pages from each of a few chapters. Do you like the tone and approach? Does the author write well, and can you follow, at least in general, what he or she is saying?

Read All About It

Some of the material in this chapter originally appeared in my column "Object-Oriented C++ from Scratch" in *C++ Report* (Recommended Reading, October, 1998).

Are there enough examples and are they explained in detail? Some people like lots of examples and find that a good example is worth five pages of theory; others don't need examples and feel they bloat the book. Find a good fit for your learning style.

Do you want exercises at the end of each chapter? If so, does this book have them and does the author supply the answers? Once again, this is a matter of personal learning style.

Before you buy, consider this: Can you find the author to ask questions—does he or she supply an email address? Sometimes, when you are stuck, one quick pointer in the right direction can make all the difference.

Finally, how comprehensive is the book? Does it cover the language from scratch, and does it cover it fully or does it gloss over key facts? Of course, you can't be sure (after all, you're not yet an expert in the language, or why do you need the book?) but reading through the table of contents can give you a good idea of where they begin and how much they cover. Compare the tables of contents among two or three books; that will give you a good sense of what ought to be in there and what might be missing.

C++ Programming

For many of the reasons described in Part 2, C++ is by far the most popular professional programming language for serious applications development. It is also one of the more complex languages and arguably one of the hardest to learn.

Obviously, I'm not objective—I have four books designed for self-study in C++. *Sams Teach Yourself C++ in 21 Days, Third Edition* (Sams, 1999, ISBN: 0-672-31070-8) is a comprehensive tutorial loaded with examples, quizzes, exercises, and answers, and it covers every aspect of the language.

My second book, *Sams Teach Yourself C++ in 24 Hours, Second Edition* (Sams, 1999, ISBN: 0-672-31067-8) breaks things down into smaller chunks, leaves out the exercises, and skips some of the most esoteric aspects of C++.

I also wrote *Sams Teach Yourself C++ in 10 Minutes* (Sams, 1999, ISBN: 0-672-31067-8), which serves as a quick introduction, divided into short, snappy chapters.

Finally, this year I'll be releasing *Jesse Liberty's C++ from Scratch,* which takes an entirely different approach to learning the language. Rather than teaching a series of skills, the *From Scratch* series takes you along as I build a project, explaining the language as I go.

There are, of course, a number of other very good books by other authors. Take your time; read a chapter or two before you buy—the primer may be the most important book you choose. Many readers like to have more than one, so that they can learn from multiple authors' presentations.

Windows C++ Programming

After you've read a primer or two on C++, you may decide that you'd like to write Windows programs. You'll be surprised to learn that support for windows, buttons, and all the other user interface widgets we've grown accustomed to are not part of the C++ language and must be learned as a separate effort.

The single most popular tool for writing C++ Windows programs are the Microsoft Foundation Classes (MFC), and there are any number of good books on learning how to program with the MFC. Three that I've found most helpful are *Beginning MFC Programming* (Wrox Press Inc.; ISBN: 1861000855) by Ivor Horton, *Programming Windows MFC* (Microsoft Press; ISBN: 1556159021) by Jeff Prosise, and *Professional MFC with Visual C++* (Wrox Press Inc.; ISBN: 1861000855) by Mike Blaszczak.

Advanced C++

C++ is a complex language, and learning to program well in C++ is not a trivial undertaking. There are a number of books on advanced topics to choose among, including, of course, my advanced C++ book, *C++ Unleashed* (Sams, 1998, ISBN: 0-672-31239-5).

One of the most important books for a C++ programmer who wants to go beyond the basics to use the language well is *Effective C++* by Scott Meyers (Addison-Wesley, September 1997, ISBN: 0201924889). This wonderful book provides 50 tips in using the language well, and should be on every C++ programmer's bookshelf. I would venture to say Meyers has done more to improve the overall quality of C++ programming with this little gem than perhaps anyone else in the industry.

For insight into how C++ was created and how it has evolved, you will want to read *The Design and Evolution of C++* by Bjarne Stroustrup (Addison-Wesley, 1994, ISBN: 0201543303).

John Lakos' *Large-Scale C++ Software Design* (Addison-Wesley, July 1996, ISBN: 0201633620) offers insight into building large, real-world, commercial software applications. This book is fairly advanced; I'd read it only after reading a number of other books on this list.

Java Programming

Although Java and C++ are very similar languages, the choices in books are very different. There was a blizzard of Java books for a while; unfortunately, not all of them are terribly good.

253

You can't go wrong with a primer from Sun, as they are the creators of Java. Their series includes a number of titles including *Core Java*, *Just Java*, and *Instant Java*. Ivor Horton also has a Java book, *Beginning Java 2* (Wrox Press Inc.; ISBN: 1861002238), which many people think is terrific, and Laura Lemay's *Sams Teach Yourself Java 1.2 in 21 Days* (Sams, 1998, ISBN: 0-672-31534-3) is very highly regarded.

I have only one primer on Java, *Java from Scratch*, which builds a Java application from scratch and teaches the language as you go (Que, 1999, Liberty and Rogers, ISBN: 0-7897-2079-5).

Internet Programming

If you decide to focus on the Internet, there are hundreds of books from which to choose to get you started. I was very impressed by *Web Programming Unleashed* (Sams, 1996, ISBN: 1575211173) by Breedlove, et al. This terrific book provides an overview and introduction to all the significant Web development technology.

For learning about building enterprisewide applications, I highly recommend *Microsoft Visual InterDev 6.0 Enterprise Developer's Workshop* (Microsoft Press; ISBN: 0735605688) by Andrew Duthie. This book not only explains the technology, but also helps provide context and background information about the issues involved in building large, robust enterprise applications to run on the Web.

To learn about ASP, I recommend *Beginning Active Server Pages 2.0* (Wrox Press Inc.; ISBN: 1861001347) by Brian Francis, et al. There are a number of books on ASP in the Wrox series, all of which are very good. Microsoft also publishes good books on ASP as do Sams and many other publishers. Again, I can recommend only from the small sample I've read.

Visual Basic Programming

There are literally dozens of excellent books on Visual Basic. The one I personally turn to is *Sams Teach Yourself Visual Basic in 21 Days* (Sams, 1998, ISBN: 0-672-31310-3) by Greg Perry.

The upcoming *Jesse Liberty's Programming from Scratch* series also includes *Visual Basic from Scratch* (Que, 1999, ISBN: 0-7897-2060-4), in which you build an application from the ground up and learn the language as you go. This book makes an excellent complement to other primers, as it focuses on building the project rather than on acquiring individual programming skills.

Assembler Programming

There are fewer books on Assembler than on other languages, as learning Assembler is not nearly as popular as it once was. The book I turn to is *The Revolutionary Guide to Assembly Language* (Software Masters; ISBN: 1874416125) by Vitalii Maliugin. This is an excellent, comprehensive introduction to Wintel-compatible Assembler programming.

Object–Oriented Analysis and Design

This field is suddenly awash in good books, although many are a bit academic for my taste. Certainly the flagship books are those by the Three Amigos: Grady Booch, Ivar Jacobson, and James Rumbaugh: the *Unified Software Development Process* (Addison-Wesley Pub Co; ISBN: 0201571692), the *Unified Modeling Language User Guide* (Addison-Wesley Pub Co; ISBN: 0201571684), and the *Unified Modeling Language Reference Manual* (Addison-Wesley Pub Co; ISBN: 020130998X).

I very much enjoyed *Object-Oriented Software Construction* by Bertran Meyer (Prentice Hall, ISBN: 0-13-629155-4), but it is not for everyone and ought not be the first book you read on OOA&D. Meyer takes a different perspective, and I found him brilliant and interesting.

¡Hola, Amigos!

I talk more about the Three Amigos in Chapter 9, "Classes and Objects."

I have written two books in this category: *Beginning Object-Oriented Analysis and Design* (Wrox Press 1998, ISBN: 1861001339) and *Clouds to Code* (Wrox Press 1997, ISBN: 1861000952). *Beginning OOA&D* is a tutorial, and covers the UML as well as analysis, design, and architectural mechanisms including persistence, concurrency, and distributed objects. *Clouds to Code* is a detailed case study, written as it happened, of the development of a real-world application. Both of these books are targeted at the working C++ programmer.

After you've read a book or two on object-oriented programming, be sure to pick up *Object-Oriented Design Heuristics* by Arthur J. Riel (Addison-Wesley, 1996, ISBN: 0-201-63385-X). This wonderful book helps you understand the difference between great designs and mediocre ones. It is filled with world-class advice and guidance and I recommend it highly.

Coding Well

There are quite a few books on programming style and writing solid, robust, and easily maintained code. Two of the best, by far, are *Code Complete* (Microsoft Press; ISBN: 1556154844) by Steve C. McConnel, and *Writing Solid Code* by Steve Maguire (Microsoft Press; ISBN: 1556155514).

High on my personal list of books to read is *The Practice of Programming* (Addison-Wesley, ISBN: 0-201-61586-X) by Kernighan and Pike. The Kernighan in Kernighan and Pike is Brian Kernighan who wrote the language C and coauthored *The C*

Programming Language by Kernighan and Ritchie. This latter book was so famous among C programmers that we referred to it as the K&R book. Kernighan also wrote the seminal book *The Elements of Programming Style* (Computing McGraw-Hill, ISBN: 0070342075) with P. J. Plauger, in 1988.

Quality Assurance

The world desperately needs a good book on Quality Assurance; I know of none. If you come across a good book on this subject, please send me email (jliberty@ libertyassociates.com) and I'll update this appendix in the next edition.

Databases and Databases on the Web

Perhaps the most exciting and rapidly growing area for commercial software development is providing access to large stores of information via the Web. There are many excellent books on databases; one of my favorites is *Inside Microsoft SQL Server 6.5* (Microsoft Press; ISBN: 1572313315) by Ron Soukup.

My newest book, *Databases on the Web* (Sams 1999) focuses on building an application that provides Web access to your data, teaching the skills required as we go. I will be focusing my attention on this important area of development in the next couple of years, as I believe strongly that this will be a fertile area of development.

Magazines

Whichever books you choose, be sure to supplement your reading with a subscription to one or more technical magazines. I've tried dozens, and I occasionally pick up something new to see whether it might be of value. The three I read religiously are *C++ Report*, *Microsoft Systems Journal (MSJ)*, and *Microsoft Internet Developer (MIND)*. Depending on which language you choose, you'll find other magazines that may better match your interests. One of the smartest programmers I've ever met, Donald Xie, highly recommends the *Visual Basic Programmer's Journal*.

Online Newsgroups and Lists

Finally, magazines and books are great for depth and detail, but when you need answers in a hurry, nothing comes close to the Internet. There are a series of Internet users' groups (for example, comp.lang.c++), that provide a wealth of information, and there are a number of email lists that can also supplement your knowledge. Contact your Internet service provider for information on how to get started with these groups and lists.

Next Steps

As I mentioned at the beginning of the appendix, this list is personal and limited; I can write about only the books I know. You will want to supplement this list by exploring in your local technical bookstore and by talking with other programmers. The field changes quickly; six months from now a whole new set of books will be on the shelves.

I regularly scan `Amazon.com`, `BarnesandNoble.com`, and `softpro.com` to see what is new and what is recommended. I recommend you keep your eyes out for new titles, and if you find something great, let me know about it; I'm always working on my recommended reading list (`jliberty@libertyassociates.com`).

Binary Math

There was a time that computer science was taught in the math department of most universities. Today, programming has become far more abstract, and you can be a world-class programmer without advanced skills in mathematics.

That said, the underlying fundamentals of programming rely on the binary and hexadecimal numbering systems, and understanding these systems can be crucial to a deep understanding of programming.

This appendix introduces the skills you need as painlessly as possible. Much of the material in this appendix is adapted from my book *Sams Teach Yourself C++ in 21 Days, Third Edition*.

Numbering Systems

You learned the fundamentals of arithmetic so long ago, it is hard to imagine what it would be like without that knowledge. When you look at the number 145, you instantly see "one hundred forty-five" without much reflection.

Understanding binary and hexadecimal requires that you reexamine the number 145 and see it not as a number, but as a code for a number.

Start small: Examine the relationship between the number three and "3." The numeral 3 is a squiggle on a piece of paper; the number three is an idea. The numeral is used to represent the number.

The distinction can be made clear by realizing that three, 3, |||, III, and *** all can be used to represent the same idea of three.

In base 10 (decimal) math, you use the numerals 0, 1, 2, 3, 4, 5, 6, 7, 8, 9 to represent all numbers. How is the number ten represented?

One can imagine that we would have evolved a strategy of using the letter A to represent ten; or we might have used IIIIIIIII to represent that idea. The Romans used X. The Arabic system, which we use, makes use of position in conjunction with numerals to represent values. The first (rightmost) column is used for "ones," and the next column is used for tens. Therefore, the number fifteen is represented as 15 (read "one, five"); that is, 1 ten and 5 ones.

Certain rules emerge, from which some generalizations can be made:

1. Base 10 uses the digits 0–9.
2. The columns are powers of ten: 1s, 10s, 100s, and so on.
3. If the third column is 100, the largest number you can make with two columns is 99. More generally, with n columns you can represent 0 to $(10^n - 1)$. Therefore, with three columns, you can represent 0 to $(10^3 - 1)$ or 0–999.

Other Bases

It is not a coincidence that we use base 10; we have 10 fingers. One can imagine a different base, however. Using the rules found in base 10, you can describe base 8:

1. The digits used in base 8 are 0–7.
2. The columns are powers of 8: 1s, 8s, 64s, and so on.
3. With n columns you can represent 0 to $8^n - 1$.

To distinguish numbers written in each base, write the base as a subscript next to the number. The number fifteen in base 10 would be written as 15_{10} and read as "one, five, base ten."

Therefore, to represent the number 15_{10} in base 8, you would write 17_8. This is read "one, seven, base eight." Note that it can also be read "fifteen" as that is the number it continues to represent.

Why 17? The 1 means 1 eight, and the 7 means 7 ones. One eight plus seven ones equals fifteen. Consider fifteen asterisks:

```
*****     *****
*****
```

The natural tendency is to make two groups, a group of ten asterisks and another of five. This would be represented in decimal as 15 (1 ten and 5 ones). You can also group the asterisks as

```
****          *******
****
```

That is, eight asterisks and seven. That would be represented in base eight as 17_8. That is, one eight and seven ones.

Around the Bases

You can represent the number fifteen in base ten as 15, in base nine as 16_9, in base 8 as 17_8, in base 7 as 21_7. Why 21_7? In base 7, there is no numeral 8. To represent fifteen, you will need two sevens and one 1.

How do you generalize the process? To convert a base ten number to base 7, think about the columns: In base 7, they are ones, sevens, forty-nines, three-hundred forty-threes, and so on. Why these columns? They represent 7^0, 7^1, 7^2, 7^3 and so forth. Create a table for yourself:

4	3	2	1
7^3	7^2	7^1	7^0
343	49	7	1

The first row represents the column number. The second row represents the power of 7. The third row represents the decimal value of each number in that row.

To convert from a decimal value to base 7, here is the procedure: Examine the number and decide which column to use first. If the number is 200, for example, you know that column 4 (343) is 0, and you don't have to worry about it.

To find out how many 49s there are, divide 200 by 49. The answer is 4, so put 4 in column 3 and examine the remainder: 4. There are no 7s in 4, so put a zero in the sevens column. There are 4 ones in 4, so put a 4 in the 1s column. The answer is 4047.

To convert the number 968 to base 6:

5	4	3	2	1
6^4	6^3	6^2	6^1	6^0
1296	216	36	6	1

There are no 1296s in 968, so column 5 has 0. Dividing 968 by 216 yields 4 with a remainder of 104. Column 4 is 4. Dividing 104 by 36 yields 2 with a remainder of 32. Column 3 is 2. Dividing 32 by 6 yields 5 with a remainder of 2. The answer, therefore, is 42526.

5	4	3	2	1
6^4	6^3	6^2	6^1	6^0
1296	216	36	6	1
0	4	2	5	2

There is a shortcut when converting from one base to another base (such as 6) to base 10. You can multiply

$$4 * 216 = 864$$
$$2 * 36 = 72$$
$$5 * 6 = 30$$
$$2 * 1 = 2$$
$$968$$

Binary

Base 2 is the ultimate extension of this idea. There are only two digits: 0 and 1. The columns are

Col:	8	7	6	5	4	3	2	1
Power:	2^7	2^6	2^5	2^4	2^3	2^2	2^1	2
Value:	128	64	32	16	8	4	2	1

To convert the number 88 to base 2, you follow the same procedure: There are no 128s, so column 8 is 0.

There is one 64 in 88, so column 7 is 1 and 24 is the remainder. There are no 32s in 24 so column 6 is 0.

There is one 16 in 24 so column 5 is 1. The remainder is 8. There is one 8 in 8, and so column 4 is 1. There is no remainder, so the rest of the columns are 0.

0	1	0	1	1	0	0	0

To test this answer, convert it back:

$$1 * 64 = 64$$
$$0 * 32 = 0$$
$$1 * 16 = 16$$
$$1 * 8 = 8$$
$$0 * 4 = 0$$
$$0 * 2 = 0$$
$$0 * 1 = 0$$
$$88$$

Why Base 2?

The greatest advantage of base 2 is that it corresponds so cleanly to what a computer needs to represent. Computers do not really know anything at all about letters, numerals, instructions, or programs. At their core they are just circuitry, and at a given juncture there either is a lot of electricity or there is very little.

To keep the logic clean, engineers do not treat this amount of juice as a relative scale (a little power, some power, more power, lots of power, tons of power), but rather as a binary scale ("enough power" or "not enough power"). Rather than saying "enough" or "not enough," they simplify it to "yes" or "no." Yes or no, or true or false, can be represented as 1 or 0. By convention, 1 means true or Yes, but that is just a convention; it could just as easily have meant false or no.

After you make this great leap of intuition, the power of binary becomes clear: With 1s and 0s you can represent the fundamental truth of every circuit (there is power or there isn't). All a computer ever knows is, "Is you is, or is you ain't?" Is you is = 1; is you ain't = 0.

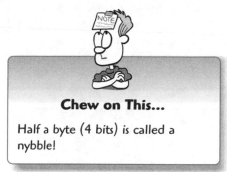

Chew on This...

Half a byte (4 bits) is called a nybble!

Bits, Bytes, and Nybbles

After the decision is made to represent truth and falsehood with 1s and 0s, binary digits (or *bits*) become very important. Because early computers could send 8 bits at a time, it was natural to start writing code using 8-bit numbers—called bytes.

With 8 binary digits, you can represent up to 256 different values. Why? Examine the columns: If all 8 bits are set (1), the value is 255. If none is set (all the bits are clear or zero), the value is 0. 0–255 is 256 possible states.

What's a KB?

It turns out that 2^{10} (1,024) is roughly equal to 10^3 (1,000). This coincidence was too good to miss, so computer scientists started referring to 2^{10} bytes as 1KB or 1 kilobyte, based on the scientific prefix of kilo for thousand.

Similarly, 1,024 * 1,024 (1,048,576) is close enough to one million to receive the designation 1MB or 1 megabyte, and 1,024 megabytes is called 1 gigabyte (giga implies one thousand million, or one billion).

Binary Numbers

Computers use patterns of 1s and 0s to encode everything they do. Machine instructions are encoded as a series of 1s and 0s and interpreted by the fundamental circuitry. Arbitrary sets of 1s and 0s can be translated back into numbers by computer scientists, but it would be a mistake to think that these numbers have intrinsic meaning.

Go ASCII Alice

ASCII stands for the American Standards Committee for Information Interchange, the organization which standardized the character set adopted by IBM for the original IBM PC computers.

For example, the Intel chip set interprets the bit pattern 1001 0101 as an instruction. You certainly can translate this into decimal (149), but that number per se has no meaning.

Sometimes the numbers are instructions, sometimes they are values, and sometimes they are codes. One important standardized code set is ASCII. In ASCII, every letter and punctuation is given a 7-digit binary representation. For example, the lowercase letter "a" is represented by 0110 0001. This is not a number, although you can translate it to the number 97 (64 + 32 + 1). It is in this sense that people say that the letter "a" is represented by 97 in ASCII; but the truth is that the binary representation of 97, 01100001, is the encoding of the letter "a," and the decimal value 97 is a human convenience.

Hexadecimal

Because binary numbers are difficult to read, a simpler way to represent the same values is sought. Translating from binary to base 10 involves a fair bit of manipulation of numbers; but it turns out that translating from base 2 to base 16 is very simple, because there is a very good shortcut.

To understand this, you must first understand base 16, which is known as *hexadecimal*. In base 16, there are sixteen numerals: 0, 1, 2, 3, 4, 5, 6, 7, 8, 9, A, B, C, D, E, and F. The last six are arbitrary; the letters A–F were chosen because they are easy to represent on a keyboard. The columns in hexadecimal are

4	3	2	1
16^3	16^2	16^1	16^0
4096	256	16	1

To translate from hexadecimal to decimal, you can multiply. Therefore, the number F8C represents

```
F * 256 = 15 * 256 = 3840
8 * 16 =           128
C * 1 = 12 * 1 =     12
3980
```

Translating the number FC to binary is best done by translating first to base 10, and then to binary:

```
F * 16 = 15 * 16 =   240
C * 1 = 12 * 1 =      12
252
```

Converting 25210 to binary requires the chart:

```
Col:        9    8    7    6    5    4    3    2    1
Power:      28   27   26   25   24   23   22   21   20
Value:      256  128  64   32   16   8    4    2    1

There are no 256s.
1 128 leaves 124
1 64 leaves 60
1 32 leaves 28
1 16 leaves 12
1 8 leaves 4
1 4 leaves 0
0
0
1    1    1    1    1    1    0    0
```

Therefore, the answer in binary is 1111 1100.

Now, it turns out that if you treat this binary number as two sets of 4 digits, you can do a magical transformation.

The right set is 1100. In decimal that is 12, or in hexadecimal it is C.

The left set is 1111, which in base 10 is 15, or in hex is F.

Thus, you have:

```
1111 1100
F    C
```

Putting the two hex numbers together is FC, which is the real value of 1111 1100. This shortcut always works. You can take any binary number of any length, and reduce it to sets of 4, translate each set of four to hex, and put the hex numbers together to get the result in hex. Here's a much larger number:

```
1011 0001 1101 0111
```

The columns are 1, 2, 4, 8, 16, 32, 64, 128, 256, 512, 1,024, 2,048, 4,096, 8,192, 16,384, and 32,768.

```
1 * 1 =      1
1 * 2=       2
1 * 4 =      4
0 * 8 =      0
```

```
1 *  16 =            16
0 *  32 =             0
1 *  64 =            64
1 * 128 =           128

1 *  256 =          256
0 *  512 =            0
0 * 1024 =            0
0 * 2048 =            0

1 *  4096 =       4,096
1 *  8192 =       8,192
0 * 16384 =           0
1 * 32768 =      32,768
Total:           45,527
```

Converting this to hexadecimal requires a chart with the hexadecimal values.

```
65536    4096    256    16    1
```

There are no 65,536s in 45,527 so the first column is 4096. There are 11 4096s (45,056), with a remainder of 471. There is one 256 in 471 with a remainder of 215. There are 13 16s (208) in 215 with a remainder of 7. Therefore, the hexadecimal number is B1D7.

Checking the math:

```
B (11) * 4096 =  45,056
1 * 256 =           256
D (13) * 16 =       208
7 * 1 =               7
Total            45,527
```

The shortcut version would be to take the original binary number, 1011000111010111, and break it into groups of 4: 1011 0001 1101 0111. Each of the four then is evaluated as a hexadecimal number:

```
1011 =
1 * 1 =       1
1 * 2 =       2
0 * 4 =       0
1 * 8 =       8
Total        11
Hex:          B

0001 =
1 * 1 =       1
0 * 2 =       0
```

266

```
0 * 4 =        0
0 * 8 =        0
Total          1
Hex:           1

1101 =
1 * 1 =        1
0 * 2 =        0
1 * 4 =        4
1 * 8 =        8
Total          13
Hex:           D

0111 =
1 * 1 =        1
1 * 2 =        2
1 * 4 =        4
0 * 8 =        0
Total          7
Hex:           7

Total Hex: B1D7
```

Index

277

INTEGRITY SERVICE SUCCESS

Permanent Placement
Matching software
professionals
to companies' software
needs

Contract Services
The right people and
the right software skills
Every time

*The Sally Silver companies provide the people and
the expertise that businesses need to succeed in the information age*

Sally Silver Companies

470 Totten Pond Road

Waltham, MA 02451

(781) 890-7272

http://www.sallysilver.com

Get **FREE** books and more...when you register this book online for our Personal Bookshelf Program

http://register.quecorp.com/

 Register online and you can sign up for our *FREE Personal Bookshelf Program...*unlimited access to the electronic version of more than 200 complete computer books—immediately! That means you'll have 100,000 pages of valuable information onscreen, at your fingertips!

 Plus, you can access product support, including complimentary downloads, technical support files, book-focused links, companion Web sites, author sites, and more!

 And you'll be automatically registered to receive a *FREE subscription to a weekly email newsletter* to help you stay current with news, announcements, sample book chapters, and special events, including sweepstakes, contests, and various product giveaways!

 We value your comments! Best of all, the entire registration process takes only a few minutes to complete, so go online and get the greatest value going—absolutely FREE!

Don't Miss Out On This Great Opportunity!

QUE® is a brand of Macmillan Computer Publishing USA.

For more information, please visit *www.mcp.com*